Banister Fletcher

The London Building Act 1894

A Text Book for the Use of Architects, Surveyors, Builders, etc. Containing the act

Printed in Extenso

Banister Fletcher

The London Building Act 1894
A Text Book for the Use of Architects, Surveyors, Builders, etc. Containing the act Printed in Extenso

ISBN/EAN: 9783337252496

Printed in Europe, USA, Canada, Australia, Japan

Cover: Foto ©Suzi / pixelio.de

More available books at **www.hansebooks.com**

THE
LONDON BUILDING ACT, 1894

A TEXT-BOOK

FOR THE USE OF

ARCHITECTS, SURVEYORS, BUILDERS, ETC.

CONTAINING THE ACT PRINTED IN EXTENSO

TOGETHER WITH A FULL ABSTRACT, GIVING ALL THE SECTIONS
OF THE ACT WHICH RELATE TO BUILDINGS, SET OUT
IN TABULAR FORM FOR EASY REFERENCE

AND

AN INTRODUCTION SHOWING THE LEADING ALTERATIONS
MADE BY THE ACT

ALSO

The Unrepealed Sections, relating to Building, of all other Acts, and the Byelaws and Regulations of the London County Council
etc. etc.

ILLUSTRATED WITH NINETEEN PLATES

SHOWING THE THICKNESS OF WALLS, PLANS OF CHIMNEYS, SHOP FRONTS,
OPENINGS AND RECESSES PERMITTED IN PARTY AND EXTERNAL WALLS;
HOW MUCH PARTY WALL MUST BE ON RESPECTIVE OWNERS'
LAND WHERE OWNERS ARE BUILDING DIFFERENT CLASS OF
BUILDING; THE WALLING NECESSARY IN CERTAIN
CASES OF LIGHTS IN ROOFS, ETC.

BY

BANISTER FLETCHER

*Professor of Architecture and Building Construction, King's College, London;
Fellow of the Royal Institute of British Architects; Fellow of King's College, London;
District Surveyor of West Newington and Part of Lambeth;
One of the Surveyors to the Board of Trade.
(Author of 'Model Houses,' 'Dilapidations,' 'Compensations,' 'Arbitrations,'
'Light and Air,' 'The Metropolitan Building Acts,' etc.)*

LONDON
B. T. BATSFORD, HIGH HOLBORN, W.C.
1895

PREFACE.

"THE LONDON BUILDING ACT," which comes into force on the 1st January 1895, supersedes the Metropolitan Building Acts, and renders obsolete my book on the subject. My Publisher has therefore desired me to prepare this book on the new Act.

I have tried to make it the text-book on the subject, by following the same methods that I have pursued in all my former works.

I specially commend to my reader's notice:

First, the Abstract of that portion of the Act which relates to Building, which will enable those designing buildings, builders, and all those in difficulty, to see at once what they must do to comply with the Act. If wishing to read the exact words at length in the Act itself, they will see that the Sections and Sub-sections are given which will enable them to do so.

Second, the coloured Plates Nos. 1 to 12, showing the thicknesses of all the walls, and enabling the reader at a glance to see the thickness of the wall required for any building under this Act.

NOTE.—This is even more necessary than before, because in this Act the thicknesses are not set out in any Schedule.

Third, the coloured Plates Nos. 13 to 19, which explain

Recesses, Chimneys and Flues in Party and External Walls, Chimneys and Hearths. The method of continuing Party Wall when Lantern Light occurs in roof. Section and plan of room in roof, showing the smallest height the Act permits. Diagram to illustrate the novel feature in the Act as to providing space at the rear of domestic buildings, and a section to illustrate Shop Front and Cornice projections.

Fourth, the existing Byelaws. These have not been repealed (see Section 216 of this Act).

Fifth, all portions of the existing Acts, so far as they relate to building, which are unrepealed by this Act and which are therefore still in force, are given *in extenso*.

Sixth, the Introduction, setting out briefly the differences between the expiring Act and this Act.

Lastly, the Table of Contents and the Index, which are, I think, complete, and will readily enable the reader to turn to what he requires.

BANISTER FLETCHER.

29 New Bridge Street, Ludgate Circus, E.C.
1st December 1894.

CONTENTS.

ABSTRACT

of that portion of the London Building Act, 1894, *relating to Building.*

TABLE	PAGE
1. Recesses and openings	3
2. Timbers in external and party walls and bressummers	3, 4
3. External walls	4, 5
4. Party walls	5, 6
5. Roofs	6
6. Chimneys and flues	7–9
7. Furnace chimney shafts	9
8. Close fires and pipes	9, 10
9. Accesses and stairs	10, 11
10. Habitable rooms	11, 12
11. Party arches over public ways	12
12. Arches under public ways	13
13. Projections	13–15
14. Separation of buildings and cubical extent	15, 16
15. Rules as to uniting buildings	16, 17
16. Additions and alterations	17
17. Conversion of buildings	17
18. Public buildings	18
19. Exempted buildings, land and hoardings	18–20
20. Fire-resisting materials	20
21. Dwelling houses on low-lying land	21
22. Open spaces about buildings	21–26
23. Heights of Buildings	27, 28

THE LONDON BUILDING ACT, 1894.

Preamble.

Part I.—Introductory.

	SEC.
Short title	1
Division of Act into Parts	2
Commencement of Act	3
Extent of Act	4
Definitions	5

Part II.—Formation and Widening of Streets.

As to making streets	6
Sanction to formation of new streets	7
Evidence of commencement of street	8
Grounds for refusal to sanction plans of streets	9
Adaptation of ways for streets	10
Grounds for refusing to sanction adaptation of ways for streets	11
Greater width of street may be required in certain cases	12
Position of new buildings with reference to streets	13
Notice to comply with preceding section	14
As to compensation in certain cases	15
As to erection of buildings at less than prescribed distance from centre of ways not being highways	16
Sanction to construction of new buildings at less than prescribed distance	17
Regulations to be printed and supplied	18
Appeal	19
As to private roads laid out by a railway company	20
Exempting certain School Board buildings	21

Part III.—Lines of Building Frontage.

Mode of proceeding with regard to buildings beyond line of street	22
Buildings projecting beyond general line when taken down to be set back	23
Notices of definition of general line	24
Appeal against certificate of architect as to general line	25
Conditions may be attached to consent to building in front of general line	26

CONTENTS.

	SEC.
Consent not to affect rest of general line	27
Effect of conditions	28
Defining in what street or way a building or structure is situate	29
Part of Act not to apply in City	30
Certain powers of railway companies not affected by this Part of Act	31

PART IV.—NAMING AND NUMBERING OF STREETS.

Notice of new name of street	32
Affixing names of streets by Local Authority	33
Altering names of streets	34
Notice of altering names of streets	35
Numbering houses	36
Power to Council to name and number streets in default of Local Authority complying with order	37
Register to be kept of alterations in names of streets	38

PART V.—OPEN SPACES ABOUT BUILDINGS, AND HEIGHT OF BUILDINGS.

Meaning of "domestic building" in this Part of Act	39
Light and ventilation of habitable basements	40
Space at rear of domestic buildings—	
Domestic buildings abutting on new streets	41
Domestic buildings abutting on old streets	41
Open space to be provided about certain buildings not on the public way	42
Saving for certain domestic buildings on old sites	43
Laying out of new streets on cleared area	44
Courts within a building	45
Superintending architect may define front or rear of buildings	46
Height of buildings limited	47
Procedure where greater height allowed	48
Heights of buildings in certain cases	49
Raising of buildings so as to comply with provisions of Act as to habitable rooms	50
As to re-erection of certain working-class dwellings of Local Authority	51
Saving for certain domestic buildings with stables in the rear	52

Part VI.—Construction of Buildings.

	SEC.
Structure and thickness of walls	53
Rules as to recesses and openings	54
Rules as to timbers in external walls	55
Rules as to bressummers	56
Heights and thicknesses of parapets to external works	57
Cases in which a wall to be deemed a party wall	58
Heights of party walls above roofs	59
Rules as to chases in party walls	60
Rules as to construction of roofs	61
Storeys in roofs	62
Means of escape at top of high buildings	63
Rules as to chimneys and flues	64
Furnace chimney shafts	65
Rules as to close fires and pipes for conveying vapour, &c.	66
Floors above furnaces and ovens	67
Rules as to recesses and stairs in certain buildings	68
Ventilation of staircases	69
Rules as to habitable rooms	70
Rules as to party arches over public ways	71
Rules as to arches under public ways	72
Rules as to projections	73
Separation of buildings	74
Cubical extent of buildings	75
Consent to larger dimensions	76
Rules as to uniting buildings	77
Construction of public buildings	78
Conversion of houses, &c. in public buildings	79
Staircases in churches and chapels	80
Application of Act to buildings under railway arches	81

Part VII.—Special and Temporary Buildings and Wooden Structures.

Application to Council for buildings to which rules of Act are inapplicable	82
Control by Council of certain temporary buildings	83
Wooden structures not to be erected without license of Council	84
Piles of loose timber not regarded as structures	85
As to structures of railway companies	86

CONTENTS.

Part VIII.—Rights of Building and Adjoining Owners.

	SEC.
Rights of owners of adjoining lands respecting erection of walls on line of junction	87
Rights of building owners	88
Rights of adjoining owners	89
Rules as to exercise of rights by building and adjoining owners	90
Settlement of difference between building and adjoining owners	91
Power for building owner to enter premises	92
Building owner to underpin adjoining owner's building	93
Security to be given by building owner and adjoining owner	94
Rules as to expenses in respect to party structures	95
Account of expenses to be delivered to adjoining owner	96
Adjoining owner may object to account	97
Building owner may recover if no appeal made	98
Structure to belong to building owner until contribution paid	99
Adjoining owner liable to expenses incurred on his requisition	100
Saving for lights in party walls, &c.	101

Part IX.—Dangerous and Neglected Structures.

Dangerous Structures.

Meaning of structure	102
Survey to be made of dangerous structures	103
Effect of this Part of Act within the City	104
Surveyor to give certificate	105
Notice to be given to owner in respect of certificate	106
Proceedings to enforce compliance with notice	107
Court may make order notwithstanding arbitration	108
Expenses	109
Provisions respecting sale of dangerous structures	110
If proceeds insufficient, land not to be built on till balance paid	111
Recovery of expenses	112
Fees to surveyor	113
Power to remove inmates from dangerous structure	114

Neglected Structures.

Removal of dilapidated and neglected buildings	115

CONTENTS.

Supplemental as to Dangerous and Neglected Structures.

	SEC.
Provision for enforcing repayment of expenses incurred by Council	116
Fees on dangerous or neglected structures to Council	117

Part X.—Dangerous and Noxious Businesses.

Regulations for building near dangerous business	118
Regulations for building near noxious business	119
Provisions as to certain old noxious businesses (Metropolitan Building Act, 1844, Secs. 54 to 58)	120
Saving for gas-works and distilleries	121

Part XI.—Dwelling-Houses on Low-Lying Land.

Dwelling houses on low-lying land	122
Power to make regulations	123
Publication and copies of regulations	124

Part XII.—Sky Signs.

Sky signs	125
District Surveyor to act for purposes of this Act	126
Prohibition of future sky signs	127
Regulations of existing sky signs	128
Renewal of license	129
Alteration of sky signs to meet surveyor's requirements	130
Notice of refusal of certificate to be sent to the Council	131
Appeal against refusal of certificate	132
Forfeiture of license	133
Removal of sky signs	134
Application of this Part of Act within the City	135

Part XIII.—Superintending Architect and District Surveyors.

Power for Council to appoint Superintending Architect	136
Power of Superintending Architect to appoint deputy	137
Buildings to be supervised by District Surveyors	138
Powers of Council as to surveyors and districts	139
Examination of candidates for office of surveyor	140
Surveyor to have an office	141

CONTENTS. xiii

SEC.

Power of surveyor to appoint deputy 142
Power to appoint assistant surveyor.. 143
Surveyor not to act in case of works under his professional
   superintendence 144
Notices to be given to surveyor by builder 145
Surveyor to enforce execution of Act 146
Notice to be evidence of intended works 147
Power of entry to inspect buildings 148
In case of emergency, works to be commenced without notice 149
As to service of notice of objection on builder or building
   owner 150
Notice by surveyor in case of irregularity 151
Notice of irregularity after completion of building 152
Summary proceedings on non-compliance with notice .. 153
Payments to surveyors for ordinary and special services .. 154
Council to pay District Surveyor in relation to formation of
   streets, &c. 155
Fees in relation to evidence before tribunal 156
Periods when surveyors entitled to fees 157
Power of Council to pay salaries to surveyors 158
Council may proceed on behalf of District Surveyor 159

Returns by District Surveyors.

Monthly returns by District Surveyor to Council 160
Return to be a certificate that works are in accordance with
   Act 161
Audit of accounts of fees charged by District Surveyor .. 162
District Surveyor to notify certain irregularities to the
   Council 163

PART XIV.—BYELAWS.

Power to Council to make byelaws 164
Saving for the City of London 165

PART XV.—LEGAL PROCEEDINGS.

Summary proceedings for offences, &c., and recovery of
   penalties 166
Proceedings by surveyor 167
Powers of and appeal from County Court 168

xiv   CONTENTS.

	SEC.
Application of penalties	169
Council may demolish buildings and sell materials, and recover expenses	170
Procedure by local authorities in case of buildings in advance of general line	171
Payment of surplus of proceeds into court	172
Payment of expenses by owners	173
As to periods for giving consents, &c. expiring in vacations	174

Tribunal of Appeal.

Constitution and powers of tribunal of appeal	175
Duration of office	176
Removal of members	177
Vacancies to be supplied	178
Remuneration of members of tribunal	179
Officers, &c. of tribunal	180
Powers for Council to support decisions of officers before tribunal	181
Tribunal may state case for opinion of High Court	182
Procedure of tribunal	183
Regulations as to procedure and fees	184
Enforcement of decision of tribunal	185
Fees, &c. to be paid to Council—expenses	186

Notices.

Notices to be in writing	187
Service of notices	188

Part XVI.—Miscellaneous.

Expenses, how borne	189
Power for Council to annex conditions	190
As to buildings of historical interest	191
Power of entry to owner, &c. to execute work	192
Limitation of time for proceedings where notice not given	193
Plans and documents to be property of Council	194
Mode of giving approval of Council to plans	195
Consent, how given on behalf of owners not to be found	196
Storing of wood and timber	197
Removal of roof not to affect proceedings	198
Preventing obstructions in streets	199

CONTENTS.

OFFENCES AGAINST ACT.

	SEC.
Offences against Act	200

APPLICATION OF ACT.

Buildings exempt from Parts of Act	201
Exemption of Government buildings	202
As to buildings for the supply of electricity	203
Exempting lands, buildings and property of Inns of Court ..	204
Saving existing rights of gas companies	205
Duration of exemption	206
Buildings not to be altered so as not to conform to Act	207
When remainder of party wall, &c. to be taken down	208
Additions to, and alterations of buildings	209
Application of Act to buildings erected before commencement of Act	210
Rules as to conversion of buildings	211
Buildings in progress	212
Saving powers of local authorities	213

REPEAL.

Repeal of Section 50 of " Metropolitan Railway Act, 1866 "..	214
Repeal of enactments in Schedule	215
Securities, byelaws, &c. under repealed Acts to remain in force	216
Saving for existing officers	217
References in Acts or documents to repealed Acts to be read as referring to this Act	218

SCHEDULES.

1st *Schedule—Preliminary to Parts* 1 *and* 2.

	PAGES
Part 1. Buildings not public, and not of the warehouse class	153–156
Part 2. Buildings of the warehouse class	157–160

2nd *Schedule.*

Character of materials	160, 161

xvi   CONTENTS.

3rd Schedule.

Part 1. Fees payable to District Surveyors, on new buildings, alterations, additions or other work, on chimneys and flues, on certifying plans, on wooden and temporary structures, on attending court 161–163

Part 2. Fees payable to District Surveyors on dangerous structures 163, 164

Part 3. Fees payable to District Surveyors for special services 164

Part 4. Fees payable to Council on dangerous structures, dilapidated or neglected buildings or structures, regulations 165, 166

4th Schedule.

Acts repealed and part repealed 166, 167

THE FOLLOWING SECTIONS OF VARIOUS ACTS, WHICH RELATE TO BUILDING, ARE STILL IN FORCE.

THE METROPOLIS MANAGEMENT ACT, 1855, 18 & 19 VICT. c. 120.

SEC.   PAGE
LXXI. Gullyholes, &c. to be trapped 168
LXXIII. Vestry or District Board in certain cases may compel owners, &c. of houses to construct drains into the common sewer. Penalty on owner, &c. for neglect 168
LXXIV. Provision for combined drainage of blocks of houses 169
LXXV. No house to be built without drains constructed to the satisfaction of the Vestry or District Board 170
LXXVI. Notice of buildings to be given to the Vestry or District Board before commencing the same 170
LXXVII. Power to branch drains into sewers constructed by Metropolitan Board, or any Vestry or District Board, under certain regulations. Penalty 171
LXXXII. Power for Vestries and District Boards to authorise inspection of drains, privies and cesspools 172
LXXXV. Vestry or District Board to cause drains, &c. to be put into proper condition, &c. where necessary 172

CONTENTS.

SEC.   PAGE
CI. Vaults and cellars under streets not to be made without the consent of the Vestry or Board 172
CII. Vaults, &c. under streets to be repaired by owners or occupiers 173
CV. Provisions for paving new streets 173
CXIX. Owners, &c. to remove future projections, on notice from Vestry or District Board. Penalty for neglect 174
CXX. Vestry or District Board may remove existing projections, and make compensation for the same 174
CXXI. Hoards to be erected during repairs. Penalty on not erecting hoards 175
CXXII. No hoard to be erected without license from Vestry or District Board 175
CXXIII. If hoard be erected, or materials be deposited in any manner otherwise than to the satisfaction of the Vestry or District Board, the same may be removed 176

BYELAWS.

CCII. Power to Metropolitan Board of Works to make byelaws. Penalty for breach of byelaws. Power to Justices to remit penalties 177
CCIII. Publication of byelaws. Evidence of byelaws 177
CCIV. Buildings not to be made over sewers without consent 178

THE METROPOLIS LOCAL MANAGEMENT ACTS AMENDMENT ACT, 1862, 25 & 26 Vict. c. 102.

LXI. Regulations respecting openings into sewers 179
LXIV. Where parties neglect to carry out works pursuant to order of Vestry, the Vestry may recover penalty or do the works 180
LXVI. Temporary provision for drainage of property where no proper sewer within 200 feet 181
LXVIII. Penalty on persons placing buildings or encroachments on sewers 181
LXIX. Penalty on persons interfering with sewers 182
LXXXVIII. Persons omitting to give notice required by Section 76 of 18 & 19 Vict. c. 120, liable to penalty 183
XCVI. Vestry or District Board may require payment of costs or expenses from owner or occupier, and occupier

SEC.		PAGE
	paying to deduct from rent. Agreements between landlord and tenant not to be affected	183
XCVII.	Deduction by owner paying rent where amount of expenses deducted from rent paid to him	184

THE METROPOLIS MANAGEMENT AND BUILDING ACTS AMENDMENT ACT, 1878, 41 & 42 Vict. c. 32.

I., II., III.	Preliminary	187
V.	Metropolis Management Acts and this part of Act to be construed as one Act	187
XI.	Power to Board in certain cases to require proprietors of theatres and certain music halls in use at the time of the passing of this Act to remedy structural defects	187
XII.	Power to Board to make regulations with respect to new theatres and certain new music halls for protection from fire	189
XIII.	Provisional license for new premises	190
XXI.	Power for architect and persons authorised by Board and District Surveyor to enter and inspect theatres, music halls, buildings and works	190
XXII.	Power to owners, &c. to enter houses, &c. to comply with notices or order .. .. :	191
XXIII.	Recovery of penalties	191
XXIV.	Exceptions from Metropolis Management Act extended to this Act	191
XXVI.	Act not to apply to the Inner and Middle Temple, &c.	192
XXVII.	Saving rights of the Crown and the Duchy of Lancaster	192

THE LONDON COUNCIL (GENERAL POWERS ACT), 1890.

XXXII.	Notice to be given to Vestry or District Board, of building or demolishing any house, building or wall	193

THE METROPOLIS MANAGEMENT AMENDMENT ACT, 1890, 53 & 54 Vict. c. 66.

I., II.	Preliminary	195
III.	Power to Vestry or District Board to repair a road or way, not being a street	195

CONTENTS.

SEC.		PAGE
IV.	Penalty for making sewers contrary to plans approved ..	196
V.	Penalty in case of connections with local sewers	197
VI.	Subsoil under a street, road, passage or way not to be removed without the consent of the Vestry or District Board or Council	198
VII.	Surveyor or other officer to see that conditions are observed	200
VIII.	Limited application of Act to City of London	200
IX.	Penalties and expenses	200
X.	Expenses of Act	200

THE PUBLIC HEALTH (LONDON) ACT, 1891,
54 & 55 Vict. c. 76.

XCVI. Provisions as to the occupation of underground rooms as dwellings 201
XCVII. Enforcement of provisions as to underground rooms 203
XCVIII. Provisions in case of two convictions for unlawfully occupying underground room 204

THE FACTORY AND WORKSHOP ACT, 1891,
54 & 55 Vict. c. 75.

VII. Provision against fire 205

LONDON COUNTY COUNCIL.
BYELAWS AND REGULATIONS IN FORCE.

BYELAWS MADE UNDER SECTION XVI. OF THE METROPOLIS MANAGEMENT AND BUILDING ACTS AMENDMENT ACT, 1878.

	PAGE
Repeal of previous byelaws	207
Foundations and sites of buildings	207
Description and quality of the substances of walls ..	208, 209
Duties of District Surveyors	209
Fees to be paid to District Surveyors	209, 210
Deposit of plans and sections	210
Penalties and dispensation	210, 211

BYELAWS UNDER SECTION XXXI. OF THE LONDON COUNCIL (GENERAL POWERS) ACT, 1890.

	PAGE
Description and quality of the substances of which plastering to be made	212
As to the mode in which and the materials with which any excavation outside the site of a building is to be filled up	212, 213
Duties of District Surveyors	213
Fees to be paid to District Surveyors	213
Penalties	213

THE METROPOLIS MANAGEMENT AND BUILDING ACTS AMENDMENT ACT, 1878. REGULATIONS MADE BY THE COUNCIL ON THE 9th FEBRUARY 1892.

Limits of regulations	214
Interpretation of " such premises "	214

PART I.—STRUCTURAL.

Applications and drawings	214, 215
Site	215
Windows overlooking site	216
Walls	216
Dressing rooms	216
No theatre under or over any other building	216
Number of tiers	217
Height of tiers	217
Floor of pit	217
Entrances and exits	217
Vestibules	217
Proscenium wall	217, 218
Proscenium opening	218
Roof over stage	218
Corridors, passages and staircases	218, 219
Staircases	219
Gangways	219
Ironwork	219
Workshops, &c.	219, 220

CONTENTS.

	PAGE
Limelight tanks, boilers and dynamos	220
Scene dock	220
Enclosures	220
Skylights	220
Gas	221
Doors and fastenings	221, 222
Ventilation	222
Warming	222, 223
Water supply	223
Addition or alteration to premises	223, 224

PART II.—GENERAL.

Oil or candle lamps	224
Fire alarm	224
Notices	224
Precautions against fire	224, 225

PART III.—ELECTRIC LIGHTING.

Certificate	225
Circuits	225
Conductors	225, 226
Conductors, fixing and protection	226, 227
External conductors	227
Switches, cut-outs, &c.	227, 228
Resistances	228
Arc lamps	228
Stage lighting	228, 229
Stage switchboard	229
Generating plant	229, 230
Batteries	230
Transformers	230
Insulation resistance	230
Supervision	230
Plan of wiring	231

PART IV.—POWER TO MODIFY OR DISPENSE WITH THESE REGULATIONS.

Person responsible	231

REGULATIONS MADE BY THE COUNCIL ON THE 23RD NOVEMBER 1894, UNDER THE LONDON BUILDING ACT, 1894.

                                                      PAGE

I.—GENERAL 232

II.—PARTICULARS AS TO DRAWINGS REQUIRED IN EACH CASE.

New streets, &c. 233
Buildings within prescribed distances, lines of frontage, &c... 233
Space at rear of domestic buildings, and open space about working-class dwellings not on the public way 234
Open space at rear of domestic buildings on old sites 234
Laying out new streets on a cleared area 234
Height of buildings 234
Timber in external walls, and furnace chimney shafts 235
Projections 235
Additional cubical extent, and buildings for the supply of electricity 235
Special and temporary buildings and wooden structures .. 235
Naming of streets and numbering of houses 236

BYELAWS MADE UNDER SECTION 39 (1) OF THE PUBLIC HEALTH (LONDON) ACT, 1891.

With respect to water-closets, earth-closets, privies, ash-pits, cesspools, and receptacles for dung, and the proper accessories thereof, in connection with buildings, whether constructed before or after the passing of this Act 238–250

INDEX 251–267

LIST OF PLATES.

BUILDINGS NOT PUBLIC AND NOT OF THE WAREHOUSE CLASS.

		PAGE
1.	{Up to 25 feet high / 25 „ 40 „}	153
2.	40 „ 50 „	154
3.	{50 „ 60 „ / 60 „ 70 „}	154
4.	{70 „ 80 „ / 80 „ 90 „}	155
5.	{90 „ 100 „ / 100 „ 120 „}	155, 156
6.	Cross Wall. Comparison as to thickness with external or party wall	160

WAREHOUSE WALLS.

7.	{Up to 25 feet high / 25 „ 30 „ / 30 „ 40 „}	157
8.	40 „ 50 „	157
9.	{50 „ 60 „ / 60 „ 70 „}	157, 158
10.	{70 „ 80 „ / 80 „ 90 „}	158
11.	{90 „ 100 „ / 100 „ 120 „}	158, 159
12.	Cross Wall. Comparison as to thickness with external or party wall	160
13.	Recesses in external and party walls, and chases in party walls	65
14.	Lantern light showing nearest position to party wall	68

LIST OF PLATES.

		PAGE
15.	Chimneys and flues in external and party walls	70
16.	Shows the least height permitted by the Act for habitable rooms wholly or partly in the roof	74
17.	Greatest projections of shop fronts and cornices in front of external wall of the building to which it belongs	77
18.	Exempted private buildings	144
19.	Illustration as to Section 41. Back yards	55

INTRODUCTION.

It is desirable shortly to mention the new provisions and to point out the leading differences between the expiring Acts and this new London Building Act, which comes into force on the 1st January next, so that those that have not followed the Bill during its progress through Parliament may have set before them some idea of the scope of the Act and the alterations. I propose doing this as briefly as possible, considering that to burden one's mind with the changes is not so successful a method of learning the new Act as studying the Act itself. I commend, therefore, the Abstract, to which I have given much consideration, and the accompanying diagrams, to the earnest attention of my readers.

The definitions have ever been the stumbling block of Acts of Parliament, and it is curious that although in this Act the definitions are much improved, we have not amongst them one of "what is a building." To show how difficult is a definition of a building, I need only quote the case of Stevens v. Gourley, which came before the magistrates, and on appeal before Chief Justice Erle and Justices Williams and Biles. That the arguments in the appeal case occupy thirteen pages of my work on the Metropolitan Building Acts serves to show the extreme difficulty of definitions. It is true that in the Bill *an attempt to define* "a building" was made, but I think this definition was struck out during its progress through Parliament. Why will not our legal friends face the difficulty rather than leave the matter open, which must

Definitions.

lead to disputes and litigations? Is it fair of the legal profession to shirk definitions, and thus leave us laymen to fight over the "*expressions*" in courts of law?

As proof that definitions can be made clear and not liable to be misunderstood, take number 26 in this Act. Here we have a definition so worded that there is no question. It includes every building that can be erected except two, which are defined in Nos. 27 and 28.

Definition 37 explains the expression "inhabited."

Definition 38 explains the expression "habitable" as a room constructed or adapted to be inhabited.

<small>Centre of roadway.</small> With regard to centre of roadways, I notice one of the professional journals does not seem to appreciate the centre remaining, notwithstanding that the *actual* centre of the roadway may have become altered by reason of the roadway having been widened on one side only, or on both sides to an unequal extent. That it should remain appears to me of much value in preventing the active owner from loss of his proper advantage. For example, the owner on either side of a road 20 feet wide, if the widening is required for carriage traffic, would have to set back each 10 feet, and therefore each owner, whom we will call respectively A and B, loses 10 feet in the depth of his land. Now, assume A desires to have a 50-feet road, and he sets back from the centre of the roadway 25 feet. B, without this regulation, need only set back 5 feet instead of 10 feet, and thus, to give a road 40 feet wide, gains 5 feet in the depth of his land; and so by delay gains an advantage and prevents A obtaining the advantage he desired. It is this difficulty which absolutely calls for a difference of position between the *legal* and *geometrical* centre of the road.

<small>Gradient.</small> The fixing of a gradient is, I think, extremely good. This is given in section 9, sub-section 6.

<small>Power of Council to vary rules.</small> I strongly dislike the power the Council have taken to vary the rules. Take as an example section 17. You will find the Council may sanction "the erection of any

building or structure at any less distance than the prescribed distance from the centre of the roadway, not being a 'highway.'"

Speaking in the discussion at a meeting of the Royal Institute of British Architects, I said, "I would call attention to a most objectionable phrase in the Bill—'the Council may permit.' The whole Bill bristled with permissions to avoid every clause in it."

I strongly advise the Council to get rid of this power as far as possible by formulating fixed rules and regulations, so that one set of rules and regulations may apply to all.

Section 9, sub-section 4, will, I think, prevent the formation in the future of circular or crescent roadways, having each end communicating with the same street. There has been much litigation, and the words now used, "laying out the same to afford direct communication between two streets," will probably prevent any question arising in the future.

The District Surveyor has more power under this Act with regard to bressummers, and it is the first time that I remember any allowance being set out for expansion of metal in a Building Act.

The bearing of 4 inches is important, because, in dealing with long wooden beams, if the builder insist on his right of only giving 4 inches, as the Act permits, the District Surveyor can, if he thinks it insufficient, require additional storey-posts or iron columns, &c. The builders, therefore, will be very willing to give sufficient bearing for safety.

In the discussion at the Royal Institute of British Architects, Mr. H. H. Statham produced a diagram showing the effect that the new restriction as to projections of cornices to only 2 feet 6 inches over the public way would have, supposing one desired to build a house with a cornice of the same projection as the Strozzi Palace, and undoubtedly his diagram was convincing that the limitation of the projection would seriously interfere with the cornices in Classic and Renaissance architecture. The restriction has now become law, and the only way a greater projection can be obtained is by setting back the front walls or obtaining the consent of the Council.

Cubical extent of warehouse buildings.

There is a slight alteration in the area permitted as to the cubic contents of warehouse buildings. It is extended from 216,000 to 250,000 cubic feet.

The new Act in clause 76 gives power to the Council (where the Superintending Architect and the Chief Officer of the Fire Brigade advise favourably) to consent, under certain conditions, to each building containing additional cubical extent; but there is a proviso that such consent shall continue in force only while the said building is actually used for the purposes of the trade or manufacture in respect of which the consent was granted.

Wood cornices, barge boards.

More latitude in the use of combustible materials is permitted by the relaxation of the provisions in the expiring Act. Under the new Act cornices and bargeboards of wood are permitted.

Openings to roof.

A new requirement is that buildings exceeding 30 feet high, used as dwellings or factories, and having a parapet, are to be provided with a dormer window or door opening on to roof, and a trap-door with proper step ladder or other proper means of access to the roof.

This requirement cannot be demanded, apparently, where there is no parapet.

Storeys in roofs.

The new Act limits the number of storeys in the roof, so that buildings like the Grosvenor Hotel cannot be repeated, and it has a provision that where the storey is above 60 feet from the street level it may not have a boarded floor, if constructed in the roof, but the upper surface of the floor shall be of fire-resisting materials.

Inclination of roofs.

The old rule as to the angle of inclination of roofs of the warehouse kind continues.

A novel feature in the Act is the fixing of an angle of inclination of roofs of other buildings; they must not incline upwards at a greater angle than 75°. This limitation does not, however, apply to towers, spires and turrets.

This Act recognises for the first time a separation of buildings by other means than party walls. It permits the separation by a party structure, and a reference to the definition shows that party structure may be a party wall, or a partition, floor or other structure, separating vertically or horizontally buildings, &c. Some district surveyors have permitted this as an interpretation of a party wall under the expiring Act, but it is very desirable to have all doubt removed by clause 74 and definition in section 5, sub-section 20. The same section 74 requires that the dwelling house shall be divided from the shop or trade portion in every building exceeding ten squares in area. *Separation of buildings.*

The rules with regard to separate sets of chambers in one building, are made more stringent, by making the area commence at 2500 square feet instead of 3500. *Chamber section.*

Section No. 75 permits one-storey buildings beyond the two-mile radius of St. Paul's to have any cubical contents, provided they are used for certain purposes. *One-storey buildings.*

The uses to which such buildings may be put are very limited (see Abstract, page 10).

The provisions as to chimneys and flues are practically the same as in the expiring Act. The only concession made is in following the same lines as building on a bressummer. If chimneys be so built, the work must be done to the satisfaction of the District Surveyor. *Chimneys and flues.*

One important alteration is set forth in the section that prevents the use of ordinary flues for trade purposes.

The provision as to marking flues, where a wall is likely to be built against, is probably useful, but I have never found any difficulty in getting this done.

One added security against smoke and fire is the provision set out in section 64, sub-section 6, that all flues are to be rendered on their outside face when passing through floor or roof. This will entail some additional expense, as the quantity of rendering through roof portion will sometimes be considerable.

Chimney openings. The backs of chimney openings can be 4½ inches in walls other than party walls (section 20, sub-section 7 of the expiring Act). The new Act has no provision.

Thickness of hearth. There is a slight reduction in the thickness of hearth, from 7 inches to 6 inches. This cannot increase the risk of fire, whilst it may give an advantage from a constructive point of view.

Chimney stacks and shafts. Another alteration is that this Act requires that the top six courses of the stack or shaft are to be built in cement. This will be most useful in maintaining the stability of the chimney shaft, and also the stability of those too often added deformities, called tall-boys, wind-guards and cowls, because they will be bedded in the courses of brickwork in cement.

The Act relieves the Council of the labour of fixing the thickness and tapering of the shafts. These are set forth in the Act. The height of the chimney shaft is limited by the width or circumference of the base (see Abstract, page 9). Many existing shafts if condemned could not be rebuilt to their present height without increasing their width at the base. I mention this to show that the present requirements will give a certainty of more substantial building.

Hollow walls. The provision with regard to "hollow walls" is likely to prevent them being built, because the wall one side of the hollow space must be of the full thickness prescribed by the Act, and therefore the hollow wall will have to be just a wall of the thickness shown in the diagrams I have given, *plus* the hollow space, *plus* the outer casing.

Recesses. The variation that no recess shall come within 13½ inches, instead of 12 inches in the old Act, is wise, as it makes a "brick measurement" of it.

An important alteration is that under the new Act there is apparently no limitation as to the quantity of openings and recesses on the *ground floor storey*. This is a most important concession, and removes a great difficulty as to shop premises. It has been contended by a professional writer that this clause might be read to mean that there shall be no openings or recesses on the ground floor storey, but I think the common-sense reading will be sure to be adopted by the courts.

This Act sets out the structural method of arching recesses which are deeper than 5 inches. It says the arching shall be by not less than two rings in brickwork the full depth of the recess in party walls, and thus defines the method more clearly than the old Act, which only said "arched over."

There is a novelty in the Act which permits recesses under 5 inches deep. These may be *corbelled* out in brickwork or stonework.

There is an exemption of hoardings from the Act, where they are placed around vacant land, provided such hoarding shall not exceed 12 feet in height. The difficulty that some anticipate is that these hoardings may be kept up after the land is occupied. This, I think, cannot arise, as the wording of the exemption is quite clear. Hoardings

A relaxation of the strict rule as to sheds I consider of much advantage to small traders. It is that "open sheds not exceeding 4 squares in area may be constructed of any substance, and in any manner approved by the District Surveyor." Sheds.

The Act gives increased height to dwelling rooms. Instead of 7 feet it must now be 8 feet 6 inches. With regard to the height of rooms in roofs one foot is added, making it 8 feet instead of 7 feet. Dwelling houses.

The Act is silent with regard to the size of lantern lights (see the last paragraph of sub-sec. *c* of sec. 70). This is wise, because a very small area is sufficient, and it is best to leave that area to the builder's discretion, otherwise it might interfere with his getting a good watertight roof. Lantern lights.

The requirement for ventilation is sufficient; it is that

the part which shall open shall be equal to one-twentieth part of the floor space.

Underground rooms.
I think it is wise that the restrictions as regards underground rooms are to be continued. I have seen a complaint that the Act has omitted to state the amount of the penalty. This is not so. It is not mentioned in section 70, sub-section 2, but it is given in section 200, sub-section 11 (*j*).

There is a Section in the Act requiring ventilation under the lowest floor, unless it be a solid wood floor on concrete.

Size of windows.
The novel provisions as to the sizes of windows to rooms (other than those in the basement) can scarcely be considered necessary, because it is the custom to build these rooms with sufficient window space. However, the requirements will have this advantage, that they will inform the builder what is considered the smallest windows he ought to make.

Windows in roofs.
The regulations with regard to the windows in the roof I think are decidedly necessary; for too often one has found windows too near the floor, solely because of the elevation; no doubt the elevation must and should give way to good sanitary planning, but I fail to see why the elevation need therefore be less well proportioned.

Classification of walls.
The change of classification of walls is an advantage. Walls classed in the expiring Act as dwelling-house walls are now described as "walls of buildings not public and not of the warehouse class." The new Act, therefore, has this advantage, that it defines the walls for *every* building.

Thicknesses of walls. Buildings not public and not of the warehouse class.
In walls of buildings, not public and not of the warehouse class, up to 40 feet, one division is left out, and we have left, the sections up to 25 feet high, and from 25 feet up to 40 feet high. This appears to me a distinct advantage.

Although it is to be wished that the $8\frac{1}{2}$-inch walls had disappeared, at least for external walls, it is an advantage that the 8½-inch thickness is limited to storeys in a wall up to 25 feet high, and to one storey up to the height of 40 feet.

Taking the next height—40 feet to 50 feet—we still have the 8½ inches thick up to 30 feet in length, but the basement or lowest storey is increased to 17½ inches thick. The 8½-inch wall disappears where the length is above 30 feet.

Dealing with the next height—50 feet to 60 feet—I think it a distinct advantage that only two sections are required instead of three, and the way it is done is good. The length up to 30 feet is omitted, such length being increased to 45 feet; therefore, instead of "up to 30 feet," "from 30 feet to 50 feet," and "above 50 feet," we have the simpler formula "up to" 45 feet and "above."

In the next height—60 feet to 70 feet—the same rule applies: two sections instead of three. The old Act being "up to 40 feet," and "40 feet to 55 feet and above 55 feet;" now "up to" 45 feet and "above."

Passing on to 70 feet to 80 feet in height, the same method is continued, and we have simply two sections of walls, with the slight thickening of one storey above 45 feet, three storeys instead of two of 17½ inches work. The old thickness for walls 40 feet long is increased in thickness for one storey to 17½ inches for walls 45 feet long, above this length there is also a slight increase in the thickness of the old wall above 60 feet long.

With regard to the next height—80 feet to 90 feet— exactly the same treatment occurs, omitting one section, retaining, however, the first division, as in the expiring Act, namely up to 45 feet, with an increase of thickness on the ground storey. The thickness for walls above 45 feet is increasing each storey 4½ inches, excepting the two topmost storeys.

From 90 feet to 100 feet the same reduction occurs, to two sections (instead of three). The first limitation in length being similar to the present, viz. 45 feet, increasing base storey to 26 inches thick, and increasing the storey next but one above to 21½ inches. The diminished thickness is given at the top of these walls.

From 100 feet to 120 feet in height the thicknesses of walls are now given, which were not given in the expiring Act.

Thicknesses of walls of public buildings.

The thicknesses of walls of public buildings are not defined in the Schedule, nor were they in the Act now expiring. They are to be built to the satisfaction of the District Surveyor, as now; the only difference is that instead of the appeal being to the Council, it is to be made to the new tribunal.

Warehouse walls.

Warehouse walls up to 25 feet, and from 25 feet to 30 feet, remain as in the expiring Act.

From 30 feet to 0 feet high, the only variation is the extension of length in the first to 35 feet, and the reduction of the second thickness of walling to 45 feet in length, making the thickest wall begin at 45 feet in length, instead of 60 feet as formerly.

Walls 40 feet to 50 feet high are practically thickened, because the length of the first wall is reduced to 30 feet, the second wall to 45 feet (instead of 70 feet), and the unlimited length begins at 45 feet.

From 50 feet to 60 feet high the number of sections is reduced from three to two; the first thickness being for walls up to 45 feet, the second above, and practically the lighter section wall is abandoned.

Walls 60 feet to 70 feet high are similarly treated. There are two sections instead of three, the lighter section wall being again abandoned.

In walls of 70 feet to 80 feet high the third section is again abandoned; but curiously enough the section abandoned is not the thinner, but the thickest, namely, that with 30 inches at its base.

Walls 80 feet to 90 feet high also have only two sections given instead of three, and here the thickest section is abandoned.

In walls 90 feet to 100 feet high we have again only two sections, the abandoned section being the thickest wall, namely, 34 inches at its base.

For walls up to 120 feet high the new table gives the thickness for walls, length up to 45 feet, as was formerly that up to 100 feet (length unlimited). It also gives the thickness for a wall the same height but above 45 feet.

There is a novelty which applies to the section of all walls where the length is 45 feet, or greater, which is that the increased thickness may be distributed in piers according to the Schedule.

The next very important alteration is the yard space, and a novel feature is the introduction of the diagonal line, limiting the height of buildings according to the depth of the back yard. Before the Bill became an Act of Parliament this diagonal line was very much discussed. It was proposed to have an angle of 45 degrees, which would have reduced the heights of buildings to a much greater extent than the angle finally adopted, which is 63½ degrees. *Yard space.*

A reference to the diagram (Plate 19) will show that where the builder desires to take full advantage of his land, and builds therefore to the extreme limit permitted by the Act, all the upper rooms will be reduced in depth. I expressed my views with regard to this in the meeting at the Institute, held to consider the Bill. The objection, I said, to the angle proposed, or to any angle, was, that it must of necessity make a building worse internally; it was impossible to get square rooms while building up to a diagonal line; any angle should cease when it touched the back wall. In the diagram referred to, I have purposely taken the back yard at the smallest depth permitted by the Act.

Directly following this Introduction is the Abstract, set out in tabular form. I think this will be found of great value in enabling the reader to find at once all the portions of the Act set out concisely under the different heads, as for example, if he will turn to Table VI. he will find every rule relating to chimneys and fireplaces, in Table I. all those relating to recesses, openings, &c.

Following these tables is the Act *in extenso*, so that if the slightest doubt arises as to the exact wording, it can at once be turned to. The section and sub-section are given in the tables. Then follow all those sections of other Acts which are still unrepealed, and which relate to building and drainage, and the byelaws of the London County Council.

ABSTRACT

OF THAT

PORTION OF THE ACT RELATING TO BUILDING.

INDEX.

TABLE		PAGE
1.	Recesses and Openings	3
2.	Timbers in External and Party Walls, and Rules as to Bresstummers	3, 4
3.	External Walls	4, 5
4.	Party Walls	5, 6
5.	Roofs	6
6.	Chimneys and Flues	7, 8, 9
7.	Furnace Chimney Shafts	9
8.	Close Fires and Pipes	9, 10
9.	Accesses and Stairs	10, 11
10.	Habitable Rooms	11, 12
11.	Party Arches over Public Ways	12
12.	Arches under Public Ways	13
13.	Projections	13, 14, 15
14.	Separation of Buildings and Cubical Extent	15, 16
15.	Rules as to Uniting Buildings	16, 17
16.	Additions and Alterations	17
17.	Conversion of Buildings	17, 18
18.	Public Buildings	18
19.	Exempted Buildings, Land and Hoardings	18, 19, 20
20.	Fire-Resisting Materials	20
21.	Dwelling Houses on Low-Lying Land	21
22.	Open Spaces about Buildings	21, 22, 23, 24, 25, 26
23.	Heights of Buildings	27, 28

B

ABSTRACT.

TABLE I.
RECESSES AND OPENINGS.

External Wall.—Backs of recesses not less than 8½ inches	PART VI., Sec. 54. Sub-sec. 1, Rule (*a*).
Area of both *above ground storey* not to exceed one-half of whole area of wall above ground storey	,, ,, ,, (*b*).
Party Walls.—Backs of recesses not less than 13 inches	,, 2 ,, (*a*).
Over recess formed an arch of at least two rings of brickwork full depth of recess to be turned on every storey, except in case of recesses formed for lifts, but where such recess does not exceed 5 inches in depth, corbelling in brick or stone may be substituted for the arching	,, ,, ,, (*b*).
Area not to exceed half of whole area of the wall of the storey in which made	,, ,, ,, (*c*).
No recess to come within 13½ inches of *inner* face of external walls (*see Plate* 13)	,, ,, ,, (*d*).
Superintending architect may consent to any modification or relaxation of the requirements of this Section	,, 3.
The word area in this Section means area of vertical face, or elevation of the wall or recess to which it refers	,, ,,

TABLE II.
TIMBERS IN EXTERNAL AND PARTY WALLS. RULES AS TO BRESSUMMERS.

Woodwork fixed in external walls, except bressummers and storey-posts under same, and frames of doors and windows of shops on ground storey shall be set back 4 inches at least from external face of wall	PART VI., Sec. 55.
Loophole frames, and *frames of doors and windows* may, however, be fixed *flush* with face of external wall	,, ,, ,, ,,
Council may by byelaws or otherwise exempt from provisions of this Section oak, teak, or other wood, provided work be constructed to satisfaction of District Surveyor	,, ,, 2 ,,

Bressummers, whether wood or metal, to have bearing 4 inches at least at end, on sufficient pier of brick or stone, or upon timber or iron storey-post fixed on solid foundation, in addition to bearing on any party or external wall. District Surveyor shall have power to require that every bressummer shall have such other storey-posts, iron columns, stanchions, or piers as may be sufficient to carry superstructure .. .. | PART VI., Sec. 56, Sub-sec. 1.

Ends of bressummers, if wood, not to be placed nearer to centre line of party wall than 4 inches .. .. | ,, ,, ,, ,,

Metallic bressummer at end shall have space left equal to $\frac{1}{4}$ inch to every 10 feet or fractional part of 10 feet of length of bressummer to allow for expansion .. .. .. | ,, ,, ,, 2.

Bond timber or wood plate not to be built into any party wall .. .. | ,, ,, ,, 3.

Ends of wooden beam or joists bearing on such walls to be 4 inches at least from centre line of party walls.. .. .. | ,, ,, ,, ,,

Bressummer bearing on party walls to be borne by templet or corbel of stone or iron tailed through half thickness of wall and full breadth of bressummer .. .. | ,, ,, ,, 4.

End of any timber not permitted to be placed in or have bearing on any party wall may be carried on corbel or templet of stone, iron, or vitrified stoneware tailed into wall a distance of at least $8\frac{1}{2}$ inches, or otherwise supported to satisfaction of District Surveyor .. .. | ,, ,, ,, 5.

TABLE III.

EXTERNAL WALLS.

The thickness and substance of walls to be as mentioned in the First Schedule of the Act, but may be varied by byelaws .. .. .. | PART VI., Sec. 53.

N.B.—The thicknesses required by the Act are set out in the sections *shown on Plates* 1 *to* 12.

Parapet at least 1 foot above highest part of gutter if formed of combustible material, and at least $6\frac{1}{2}$ inches in thickness .. .. .. | ,, ,, ,, 57.

Where external wall not in conformity with this Act is taken down, burnt, or destroyed

to extent of one half, measured in superficial feet, every remaining portion not in conformity with Act shall be made to conform therewith, or be taken down before rebuilding thereof, unless Council otherwise allow..	PART XVI., Sec. 208.

TABLE IV.
PARTY WALLS.

The thickness and substance of walls to be as mentioned in the First Schedule of the Act, but may be varied by bye-laws	PART VI., Sec. 53.
N.B.—The thicknesses required by the Act are set out in the sections *shown on Plates* 1 to 12.	
Party wall to be carried up in a building of warehouse class equal to thickness of wall in topmost storey, any other building 8½ inches to such a height as will give a distance of 3 feet in a building of warehouse class (exceeding 30 feet in height), 15 inches in height any other building above highest part of any roof, flat or gutter .. .. .. :	,, 59, Sub-sec. 1.
If dormer, turret, lantern light, &c. within 4 feet from this wall, wall shall extend at least 12 inches higher and wider on each side. If roof within 4 feet, then this wall shall go above (*see Diagram, Plate* 14)	,, ,, ,, 2.
No chase wider than 14 inches nor deeper than 4½ inches from face of wall, nor leave less than 8½ inches thick, nor be within 7 feet of another chase on same side of wall, nor within 13 inches from an external wall (*see Plate* 13)	,, 60.
No chase to be made in wall of less thickness than 13 inches	,, ,,
Where party wall not in conformity with this Act is taken down, burnt, or destroyed to extent of one half, measured in superficial feet, every remaining portion not in conformity with Act shall be made to conform therewith or be taken down before rebuilding thereof, unless Council otherwise allow ..	PART XVI., Sec. 208.

Cases in which a wall to be deemed a PARTY WALL.

(a) When a wall is after the commencement of this Act built as a party wall in any part; or	PART VI., Sec. 58.

(b) Where a wall built before or after the commencement of this Act becomes after the commencement of this Act a party wall in any part
    the wall shall be deemed a party wall for such part of its length as is so used .. Part VI., Sec **58**.

TABLE V.
Roofs.

Every part of covering must be externally covered with slate, tiles, metal, or other incombustible materials, except wooden cornices and barge boards to dormers not exceeding 12 inches in depth, and the doors, door frames, window, and window frames of such dormers, turrets, lantern lights, skylights, or other erections	Part VI., Sec. **61**, Sub-sec. 1.
Buildings exceeding 30 feet high, used wholly or in part as a dwelling or factory, having a parapet shall be provided—	
(a) With a dormer window or door opening on to the roof; or	„ „ „ 2.
(b) Trap door furnished with fixed or hinged step ladder leading to roof; or	
(c) Other proper means of access to roof.	
If building of warehouse class, plane of surface of roof not to incline from external or party wall upwards at greater angle than 47° with horizon. This Sub-section shall not apply to towers, turrets, or spires	„ „ „ 3.
Any other building, plane of surface of roof not to incline from external or party walls upwards at greater angle than 75° with horizon. This Sub-section shall not apply to towers, turrets, or spires	„ „ „ 4.
Not more than two storeys to be constructed in roof of domestic building	„ **62** „ 1.
If storey constructed in roof of domestic building, the upper surface of floor of which storey is 60 feet from street level, shall be constructed of fire-resisting material throughout	„ „ „ 2.
Means of escape in case of fire to be provided for persons dwelling or employed in storeys, the upper surface of floor whereof is above 60 feet from street level. No such storeys shall be occupied until certificate issued by Council	Sec. **63**.

TABLE VI.

CHIMNEYS AND FLUES.

Chimneys on corbels of brick, stone, or other incombustible materials must not exceed in projection more than thickness of wall measured immediately below corbel. All other chimneys must be on solid foundations, with footings similar to footings of wall, unless carried on iron girders with direct bearings on party, external, or cross walls to satisfaction of District Surveyor	PART VI., Sec. 64, Sub-sec. 1.
Chimneys and flues having soot doors not less than 40 square inches, may be at any angle, but in no other case shall flue be inclined at less angle than 45° to horizon, and to be properly rounded. All soot doors 15 inches distant from any woodwork	,, ,, ,, 2.
An arch of brick or stone, or bar of wrought iron of sufficient strength shall be built over opening of every chimney to support breast. If breast projects more than 4 inches, and jamb less width than 17½ inches, abutments shall be tied in by iron bar or bars turned up and down at ends, and built into jambs at least 8½ inches (*see Plate* 15)	,, ,, ,, 3.
Flue not to be adapted to or used for any new oven, furnace, cockle, steam boiler, or close fire used for any purpose of trade or business, or for range or cooking apparatus of any hotel, tavern, or eating house, unless flue surrounded with brickwork at least 8½ inches thick from floor on which such oven, furnace, cockle, steam-boiler, or close fire is situate to level of ceiling of room next above same ..	,, ,, ,, 4.
Flue not to be used in connection with steam boiler or hot-air engine unless flue is at least 20 feet in height, measured from level of floor on which engine placed	,, ,, ,, 5.
Inside of flue, and outside where passing through floor or roof, or behind or against any woodwork, to be rendered	,, ,, ,, 6.
Position and course of every flue shall be distinguished on outside of work, as it is carried up, by outline marks, except when exterior face of flue forms part of external wall not likely to be built against	,, ,, ,, 7.

8 ABSTRACT OF THAT PORTION OF THE ACT

Jambs to be at least 8½ inches wide each side of opening	PART VI., Sec. 64, Sub-sec. 8.
Breast and brickwork surrounding every smoke flue to be 4 inches thick	,, ,, ,, 9.
Back of fire place in party wall from hearth to 12 inches above mantel shall be at least 8½ inches thick	,, ,, ,, 10.
Thickness of upper side of every flue when angle of less than 45° must be 8½ inches ..	,, ,, ,, 11.
Shafts at least 4 inches thick to a height of not less than 3 feet above roof, flat, or gutter, measured at highest point of juncture	,, ,, ,, 12.
Highest six courses of shaft or stack shall be built in cement	,, ,, ,, 13.
No shaft to be higher above roof, flat, or gutter, and from highest point than six times the least width, unless built with and bonded to another shaft not in same line, or otherwise rendered secure*	,, ,, ,, 14.
Slab to be of stone, slate, or other incombustible material, 6 inches longer than opening on each side and 18 inches wide in front of breast (see *Plate* 15)	,, ,, ,, 15.
Slab to be laid wholly on stone or iron bearers or brick trimmers, or other incombustible materials, but on lowest floor may be bedded on concrete covering the site..	,, ,, ,, 16.
Hearth or slab to be solid for a thickness of 6 inches at least beneath upper surface ..	,, ,, ,, 17.
Flue not to be built against any party structure unless surrounded with new brickwork 4 inches thick, properly bonded	,, ,, ,, 18.
No chimney breast or shaft, with or in any party wall to be cut away unless District Surveyor certifies, &c.	,, ,, ,, 19.
Chimney shaft, jamb, breast, or flue, can only be cut into for three purposes (*a*) (*b*) (*c*)	,, ,, ,, 20.
Timber or Woodwork:— (*a*) Not to be nearer than 12 inches to inside of flue or chimney opening. (*b*) Not to be within 10 inches from upper surface of hearth of chimney opening. (*c*) Not to be within 2 inches from face of brickwork or stonework about chimney or flue where the work is less than 8½ inches thick, unless face rendered.	,, ,, ,, 21.

---

* Except furnace of steam engine, brewery, distillery, or manufactory.

Wooden plugs must not be nearer than 6 inches to the inside of flue or chimney opening, nor any iron holdfast or other iron fastening nearer than 2 inches .. .. :	Part VI., Sec. 64, Sub-sec. 22.

TABLE VII.
Furnace Chimney Shafts.

Unless Council otherwise permit shall be constructed as follows	Part VI., Sec. 65.
Carried up throughout in brick and mortar of best quality, and if detached shall taper from base to top at least 2½ inches in 10 feet of height	,, ,, Sub-sec. 1.
Thickness of brickwork at top and for 20 feet below to be at least 8½ inches, and increased one-half brick for every additional 20 feet, measured downwards	,, ,, ,, 2.
Every cap, cornice, pedestal, plinth, string course, or other variation from plain brickwork shall be in addition to thickness of brickwork required, and every cap shall be constructed and secured to satisfaction of District Surveyor	,, ,, ,, 3.
Foundation to be made to satisfaction of District Surveyor	,, ,, ,, 4.
Footings to spread all round base by regular offsets to a projection equal to the thickness of enclosing brickwork at base of shaft, and space enclosed by footings to be filled in solid as work proceeds	,, ,, ,, 5.
Width of base of shaft if square shall be at least one-tenth, or if round one-twelfth, height of shaft	,, ,, ,, 6.
Firebricks built inside lower portion of shaft to be additional to thickness of brickwork and not bonded therewith	,, ,, ,, 7.

TABLE VIII.
Close Fires and Pipes.

Floor under copper, steam boiler, or stove not heated by gas, and floor around same shall for a space of 18 inches be formed of incombustible material not less than 6 inches thick	Part VI., Sec. 66, Sub-sec. 1.

No pipe conveying smoke, &c. to be fixed against any building on the face next street, &c.	PART VI., Sec. 66, Sub-sec. 2.	
No pipe for conveying smoke, &c., to be fixed nearer than 9 inches to any combustible materials	,, ,, ,,	3.
No pipe for heated air or steam nearer than 6 inches to any combustible material	,, ,, ,,	4.
No pipe for hot water nearer than 3 inches	,, ,, ,,	5.
Restrictions imposed by this Section shall not apply to hot water or steam pipes at low pressure	,, ,, ,,	,,
For the purpose of this Section hot water or steam shall be deemed to be at low pressure when provided with a free blow off	,, ,, ,,	,,
Floor over any room or enclosed space in which a furnace is fixed, and any floor within 18 inches from crown of an oven shall be constructed of fire-resisting materials	,, 67.	

TABLE IX.
ACCESSES AND STAIRS.

Public buildings and those having more than 125,000 cubic feet, and adapted or constructed as a dwelling house for separate families, the floors of lobbies, corridors, passages, landings, and flights of stairs to be of fire-resisting materials and carried by supports of fire-resisting materials	PART VI., Sec. 68.	
Buildings constructed or adapted to be occupied by more than two families, the principal staircase used in common shall be ventilated on every storey above ground storey by windows or skylights opening directly into external air, &c.	,, 69, Sub-sec.	1
Principal staircase in every dwelling house not subject to provisions of foregoing Sub-section shall be ventilated by window or skylight, &c.	,, ,, ,,	2.
Staircases in Churches, Chapels, or PUBLIC *places of Assembly.*		
To be supported and enclosed by brick walls 9 inches thick. Rule (a)	,, 80.	
The treads of each flight to be of uniform width. Rule (a)	,, ,,	

No staircase, internal corridor, or passage way to be less than 4 feet 6 inches wide, except where not more than 200 persons accommodated, the width may be 3 feet 6 inches. Rule (b) .. .. PART VI., Sec. 80.
Every staircase, corridor, or passage way communicating with any portion of the building intended to accommodate larger number of public than 400, to be increased in width 6 inches for every additional 100 persons until maximum width of 9 feet obtained. Rule (c) .. .. ,,   ,,   ,,   ,,
Where staircases 6 feet wide and upwards, handrail to divide.
In lieu of single staircase, corridor, or passage way of width prescribed by this Sub-section two may be substituted at least equal to two-thirds of the width prescribed in this Sub-section for single staircase, corridor, or passage way, but neither of such two shall be less than 3 feet 6 inches wide. Rule (c) .. .. ,,   ,,   ,,   ,,
Where portion of public to be accommodated over or at higher level than others of the public, separate means of exit communicating with street or open space to be provided from each floor or level. Rule (d) .. .. .. ,,   ,,   ,,   ,,
All doors and barriers to open outwards, and no outside locks or bolts affixed thereto. Rule (e) .. .. ,,   ,,   ,,   ,,

TABLE X.

HABITABLE ROOMS.

Every part (except rooms wholly or partly in roof) to be 8 feet 6 inches high from floor to ceiling. Rule (a) .. .. PART VI., Sec. 70, Sub-sec. 1.
In roofs at least 8 feet high, and such height not less than half the area of room. Rule (b) (see Plate 16) .. .. ,,   ,,   ,,   ,,
Every room to have one or more windows opening into external air or into conservatory, with total superficies, clear of sash frames, &c., equal to one-tenth floor area of room, and so constructed that one-twentieth of floor area can be opened, and opening shall extend at least 7 feet above the floor level ; but room having no external wall or constructed in

whole or part in roof, to be lighted through roof by dormer window, with total superficies, clear of sash frames &c., to light equal to one-twelfth of floor area of room, so constructed that a portion of such window equal to one twenty-fourth of floor area can be opened. The opening in each case shall extend to at least 5 feet above floor level; or such room may be lighted by lantern light, a portion of which, equal to one-twentieth of floor area, can be opened. Rule (c)	Part VI., Sec. **70**, Sub-sec.	1.
Basement rooms having wooden floor other than wood block on concrete to have sufficient space between ground and floor surfaces for ventilation, &c. Rule (d)	,, ,, ,,	,,
If constructed over stable, floor to have in every part not occupied by joist or girders concrete pugging or other solid construction 3 inches thick, smoothed on upper surface and properly supported. Underside of such floor shall be ceiled with lathe and plaster, &c. Rule (e)	,, ,, ,,	,,
Staircase, gallery, or structure by which such rooms approached, to be separated from stable by brick wall not less than 9 inches thick ..	,, ,, ,,	,,
Nothing in this Act shall affect, alter, or repeal The Public Health (London) Act, 1891, as to underground rooms. Rule (f)	,, ,, ,,	,,
Penalty to be inflicted for allowing rooms to be occupied unless complying with this Section	,, ,, ,,	2.

TABLE XI.

Party Arches over Public Ways.

Every party arch, &c., and every arch or floor over public way, or passage leading through or under a building to premises in other occupation, shall be of brick or stone, &c. ..	Part VI., Sec. **71**, Sub-sec.	1.
Thickness 8½ inches at least if brick or stone, and rise one inch every foot of span, &c. ..	,, ,, ,,	2.
Construction in other materials as District Surveyor may approve	,, ,, ,,	3.

TABLE XII.
ARCHES UNDER PUBLIC WAYS.

To be formed of brick, stone or other hard and incombustible materials	PART VI., Sec. **72**, Sub-sec.	1.
If brick or stone used :— (*a*) Span not exceeding 10 feet thickness, 8½ inches. (*b*) Span not exceeding 15 feet thickness, 13 inches.		
(*c*) Beyond as District Surveyor may approve	,, ,, ,,	2.
Construction in other materials as District Surveyor may approve	,, ,, ,,	3.

TABLE XIII.
PROJECTIONS.

All to be of brick, tile, stone, artificial stone, slate, cement, or other fireproof materials, except the cornices and dressing to window, fronts of shops, and eaves, barge boards and cornices to detached and semi-detached dwellings, houses, and other dwelling houses in which party walls are corbelled out so as to project 4 inches beyond same, except with consent of Council. A pair of semi-detached houses one building for the purposes of this Sub-section	PART VI., Sec. **73**, Sub-sec.	1.
Balcony, cornice, or other projection to be tailed into wall and weighted or tied down to satisfaction of District Surveyor. Projection not to exceed 2 feet 6 inches over public way .. In streets or ways less than 30 feet shop front may project beyond external wall not more than 5 inches, and any cornice 13 inches. If wider than 30 feet, shop front may project 10 inches and cornice 18 inches over ground of the owner of the building (*see Plate* 17).	,, ,, ,,	2.
NOTE.—This provision does not authorise projection of shop front other than cornice over public way or land to be given up to public way	,, ,, ,,	3.
Woodwork of shop front not to be fixed higher than 25 feet above pavement of footpath in front of shop. No part of any woodwork of shop front shall be fixed nearer than 4 inches		

to centre of party wall, &c., or nearer than 4 inches to face of wall of adjoining premises, where adjoining premises have separate wall, unless a pier or corbel 4 inches wide at least be placed as high as such woodwork, and projecting throughout an inch at least in front between such woodwork and centre line of party or separate wall, &c. .. .. | PART VI., Sec. **73**, Sub-sec. 4.

Bay windows to dwelling houses may be erected on land belonging to owner of the building in a street not less than 40 feet in width, or to a building, the front wall of which is not less distance than 40 feet from opposite boundary of the street, notwithstanding the rules in this Act as to buildings beyond general line of buildings as follows :—

(*a*) Not to exceed three storeys in height above footway.

(*b*) Not to project more than 3 feet from main wall.

(*c*) Not to project in any part within prescribed distance from centre of roadway.

(*d*) Not to be nearer to centre of nearest party wall than extreme amount of their projection from main wall.

(*e*) Taken together, not to exceed in width three-fifths of frontage of building, &c.

(*f*) Not to be constructed on public way or land agreed to be given up to public way,

(*g*) Not to be used for trade purposes.

Bay windows to which foregoing rules do not apply to receive consent of Council. .. .. | ,, ,, ,, 5.

Oriel windows or turrets may be constructed in a street not less than 40 feet, or to a building, the front wall of which is not at a less distance than 40 feet from opposite boundary, provided—

(*a*) No part extend more than 3 feet from face of building, or more than 12 inches over public way.

(*b*) No part less than 10 feet above footway.

(*c*) No part (where it overhangs public way) within 4 feet from centre of nearest party wall.

(*d*) On no floor shall total width taken together exceed three-fifths length of wall of building on level of that floor.

(e) Construction to be to the satisfaction of District Surveyor, &c. Oriel windows and turrets to which foregoing rules do not apply to receive consent of Council	Part VI., Sec. 73, Sub-sec. 6.
Roof, flat, or gutter of every building and every balcony, verandah, shop front, or similar projection arranged so water does not drop on public way	,, ,, ,, 7.
Except in case of shop fronts and projecting windows and water-pipes, copings, string courses, cornices, fascias, window-dressings, and other architectural decorations, no projection without consent of Council	,, ,, ,, 8.

TABLE XIV.

SEPARATION OF BUILDINGS AND CUBICAL EXTENT.

Every building shall be separated by external or party wall or party structure from adjoining building or buildings	Part VI., Sec. 74, Sub-sec. 1.
Every building exceeding ten squares in area, used part for trade or manufacture and part as dwelling house, the part used for trade or manufacture to be separated from that used as dwelling house by walls and floors of fire-resisting materials, including passages, staircases and other means of approach. The part used for trade or manufacture (if extending to more than 250,000 cubic feet) be subject to provisions of this Act relating to cubical contents of buildings of warehouse class	,, ,, ,, 2.
Doorways necessary for communication may be constructed in walls of such staircases and passages, and there may be formed in any walls of such building openings fitted with fire-resisting doors	,, ,, ,, ,,
Buildings exceeding twenty-five squares in area containing separate sets of chambers &c., to have floors and principal staircases of fire-resisting materials	,, ,, ,, 3.
No warehouse building shall extend to more than 250,000 cubic feet unless divided by party walls in such manner that no division extend more than 250,000 cubic feet	,, 75.

ABSTRACT OF THAT PORTION OF THE ACT

No addition to be made to warehouse so that cubical extent exceed 250,000 cubic feet ..	PART VI., Sec. 75.
Cubical contents under this section shall not apply to buildings at greater distance than two miles from St. Paul's Cathedral, and used wholly for manufacture of machinery, boilers of steam vessels, retort house, manufacture of gas, or for generating electricity, provided they consist of one floor only and constructed of brick, stone, iron, and other incombustible material throughout, and not used for any other purpose. Such building, with respect to special buildings under this Act, be deemed building to which general rules of this Act inapplicable	„ 76
Council may consent to additional cubical extent under certain conditions	„ „ Sub-secs. 1, 2 and 3.

TABLE XV.

RULES AS TO UNITING BUILDINGS.

No building shall be united unless wholly in one occupation, or constructed or adapted to be so	PART VI., Sec. 77, Sub-sec. 1.
Nor if so done it shall be contrary to Act ..	„ „ „ 2.
No opening to be made in any party wall or in two external walls dividing buildings which if taken together would extend to more than 250,000 cubic feet except .. .. such opening shall not exceed in width seven feet, or height eight feet. Such openings taken together not to exceed one-half the length of party wall on each floor they occur. Rule (*a*)	„ „ „ 3.
	„ „ „ „
Such opening shall have floor jambs and head of brick, stone, or iron, and closed by two wrought-iron doors, each one-fourth of an inch thick in panel, distant from each other full thickness of wall, fitted to rebate frames without woodwork, or by wrought-iron sliding doors or shutters properly constructed, fitted into grooved or rebated iron frames. Rule (*b*)	„ „ „ „
If thickness of wall not less than 24 inches, or doors placed at a distance from each other of 24 inches, such opening may be 9 feet 6 inches high. Rule (*c*)	„ „ „ „

When ceased to be in one occupation must again be divided and openings bricked up, &c.	PART VI., Sec. 77, Sub.-sec. 4.
Notice to be given to District Surveyor when united buildings cease to be in one occupation	,, ,, ,, 5.

TABLE XVI.
ADDITIONS AND ALTERATIONS.

Every addition to or alteration of a building, and any other work made or done for any purpose in, to or upon a building (except that of necessary repair not affecting the construction of any external or party wall) shall be subject to provisions of this Act and byelaws thereunder relating to new buildings ..	PART XVI., Sec. 209
This Act does not apply to new buildings or alterations commenced and in progress before 1st January 1895..	,, ,, ,, 212
No alteration (except with consent of Council), to be made unless in conformity with this Act applicable to new buildings	,, ,, ,, 207

TABLE XVII.
CONVERSION OF BUILDINGS.

Unless Council otherwise permit.—No power to convert into a dwelling house any building or part not originally constructed for human habitation	PART XVI., Sec. 211, Sub-sec. 1.
No power to convert into one dwelling house two or more dwelling houses constructed originally as separate dwelling houses	,, ,, ,, 2.
No power to convert into or use as two or more dwelling houses any building originally constructed as one dwelling house	,, ,, ,, 3.
No power to convert a building, which when originally erected was exempt from Act or byelaws, into a building which, had it been originally erected in its converted form, would have been within the operations of these enactments or byelaws	,, ,, ,, 4.
No power to convert into a dwelling house any building discontinued or appropriated for any purpose except a dwelling house	,, ,, ,, 5.

18 ABSTRACT OF THAT PORTION OF THE ACT

No power to convert into or use as a dwelling any room or part of a room used as a shop ..	PART XVI., Sec. 211, Sub-sec. 6.
No power to convert a dwelling house or any part into a shop in such manner that the building or part so constructed will be contrary to this Act, relating to the class of buildings which the building when so converted will belong	,, ,, ,, 7.

TABLE XVIII.
PUBLIC BUILDINGS.

Walls, roofs, floors, galleries, and staircases, and every structure and work shall be constructed in such manner as may be approved by District Surveyor, or in event of disagreement by the Tribunal of Appeal.* Not to be used until District Surveyor or Tribunal of Appeal shall have declared approval of construction. After approval granted, no work to be done without the approval of District Surveyor, or such certificate as aforesaid.	PART VI., Sec. 78.
No conversion of houses, &c. into public building unless the alteration or conversion to approval of District Surveyor or Tribunal of Appeal	,, ,, ,, 79.

*NOTE.—Tribunal of Appeal shall be constituted as follows:—
    One member shall be appointed by Secretary of State.
    One member shall be appointed by Council of R.I.B.A.
    One member shall be appointed by Council of Surveyor's Institution.
No member or officer of the Council shall be a member of the Tribunal of Appeal.
	PART XVI., Sec. 175.

TABLE XIX.
EXEMPTED BUILDINGS, LAND AND HOARDINGS.

Government Buildings.—Buildings for public purposes, occupied by Justices of the Peace for the counties of Middlesex, London, and City of London, or by County Councils of London and Middlesex	PART XVI., Sec. 201, Sub-sec. 5.

RELATING TO BUILDING. 19

	PART XVI.,
Mansion House	Sec. 201, Sub-sec. 2.
Guildhall	,, ,, ,, ,,
Royal Exchange	,, ,, ,, ,,
Metropolitan Cattle Markets and the Cattle Market at Deptford	,, ,, ,, 7
Covent Garden. Buildings built with sanction of Commissioners for the Exhibition of 1851 on their land	,, ,, ,, 4
Buildings belonging to Canal Companies	,, ,, ,, 8
Buildings belonging to Railway Companies	,, ,, ,, ,,
Buildings belonging to Gas Companies	,, ,, ,, ,,
Buildings belonging to Dock Companies	,, ,, ,, 9
Buildings not exceeding 30 square feet in area, and not exceeding 5 feet high in any part, at least 5 feet from any other building or street, and not having any stove, flue, fireplace, hot-air pipe, hot-water pipe, or other apparatus for warming and ventilating the same, provided no portion of the building extends beyond general line of buildings in any street	,, ,, ,, 10.
Not exceeding 30 feet high from footings, and not exceeding 125,000 cubic feet, and not being public buildings wholly in one occupation, 8 feet from street, 30 feet from nearest building, or ground of adjoining owner (see *Plate* 18)	,, ,, ,, 11.
NOTE.—If public building may have within 30 feet, if other than public building may have within 60 feet, stables or offices used in connection with such buildings	,, ,, Sub-secs. 11 & 12.
Not exceeding 250,000 cubic feet, not public buildings, 30 feet from nearest street, 60 feet from nearest building, or ground of adjoining owner	,, ,, ,, 12.
Party fence walls not exceeding 7 feet high measured from top of footings	,, ,, ,, 13.
Greenhouses if *not* attached to other buildings	,, ,, ,, 14.
Woodwork only of sashes, doors, and frames of greenhouses attached to buildings	,, ,, ,, 15.
Cases of metal and glass for holding plants fastened to woodwork of sill and lower sash, not projecting over public way or more than 12 inches from external face of wall of building	,, ,, ,, 16.
Openings in walls or flues for ventilating valves, not exceeding 40 square inches, not nearer than 12 inches to any timber, &c.	,, ,, ,, 17.
Inns of Court land and buildings, &c.	,, 204 ,, 1, 2, 3, 4.

Hoardings to vacant land not more than 12 feet high .. .. NOTE.—By Section 206 any buildings so exempted shall only so remain whilst used for the purpose, or retaining the character, which gave it its exemption or privilege.	PART VII., Sec. 84, Sub-sec. 1.

TABLE XX.

FIRE-RESISTING MATERIALS.

The following are so deemed in the Act :— 1. *Brickwork*, good, well burnt, hard, and sound, properly bonded and solidly put together (a) With good mortar, compounded of good lime, sharp, clean sand, hard, clean, broken brick, broken flint, grit, or slag; or (b) With good cement ; or (c) With cement and sharp, clean sand, hard, clean, broken brick, broken flint, grit, or slag. 2. Granite and other stone suitable for building by reason of its solidity, &c. 3. Iron, steel, and copper 4. Oak, teak, and other hard timber when used for beams, posts, or in combination with iron, the timber and iron (if any) to be protected by plastering in cement, or incombustible or non-conducting external coating. In the case of doors— Oak, teak, or other hard timber 2 inches thick at least. In the case of staircases— Oak, teak, or other hard timber with treads, strings and risers not less than 2 inches thick. 5. Slates, tiles, brick, and terra-cotta when used for coverings or corbels. 6. Flagstones for floors over arches not exposed on underside, and not supported at ends only. 7. Concrete composed as required by Act when used for filling in between joists of floors. 8. Any material approved from time to time by the Council.	2nd Schedule.

TABLE XXI.

DWELLING HOUSES ON LOW-LYING LAND.

Not to be erected on land if surface is below Trinity high-water mark, and which will not admit of being drained by gravitation into an existing sewer of the Council, &c., except with permission of the Council— And the Council may (subject to appeal as hereinafter provided). (i.) Prohibit the erection or adaptation of any such buildings. (ii.) Regulate the erection or adaptation of the same. (iii.) Prescribe the level of underside of lowest floor, and as to provisions as to the proper drainage, &c. Application to be made to the Council for a license to erect such building, &c.	PART XI., Sec. 122.
The Council, with concurrence of Tribunal of Appeal, may make regulations to be followed in making applications under this part of the Act	,, 123.
Printed copies of any regulations under this part of the Act shall be kept at the County Hall and supplied free of charge to any person concerned who may apply for same	,, 124, Sub-sec. 2.

TABLE XXII.

OPEN SPACES ABOUT BUILDINGS.

Domestic buildings shall not include buildings used wholly or principally as offices or counting houses for the purposes of this Part of the Act	PART V., Sec. 39.
Domestic buildings erected after commencement of this Act having habitable basement, shall have in the rear an open space not less than 100 sq. feet, free from any erection above level of adjoining pavement	,, 40.
With respect to domestic buildings erected after commencement of this Act and abutting on a street formed or laid out after the commencement of this Act, the following provisions shall have effect :—	,, 41, Sub-sec. 1.

(i.) There shall be provided an open space in rear not less than 150 sq. feet. Where basement storey has open space provided by preceding Section irrespective of use to which ground storey appropriated, or where no basement, or where ground storey not constructed or adapted to be inhabited, the open space by this Section may be above level of ceiling of ground storey, or a level of 16 feet, exclusive of lantern lights, measured from adjoining pavement.

In all other cases open space shall be free from any erection above level of adjoining pavement except a water closet, earth closet, or privy, &c. and enclosing walls, none of which erections shall exceed 9 feet in height.

(ii.) Such open space to be full width of building, and a depth in every part at least 10 feet from such building.

(iii.) The height of such building in relation to space required in rear shall be fixed and ascertained as follows:—

(*a*) An imaginary line (hereafter called horizontal line) shall be drawn at right angles to roadway in front of building and through front of centre of the face of building.

(*b*) The horizontal line shall intersect boundary of open space furthest from such roadway.

(*c*) The horizontal line shall be drawn throughout at level of pavement, unless site of building inclines towards roadway, in which case the horizontal line shall be drawn directly over the said point in front of centre of face of building at the level throughout of the ground at boundary of space furthest from roadway, where boundary is intersected by horizontal line.

(*d*) A second imaginary line (called the diagonal line) shall be drawn in direction of building above and in same vertical plane with horizontal line at an angle of $63\frac{1}{2}°$, and meeting horizontal line where it intersects boundary of space furthest removed from such roadway (*see Plate* 19).

(*e*) No part of building to extend above diagonal line except chimneys, dormers, gables, turrets, &c., aggregating in all not more than one-third width of rear elevation.

PART V., Sec. 41, Sub-sec. 1.

(*f*) When pavement in front of building not all one level, mean level shall be deemed the level thereof. Where boundary of space at rear of building not parallel with rear wall of building, a horizontal line shall be drawn to a point distant from such rear wall the mean distance from such wall of the boundary of space at rear, whether such point be beyond said boundary or not.

(*g*) When boundary of space at rear so irregular in shape that doubt arises how measurement to be taken, application to be made to Council, and applicant if dissatisfied may appeal to Tribunal of Appeal.

(*h*) When land at rear of such building, and exclusively belonging thereto, abuts immediately upon a street or open public space, or maintenance of which as an open space is secured permanently or to satisfaction of Council by covenant or otherwise, the horizontal line shall be produced, and diagonal line may be drawn from horizontal line at centre of roadway of such street at level of surface thereof, or at further boundary of such open space, and it shall not be necessary to provide any open space at the rear of such building .. .. | PART V., Sec. 41.

(iv.) (*a*) If building at corner abutting upon two streets; or

(*b*) A building at corner, one side abutting upon a street, and on another side upon open space not less than 40 feet wide, &c.

The Council may permit erection of buildings not exceeding 30 feet high upon such part of space in rear as they may think fit, provided they be satisfied that such building be so placed as not to interfere unduly with access of light and air to neighbouring buildings. When Council refuse any application under this Sub-section, applicant if dissatisfied may appeal to Tribunal of Appeal.

(v.) In case of buildings at corner, as hereafter described, nothing in this part as to determination of height by diagonal line shall prevent return front being carried up to full height of front elevation for distance of 40 feet, or such less distance as requirements of open space at rear may demand.

(vi.) In exceptional cases, where land irregular

shape, to which preceding provisions of this Section cannot be applied, Council may allow modifications.	
All persons dissatisfied with determination of Council may appeal to Tribunal of Appeal ..	Part V., Sec. 41, Sub-sec. 2.
Domestic buildings erected after commencement of this Act, abutting upon a street formed or laid out before commencement of this Act, provisions of this Section shall apply with this modification—that horizontal line shall be drawn at a level of 16 feet above level of adjoining pavement, and in any such case (except in cases of dwelling houses to be inhabited or adapted to be inhabited by persons of the working class) the open space to be provided by paragraphs (i.) and (ii.) of Sub-section 1 of this Section may be provided above level of ceiling of ground storey, or 16 feet (exclusive of lantern lights) above level of adjoining pavement.	
Notwithstanding preceding provisions of this part of this Act, any part of domestic building may extend above diagonal line provided Council or Tribunal of Appeal shall be satisfied that an open cubic space of air will be provided at rear of such building equal to the open cubic space which would have been provided at rear of such building if such diagonal line had been drawn from ground level in manner provided in Sub-section 1 (iii.) of this Section, and if no part (except as permitted) had extended above such diagonal line. Applicant if dissatisfied with determination of the Council may appeal to Tribunal of Appeal.	
Nothing in this Section shall apply to houses abutting in the rear on River Thames, public park or open space not less than 80 feet deep and dedicated to the public, &c.	,, ,, ,, ,,
Rules as to dwelling houses to be inhabited or adapted to be inhabited by persons of the working class, erected after the commencement of this Act	,, 42.
Sufficient plans showing extent and height in several parts, and position in relation to other building existing or in course of erection which is adjacent thereto, to be delivered at the County Hall one month before commencing to erect	,, ,, Sub-sec. (i.).

If Council dissatisfied with sufficiency of open spaces for admission of light and air, it shall be lawful for them to refuse to sanction such plans within one month from delivery of same. Nothing in the Sub-section shall authorise the Council to refuse sanction if open spaces for admission of light and air is or are equivalent to open spaces which would have been provided under the provisions of this Act, in case the same had been erected after commencement of this Act, abutting upon a street or way formed or laid out before commencement of this Act .. .. .. | Part V., Sec. 42, Sub-sec. (ii).

No erection of such dwelling house to be commenced without sanction of Council .. .. | ,, ,, ,, (iii).

If after delivery of plans Council do not give notice of their disapproval, sanction shall be deemed to have been given .. .. | ,, ,, ,, (iv).

If refusal of Council considered unreasonable, appeal may be made to Tribunal of Appeal .. | ,, ,, ,, (v).

For domestic buildings (not being a dwelling house inhabited by persons of working class) abutting on a street on the site of domestic buildings existing at commencement of this Act, or on a site vacant at commencement of this Act, but occupied by a domestic building any time within seven years previous to commencement of this Act, the following provisions shall have effect:— .. .. .. | ,, 43.

Before commencing to build, plans to be prepared showing extent of previously existing domestic building (if building taken down before commencement of this Act, or accidentally destroyed, best plans available), and to submit to District Surveyor who shall, if satisfied, certify as to correctness.

Such person may then erect domestic building, but no more land shall be occupied by newly erected building than was occupied by previously existing domestic building.

For failing to submit plan to District Surveyor, or the District Surveyor or Tribunal of Appeal refuse to certify the accuracy of same, person rebuilding shall be bound by preceding provisions of this Part of this Act, &c. .. .. | ,, ,, Sub-sec. (i).

If a person desires to deviate from plans as certified by District Surveyor, it shall be legal

for him to apply to Council to sanction such deviation, &c.	Part V., Sec. 43, Sub-sec. (ii).
A person dissatisfied with any decision of the Council or District Surveyor, he may appeal to Tribunal of Appeal	,, ,, ,, (iii).
When a person desires to lay out new streets on a cleared area, he may make application to the Council, and the Council may, if they think desirable, modify or relax any of the foregoing provisions of this Part of this Act, &c.	,, 44.
Courts within a building.—When a court, wholly or part open at top, but enclosed on every side, &c., and the depth of such court from eaves or top of parapet to ceiling of ground floor storey exceeds the length or breadth of such court, adequate provision for the ventilation shall be made and maintained by owner by means of communication between lower end of court and the outer air. No habitable room not having window directly opening into external air, otherwise than into a court enclosed on every side, shall be constructed in any building unless width of such court, measured from such window to opposite wall, shall be equal to half the height, measured from the sill of such window to eaves or top of parapet of opposite wall. A court of which the greater dimension does not exceed twice the less dimension, shall be held to comply with this Section if a court of same area but square in shape would comply therewith. No habitable room above ground storey, not having window directly opening in external air otherwise than into a court open on one side, the depth whereof, measured from open side, exceed twice the width, shall be constructed in any building unless every window be placed not nearer to opposite wall of such court, or to any other building, than one-half the height of top of such wall or building above level of sill of such window	,, 45.
Superintending architect may define front or rear of buildings when necessary, &c.	,, 46.

TABLE XXIII.
Heights of Buildings.

A building (not being a church or chapel) shall not be erected or subsequently increased to a greater height than 80 feet (exclusive of two storeys in roof, &c.) without consent of Council, except where contract lawfully made previously to passing of this Act, &c.	
This Section shall not apply to rebuilding same height at present of any building existing at passing of this Act of greater height than 80 feet.	
Where existing buildings forming part of continuous block, &c. exceed height prescribed by this Section, nothing in this Section shall prevent any other buildings in same block or row, belonging at date of passing this Act to same owner, from being carried to height equal to but not exceeding that of existing buildings.	
Nothing in this Section shall affect powers conferred upon railway companies, &c.	Part V., Sec. 4 *l*.
When Council consent to erection of any building of greater height than that prescribed by this Act, notice of such consent shall, within one week after consent given, be published and served in a manner directed by the Council, and the consent shall not be acted on until 21 days after such publication, or service, or in event of any appeal against consent, until after determination of such appeal	„ 48, Sub-sec. 1.
(*a*) The owner or lessee of any building or land within 100 yards of the site of any intended building, who may deem himself aggrieved by grant of such consent in respect of the last mentioned building ; or	„ „ „ 2.
(*b*) Any applicant for consent which has been refused, may respectively, within 21 days after publication of notice of consent or after date of refusal, appeal to Tribunal of Appeal	„ „ „ „
Whenever consent refused and applicant intends to appeal against same, such applicant shall give notice, within 21 days of such refusal, in such manner as Council may direct to owner or lessee of any building or land within 100	

28 ABSTRACT OF ACT RELATING TO BUILDING.

yards of site of building to which refusal relates, that he intends to appeal from such refusal	PART V., Sec. 48, Sub-sec. 3.
In the case of appeal against refusal of consent, any owner or lessee of any building or land within 100 yards of site of intended building may appear and be heard before Tribunal of Appeal against application to reverse or vary refusal	,, ,, ,, 4.
After commencement of this Act no existing building (other than church or chapel) on site of a street formed or laid out after 7th August 1862, and of less width than 50 feet, shall without consent of Council be raised, and no new building shall without consent of Council be erected on side of any such street, so that height shall exceed the distance of the front or nearest external wall of such building from opposite side of such street. Where such building is erected or intended to be erected on corner plot, so as to abut upon more than one street, the height of the building shall (unless Council otherwise consent), be regulated by the wider of such streets, &c., and also so far as it abuts &c. upon the narrower of such streets to a distance of 40 feet from the wider street. Any building erected or raised before commencement of this Act to a height to which no objection could have been taken under any law then in force, although exceeding the height provided in this Section, may be re-erected to its existing height.	
This Section not to affect rights of any railway company	,, 49.
Nothing in this part of Act shall prevent raising of any building by increasing height of topmost storey for purpose of bringing habitable rooms in such topmost storey in conformity with provisions of this Act relating to habitable rooms	,, 50.
Nothing in this part of Act shall prevent the re-erection on the same site and of not greater dimensions of any dwelling house inhabited or adapted to be inhabited by persons of the working class, erected by a Local Authority previously to the passing of this Act	,, 51.

CHAPTER CCXIII.

An Act to consolidate and amend the Enactments relating to Streets and Buildings in London.

[25th August 1894.]

WHEREAS enactments relative to streets and buildings in the administrative county of London are contained in the following Acts, viz.:—

The Metropolitan Building Act, 1844.	Public Act.
The Metropolis Management Act, 1855.	Public Act.
The Metropolitan Building Act, 1855.	Public Act.
The Metropolitan Building Act (Amendment), 1860.	Public Act.
The Metropolitan Building Amendment Act, 1861.	Public Act.
The Metropolis Management Amendment Act, 1862.	Public Act.
The Metropolitan Building Act, 1869.	Public Act.
The Metropolitan Building Act, 1871.	Public Act.
The Metropolis Management and Building Acts Amendment Act, 1878.	Public Act.
The Metropolis Management and Building Acts (Amendment) Act, 1882	Public Act.
The London Council (General Powers) Act, 1890.	Local and Personal Act.
The London Sky Signs Act, 1891.	Local and Personal Act.
The London County Council (General Powers) Act, 1893.	Local and Personal Act.

And whereas the existing provisions of the said Acts are complicated, and in some respects doubtful, and are insufficient to secure the construction and maintenance of streets and buildings in a satisfactory manner:

And whereas it will conduce to the public convenience that the said Acts should be repealed to the extent set forth in this Act, and that further provisions should be made, and powers conferred, in order to secure a proper width and direction of streets, the sound construction of buildings, the diminution of the danger arising from fire, the securing of more light, air and space round buildings, and generally with respect to the control and regulation of streets and buildings, and otherwise as in this Act set forth:

And whereas the purposes aforesaid cannot be effected without the authority of Parliament:

May it therefore please Your Majesty, that it may be enacted, and be it enacted by the Queen's most Excellent Majesty, by and with the advice and consent of the Lords Spiritual and Temporal and Commons, in this present Parliament assembled, and by the authority of the same as follows (that is to say):—

Part I.

INTRODUCTORY.

Short title. **1**—This Act may be cited as the London Building Act, 1894.

Division of Act into Parts. **2**—This Act shall be divided into Parts as follows:—
Part I. Introductory.
„ II. Formation and Widening of Streets.
„ III. Lines of Building Frontage.
„ IV. Naming and Numbering of Streets.
„ V. Open Spaces about Buildings and Height of Buildings.
„ VI. Construction of Buildings.
„ VII. Special and Temporary Buildings and Wooden Structures.
„ VIII. Rights of Building and Adjoining Owners.
„ IX. Dangerous and Neglected Structures.

Part X. Dangerous and Noxious Businesses.
„ XI. Dwelling Houses on Low-Lying Land.
„ XII. Sky Signs.
„ XIII. Superintending Architect and District Surveyors.
„ XIV. Byelaws.
„ XV. Legal Proceedings.
„ XVI. Miscellaneous.

3—This Act shall come into operation on, and shall take effect from the first day of January next after the passing thereof, which date is in this Act referred to as the commencement of this Act. Commencement of Act.

4—This Act shall, save so far as is otherwise provided, extend to London and no further: Extent of Act.
Provided always, that in addition to any exemption referring to the Commissioners of Sewers contained in this Act, nothing in this Act contained shall in any way take away, alter, prejudice or affect any of the powers, privileges, exemptions, jurisdictions or authorities given to or vested in the Commissioners of Sewers, by or under any Act of Parliament, and existing immediately before the passing of this Act, notwithstanding the repeal of the Acts specified in the Fourth Schedule hereto.

5—In this Act, unless the context otherwise requires— Definitions.
1. The expression "street" means and includes any highway and any road, bridge, lane, mews, footway, square, court, alley, passage, whether a thoroughfare or not, and a part of any such highway, road, bridge, lane, mews, footway, square, court, alley or passage.
2. The expression "way" includes any public road, way or footpath, not being a street, and any private road, way or footpath which it is proposed to convert into a highway, or to form, lay out or adapt as a street.
3. The expression "roadway," in relation to any street or way, means and includes the whole space open for traffic, whether carriage traffic and foot traffic or foot traffic only.
4. The term "centre of the roadway" means—

(a) In relation to any street or way of which the centre of the roadway has been ascertained or defined by the Council or the superintending architect previously to or after the commencement of this Act, the centre of the roadway as so ascertained or defined;

(b) In relation to any street or way of which the centre of the roadway shall not have been ascertained or defined by the Council or the superintending architect, where the roadway opposite the site of the building in question shall, since the twenty-second day of July, one thousand eight hundred and seventy-eight, have been widened, the centre of the roadway as existing immediately before the date of such widening, or where it shall not have been so widened, the actual centre of the existing roadway:

For the purpose of any enactment in this Act referring to the centre of the roadway, the superintending architect may at any time define the line constituting the centre of the roadway, in the case of a street formed or laid out after the eighteenth day of August, one thousand eight hundred and ninety, and the line so defined shall continue to be deemed the centre for such purpose, notwithstanding that the actual centre of the roadway may have become altered by reason of the roadway having been widened either on one side only, or on both sides to an unequal extent.

5. The expression "the prescribed distance" means twenty feet from the centre of the roadway where such roadway is used for the purpose of carriage traffic, and ten feet from the centre of the roadway where such roadway is used for the purposes of foot traffic only.

6. The expression "new building" means and includes—

Any building erected after the commencement of this Act;

Any building which has been taken down for

LONDON BUILDING ACT, 1894. 33

more than one-half of its cubical extent, and re-erected or commenced to be re-erected, wholly or partially, on the same site after the commencement of this Act;

Any space between walls and buildings which is roofed or commenced to be roofed after the commencement of this Act.

7. The expression "bressummer" means a wooden beam or a metallic girder which carries a wall.
8. The expression "level of the ground" means the mean level of the ground as determined by the district surveyor, or, in the event of disagreement, by the superintending architect, or on appeal, by the tribunal of appeal.
9. The expression "foundation" applied to a wall having footings means the solid ground or artificially formed support on which the footings of the wall rest, but in the case of a wall carried by a bressummer means such bressummer.
10. The expression "base" applied to a wall means the underside of the course immediately above the footings, if any, or in the case of a wall carried by a bressummer, above such bressummer.
11. The expression "ground storey" means that storey of a building to which there is an entrance from the outside on or near the level of the ground, and where there are two such storeys, then the lower of the two:

Provided that no storey of which the upper surface of the floor is more than four feet below the level of the adjoining pavement shall be deemed to be the ground storey.

12. The expression "basement storey" means any storey of a building which is under the ground storey.
13. The expression "first storey" means that storey of a building which is next above the ground storey, the successive storeys above the first storey being the second storey, the third storey, and so on to the topmost storey.
14. The expression "topmost storey" means the uppermost storey in a building, whether constructed wholly or partly in the roof or not.
15. The expression "external wall" means an outer

D

wall or vertical enclosure of any building not being a party wall.

16. The expression "party wall" means—
    (a) A wall forming part of a building, and used or constructed to be used for separation of adjoining buildings belonging to different owners, or occupied, or constructed, or adapted to be occupied by different persons; or
    (b) A wall forming part of a building and standing to a greater extent than the projection of the footings on lands of different owners.

17. The expression "cross wall" means a wall used, or constructed to be used, in any part of its height as an inner wall of a building for separation of one part from another part of the building, that building being wholly in, or being constructed or adapted to be wholly in, one occupation.

18. The expression "party fence wall" means a wall used, or constructed to be used, as a separation of adjoining lands of different owners, and standing on lands of different owners, and not being part of a building, but does not include a wall constructed on the land of one owner, the footings of which project into the land of another owner.

19. The expression "party arch" means an arch separating adjoining buildings, storeys, or rooms belonging to different owners, or occupied, or constructed, or adapted to be occupied by different persons, or separating a building from a public way or a private way leading to premises in other occupation.

20. The expression "party structure" means a party wall, and also a partition floor or other structure, separating vertically or horizontally buildings, storeys, or rooms approached by distinct staircases or separate entrances from without.

21. The expression "height" in relation to any building means the measurement taken from the level of the footway, if any, immediately in front of the centre of the face of the building, or, where there is no such footway, from the level of the ground,

before excavation, to the level of the top of the parapet, or where there is no parapet, to the level of the top of the external wall, or, in the case of gabled buildings, to the base of the gable.

22. The expression "area" applied to a building means the superficies of a horizontal section thereof made at the point of its greatest surface, inclusive of the external walls and of such portions of the party walls as belong to the building.

23. The expression "square" applied to the measurement of the area of a building means the space of 100 superficial feet.

24. The expression "cubical extent" applied to the measurement of a building means the space contained within the external surfaces of its walls and roof and the upper surface of the floor of its lowest storey.

25. The expression "dwelling-house" means a building used, or constructed, or adapted to be used wholly or principally for human habitation.

26. The expression "domestic building" includes a dwelling-house and any other building not being a public building, or of the warehouse class.

27. The expression "public building" means a building used, or constructed or adapted to be used as a church, chapel or other place of public worship, or as a school, college or place of instruction (not being merely a dwelling-house so used), or as a hospital, workhouse, public theatre, public hall, public concert-room, public ball-room, public lecture-room, public library or public exhibition-room, or as a public place of assembly, or used or constructed, or adapted to be used for any other public purpose, also a building used or constructed, or adapted to be used as an hotel, lodging-house, home, refuge or shelter, where such building extends to more than two hundred and fifty thousand cubic feet, or has sleeping accommodation for more than one hundred persons.

28. The expression "building of the warehouse class" means a warehouse, factory, manufactory, brewery or distillery, and any other building

exceeding in cubical extent one hundred and fifty thousand cubic feet which is neither a public building nor a domestic building.

29. The expression "owner" shall apply to every person in possession or receipt either of the whole or of any part of the rents or profits of any land or tenement, or in the occupation of any land or tenement otherwise than as a tenant from year to year or for any less term or as a tenant at will.

30. The expression "occupier" does not include a lodger, and "occupy" and "occupation" do not refer to occupation by a lodger.

31. The expression "building owner" means such one of the owners of adjoining land as is desirous of building, or such one of the owners of buildings, storeys, or rooms separated from one another by a party wall or party structure, as does, or is desirous of doing a work affecting that party wall or party structure.

32. The expression "adjoining owner" means the owner or one of the owners, and "adjoining occupier" means the occupier or one of the occupiers of land, buildings, storeys or rooms adjoining those of the building owner.

33. The expression "builder" means the person who is employed to build or to execute work on a building or structure, or where no person is so employed the owner of the building or structure.

34. The expression "superintending architect" means the superintending architect of metropolitan buildings for the time being.

35. The expression "district surveyor" means every such surveyor who is appointed in pursuance of this Act, or whose appointment is hereby confirmed, and shall include any deputy or assistant surveyor appointed under this Act.

36. The expression "fire-resisting material" means any of the materials and things described in the Second Schedule to this Act.

37. The expression "inhabited" applied to a room means a room in which some person passes the night, or which is used as a living room, in-

cluding a room with respect to which there is a probable presumption (until the contrary is shown) that some person passes the night therein, or that it is used as a living room.

38. The expression "habitable" applied to a room means a room constructed or adapted to be inhabited.
39. The expression "the Metropolis Management Acts" means the Metropolis Management Act, 1855, and the Acts amending the same, or any one or more of those Acts.
40. The expression "London" means the administrative county of London.
41. The expression "the Council" means the London County Council.
42. The expression "local authority" means the Vestry or District Board of Works under the Metropolis Management Acts, within whose parish or district the building, structure, place, land or thing referred to is, or will be, or in the City the Commissioners of Sewers, or in the parish of Woolwich the Woolwich Local Board of Health.
43. The expression "the City" means all parts now within the jurisdiction of the Commissioners of Sewers.
44. The expression "Corporation" means the mayor, aldermen and commons of the City of London.
45. The expression "Guildhall" means the land, offices, courts and buildings commonly called the Guildhall, and the offices, courts and buildings adjoining or appurtenant thereto, which now are used by, or may hereafter be erected for the use of the Corporation, or of any committee, commission or society appointed by them.
46. The expression "Commissioners of Sewers" means the Commissioners of Sewers of the City of London.
47. The expression "the tribunal of appeal" means the tribunal of appeal constituted by this Act.

Part II.
FORMATION AND WIDENING OF STREETS.

6—From and after the commencement of this Act streets shall not be made and ways shall not be widened, altered or adapted so as to form streets, otherwise than subject to and in accordance with the provisions set forth in this Part of this Act. Provided that this Act shall not affect the powers of any local authority to widen, alter or improve any street.

7—Before any person commences to form or lay out any street, whether intended to be used for carriage traffic or for foot traffic only, such person shall make an application in writing to the Council for their sanction to the formation or laying out of such street, either for carriage traffic or for foot traffic (as the case may be):

Every such application shall be accompanied by plans and sections, with such particulars in relation thereto, as may be required by printed regulations issued by the Council, and the Council shall forthwith communicate every such application to the local authority:

And no person shall commence to form or lay out any street for carriage traffic or for foot traffic without having obtained the sanction of the Council.

8—For the purposes of this Part of this Act a person shall be deemed to commence to form or lay out a street if he erect a fence or other boundary, or lay down lines of kerbing, or level the surface of the ground so as to define the course or direction of a street, or if he form the foundations of a house in such manner and in such position as that such house will or may become one of three or more houses abutting on or erected beside land on which a street is intended to be, or may be thereafter laid out or formed. Provided that no person shall be deemed to commence to form or lay out a street if he do any of the acts in this section mentioned for some purpose other than that of forming or laying out a street.

9.—In any of the cases following but in no other case (that is to say):—

1. Where any street is proposed to be formed or laid

out for carriage traffic, without being of or being widened to the full width of forty feet clear, or such other width as may be required under the provisions of this Act;

2. Where any street is proposed to be formed or laid out for foot traffic only, without being of or being widened to the full width of twenty feet clear;

3. Where any street exceeding sixty feet in length or any street not exceeding sixty feet in length, of which the length is greater than the width, is proposed to be formed or laid out without being open at both ends from the ground upwards;

4. Where any street not being within the City is proposed to be formed or laid out in such manner that such street will not, at and from the time of forming and laying out the same, afford direct communication between · two streets, such two streets being (where it is intended to form or lay out such street for carriage traffic) streets formed and laid out for carriage traffic;

5. Where it is proposed to form or lay out any street, not being within the City, for foot traffic only, and it appears to the Council that such street should not be formed or laid out for foot traffic only, or that such street should be formed or laid out for foot traffic only subject to conditions;

6. Where the street is proposed to be formed or laid out for carriage traffic with any gradient steeper than one in twenty;

7. Where it is proposed to form or lay out any street in such manner as to be in contravention of any bye-law of the Council;

it shall be lawful for the Council by order at any time within the period of two months after the receipt of the application, to refuse to sanction, or to sanction subject to such conditions as they may by such order prescribe, the formation or laying out of such street for carriage traffic or for foot traffic only, as the case may be, provided that the Council shall within such period give notice to the applicant of such order, stating fully all their reasons for such refusal or the imposition of such conditions, as the case may be:

Provided that if within the said period of two months the Council fail to give notice of their refusal to sanction the formation or laying out of such street, or of their disapproval of any such plan or section, they shall be deemed to have given their sanction thereto.

<small>Adaptation of ways for streets</small>

10—1. Before any person commences—

(a) To adapt for carriage traffic any street or way not previously so adapted, or to use or permit to be used for carriage traffic any street or way not previously so adapted;

(b) To adapt as a street for foot traffic only or as a public footway any way not previously so adapted;

such person shall make an application in writing to the Council for their sanction thereto, and such application shall be accompanied by plans and sections and such particulars in relation thereto as may be required by printed regulations issued by the Council, and the Council shall forthwith communicate every such application to the local authority, and no person shall commence to execute any such work without having obtained the sanction of the Council.

2. Within two months after the receipt of any such application the Council shall either sanction the plans and sections or give notice to the applicant of their disapproval thereof, stating fully all their reasons for such disapproval. Provided that if within the said period of two months the Council fail to give notice of their disapproval of any such plan or section, they shall be deemed to have given their sanction thereto.

3. A person shall be deemed for the purposes of this Part of this Act to commence to execute a work within the meaning of this section if he erect a fence or other boundary or lay down lines of kerbing or level the surface of the ground so as to define the course or direction of a work within the meaning of this section, or if he form the foundations of a house in such manner and in such position as that such house will or may become one of three or more houses abutting on or erected beside land on which

a street is intended to be or may be thereafter laid out or formed. Provided that no person shall be deemed to commence to execute a work within the meaning of this section if he do any of the acts in this sub-section mentioned, for some purpose other than that of executing a work within the meaning of this section.

4. Before any person commences to widen on either side to a less extent than the prescribed distance any part of a street or way which (being adapted for carriage traffic) is less than forty feet in width or (being adapted for foot traffic only) is less than twenty feet in width, he shall give notice in writing to the Council, accompanied by a plan showing the extent of the proposed widening, and no person shall commence to execute any such widening until after the expiration of two months from the date of such notice, unless with the previous sanction of the Council.

11—In any of the cases following, but in no other case (that is to say):— Grounds for refusing to sanction adaptation of ways for streets.

1. Whenever it is proposed to adapt for carriage traffic any street or way (not previously so adapted) where there are houses or buildings either on both sides thereof or only on one side thereof, without a distance of at least twenty feet clear being left between the centre of the roadway and the nearest external wall of the houses or buildings on the side of the street or way to which the measurement is taken, or (if there be forecourts or other spaces left between such external wall and the roadway) without there being a distance of at least twenty feet clear between the centre of the roadway and the external fences or boundaries of such forecourts or other spaces;
2. Where it is proposed to adapt as a street for foot traffic only or as a public footway any way not previously so adapted, without the same being of or being widened to the full width of twenty feet clear, measured as aforesaid;
3. Where any such adaptation would result in the formation of a street exceeding sixty feet in length, or a street not exceeding sixty feet in length, of which the length is greater than the

width, and in either case not being open at both ends from the ground upwards;

4. Where any such adaptation would result in the formation of a street, not being within the City and not affording direct communication between two streets, such two streets being (where it is intended to form or lay out such street for carriage traffic) streets formed and laid out for carriage traffic;

5. Where the adaptation will result in the formation or laying out of a street, not being within the City, for foot traffic only, and it appears to the Council either that such street should not be formed or laid out for foot traffic only, or that such street should be formed or laid out for foot traffic only subject to conditions;

6. Where the adaptation would result in the formation of a street for carriage traffic with any gradient steeper than one in twenty;

7. Where the adaptation is proposed to be made in such a manner as to be in contravention of any bye-law of the Council;

it shall be lawful for the Council by order at any time, within the said period of two months after the receipt of the application, to refuse to sanction or to sanction (subject to such conditions as they may by such order prescribe) the adaptation proposed by the application. Provided that the Council shall within such period give notice to the applicant of such order, stating fully all their reasons for such refusal or the imposition of such conditions, as the case may be. Provided also that if within the said period of two months the Council fail to give notice of their refusal to sanction such adaptation or of their sanction of the adaptation subject to conditions, they shall be deemed to have given their sanction thereto.

Greater width of street may be required in certain cases.

12—In any case where it is intended—

(a) To form or lay out any street, not being within two miles of Saint Paul's Cathedral, for carriage traffic;

(b) To adapt or permit to be used for carriage traffic any street or way (not being within two miles of Saint Paul's Cathedral) not previously so adapted;

and the Council shall deem it expedient in the public interest that the street or way should, by reason of its length or importance, or in consequence of its forming, or being so situate as to be likely to form, part of an important line of communication, or for other sufficient reason, be of a greater width than forty feet clear, they may make it a condition of their sanction that the street or way shall be throughout, or in such part as they may direct, of a greater width than forty feet, but nothing in this section shall authorise the Council to require a greater width than sixty feet:

And before requiring that any street or way shall be wider than forty feet the Council shall give notice of their intention to the local authority, in order that the local authority if they think fit may make a representation to the Council.

13—1. No person shall erect any new building or new structure or any part thereof, or extend any building or structure or any part thereof in such manner that any external wall of any such building or structure, or (if there be a forecourt or other space between such external wall and the roadway) any part of the external fence or boundary of such forecourt or other space, shall, without the consent in writing of the Council, be in any direction at a distance less than the prescribed distance from the centre of the roadway of any street or way (being a highway).

Position of new buildings with reference to streets.

2. Where the Council after consulting the local authority shall deem it expedient in the public interest, either by reason of the length or importance of the street or way, or by reason of the street or way forming, or being so situate as to be likely to form, part of an important line of communication, or for other sufficient reason, that the prescribed distance from the centre of the roadway of any such street or way should, where such roadway is used for the purpose of carriage traffic, be greater than twenty feet, it shall be lawful for the Council to determine that the prescribed distance shall be such greater distance not exceeding thirty feet from the centre of the roadway of such street or way on either side or both sides as the Council shall see fit to determine. This sub-section shall not apply to any street or way within two miles of Saint Paul's Cathedral.

3. In case the person intending to erect, form or extend any such building, structure, forecourt or space shall be dissatisfied with the determination of the Council that the prescribed distance shall be greater than twenty feet from the centre of the roadway, he may appeal to the tribunal of appeal against such determination of the Council.

4. The Council may in any case where they think it expedient consent to the erection, formation or extension of any building, structure, forecourt or space at a distance less than the prescribed distance from the centre of the roadway of any such street or way, and at such distance from the centre of such roadway and subject to such conditions and terms (if any) as they may think proper to sanction. Provided that the giving of such consent by the Council shall not in any way affect any rights of the owners of adjoining land. Before giving such consent the Council shall communicate to the local authority their intention to give the same. Any person dissatisfied with the determination of the Council under this sub-section may appeal to the tribunal of appeal.

5. Provided that where any person intends to alter or re-erect a building or structure existing either at the commencement of this Act, or at any time within seven years previously, and which shall not be or shall not have been in conformity with the provisions of this section relating to new buildings and structures, such person may cause to be prepared plans showing the extent of such building or structure (or in the event of such building or structure having ceased to exist before the commencement of this Act or having been accidentally destroyed, the best plans available under all the circumstances of the case), and the extent of the forecourt or other open space (if any) between any external wall of such building or structure and the roadway, and may cause such plans to be submitted to the district surveyor, who shall (if reasonably satisfied with the evidence of their accuracy) certify the same under his hand, and such certificate shall be taken to be conclusive evidence of the correctness of the plans. Thereupon it shall be lawful for such person to alter or re-erect such building or structure, but so that no land within the prescribed distance shall be occupied by the re-erected building or structure, or the forecourt or such other open space as aforesaid (if any), except that

which was occupied within the prescribed distance by the previously existing building, structure, forecourt or open space :

If such person should fail to submit such plans to the district surveyor, or the district surveyor or the tribunal of appeal should refuse to certify the accuracy of the same, such person shall, in altering or rebuilding the said building or structure, be bound by the preceding provisions of this section in all respects, as though no building or structure had previously existed upon the land within the period aforesaid. Provided always that no dwelling-house to be inhabited or adapted to be inhabited by persons of the working class shall without the consent of the Council be erected or re-erected within the prescribed distance to a height exceeding the distance of the front or nearest external wall of such building from the opposite side of such street, and that no building or structure shall be converted into such dwelling-house within the prescribed distance so as to exceed such height :

Provided that this section shall not prevent the re-erection of any such dwelling-house erected previously to the passing of this Act by a local authority.

6. Nothing in this section shall affect the exercise of any powers conferred upon any railway company by any special Act of Parliament for railway purposes.

14—In every case where any new building or new structure is erected at a distance in any direction from the centre of the roadway of any street or way less than the distance permitted under this Part of this Act, or contrary to the conditions and terms (if any) subject to which the Council or the tribunal of appeal has sanctioned the erection of such building, the Council may serve a notice upon the owner or occupier of the said building or structure, or upon the builder, requiring him to cause such building, structure, forecourt or space, or any part thereof, to be set back so that every part of any external wall of such building or structure, or of the external fence or boundary of such forecourt or space, shall be at a distance in every direction from the centre of the roadway of such street or way not less than the distance so permitted, and shall be in accordance with such conditions and terms (if any) as the Council or the tribunal of appeal may have prescribed.

Notice to comply with preceding section.

15—In any case where—
1. The Council under this Part of this Act make it a condition of their sanction to—
    (*a*) the formation or laying out of any street for carriage traffic over land which, either at the commencement of this Act or at any time within seven years previously, has or shall have been occupied by buildings or by market gardens; or
    (*b*) the adaptation or use for carriage traffic of any street or way not previously so adapted or used

    that the street or way shall be throughout or in any part of a greater width than forty feet; or
2. The Council determine that the prescribed distance from the centre of the roadway shall be greater than twenty feet;

the Council shall be liable to pay to the owner of land or buildings required for such greater width or such greater prescribed distance compensation for the loss or injury (if any) sustained by him by such requirement. The amount of such compensation, if not agreed within two months from the time of such condition being made or determination arrived at, may (unless the Council waive the condition or determination) be recovered in a summary manner except where the amount of compensation exceeds fifty pounds, in which case the amount thereof shall be settled by arbitration according to the provisions contained in the Lands Clauses Acts, which are applicable where questions of disputed compensation are authorised or required to be settled by arbitration, and for that purpose those Acts so far as applicable shall be deemed to be incorporated with this Act:

Provided always that within two months from the time of such condition or determination being made or arrived at, if the amount of such compensation has not been settled before the expiration of such time, it shall be lawful for the Council to waive such condition or determination. Provided also that if the Council waive such condition or determination they shall pay to the owner the reasonable costs, charges and expenses incurred by him in consequence of such condition or determination, and in connection with the negotiations for the settlement of the amount of compensation:

For the purpose of this section the expression "owner" has the same meaning as in the Lands Clauses Acts.

16—Where after the commencement of this Act— *As to erection of buildings at less than prescribed distance from centre of ways not being highways.*
(i.) Any new building or structure is erected or commenced in such a manner that—
    (a) any part of any external wall of any such building or structure; or
if there be between such external wall and the roadway any forecourt or other space—
    (b) any part of the external fence or boundary of such forecourt or space
is or will be in any direction distant from the centre of the roadway of any way (not being a highway) less than the prescribed distance, or less than such other distance as may have been sanctioned by the Council or the tribunal of appeal; or
(ii.) Any conditions or terms subject to which the sanction of the Council or the tribunal of appeal in relation to any such building, structure, forecourt or space was obtained have not been complied with; or
(iii.) The time during which such sanction was limited to continue has expired;
the way shall not become a highway except subject to the following provisions:—
  (i.) A written notice shall be served upon the Council of the proposal to make the way a public highway;
  (ii.) The Council may at any time within two months after the receipt of such notice serve a notice upon the owner of such building, structure, forecourt or space, or the builder, requiring him to cause the same or any part thereof to be set back so that every part of any external wall of such building or structure, or of the external fence or boundary of such forecourt or space, shall be in every direction at a distance not less than the prescribed distance from the centre of the roadway of such way, or at such distance and according to such conditions and terms (if any) as the Council or the tribunal of appeal may have sanctioned and prescribed;

(iii.) Unless and until such first-mentioned notice has been given to the Council and such last-mentioned notice (if any) has been complied with the way shall not become a highway:

Provided that this section shall not affect the erection or extension of any building or structure within the limits of any area which may have been lawfully occupied by any building or structure at any time within two years before the twenty-second day of July, one thousand eight hundred and seventy-eight, or the erection or extension of any building or structure lawfully in course of erection or extension on the said twenty-second day of July.

Sanction to construction of new buildings at less than prescribed distance.

17—The Council may sanction the erection of any new building or structure at any less distance than the prescribed distance from the centre of the roadway of any way (not being a highway), to be specified in such sanction, or the continuance of any new building or new structure erected at such less distance, or the continuance thereof for a limited time only to be specified in such sanction, in such cases and subject to such terms and conditions (if any) as they may think proper. And any such sanction may be framed in such manner as to apply to all new buildings in any such way or any part thereof. Provided that the giving of such sanction by the Council shall not in any manner affect any rights of the owners of adjoining land.

Regulations to be printed and supplied.

18—Copies of the printed regulations of the Council issued for the purposes of this Part of this Act shall be kept at the county hall and supplied at all reasonable times without charge to any applicants for the same.

Appeal.

19—Whenever any applicant, under Part II. of this Act, for the sanction of the Council to the formation or laying out of a street, or the adaptation of a street or way for carriage or foot traffic, or for the certificate of a district surveyor, is dissatisfied with the refusal or conditional grant of such sanction, or with any condition imposed by the Council, or with the refusal of such certificate as aforesaid, he may appeal to the tribunal of appeal.

As to private roads laid out by a railway company.

20—Nothing in this Part of this Act shall extend or apply to any private road formed or laid out by a railway company, and used as an approach to a station or station yard, or as an approach to land used for railway purposes.

21—Notwithstanding anything in this Act, any buildings to be erected upon any lands now belonging to the School Board for London, or over which they have powers of compulsory purchase, or may acquire such powers in the present session of Parliament, may be erected in accordance with the provisions of any Act in force immediately before the passing of this Act.

Exempting certain School Board buildings.

Part III.
LINES OF BUILDING FRONTAGE.

22—1. No building or structure shall, without the consent in writing of the Council, be erected beyond the general line of buildings in any street or part of a street, place, or row of houses, in which the same is situate, in case the distance of such line of buildings from the highway does not exceed 50 feet, or within 50 feet of the highway, when the distance of the line of buildings therefrom amounts to or exceeds 50 feet, notwithstanding there being gardens or vacant spaces between the line of buildings and the highway. Such general line of buildings shall, if required, be defined by the superintending architect by a certificate, such certificate to be issued within one month from the date of the application therefor.

Mode of proceeding with regard to buildings beyond line of street.

2. This section shall not apply to any building or structure erected after the commencement of this Act upon land which either at the commencement of this Act, or at any time within seven years previously has or shall have been lawfully occupied by a building or structure.

23—1. In case any building or structure which shall in any part thereof project beyond the general line of buildings in a street, or beyond the front of the building, wall or railing on either side thereof, shall at any time be taken down to an extent exceeding one-half of the cubical extent of such building or structure, or shall be destroyed by fire or other casualty, or demolished, pulled down or removed from any other cause to the extent aforesaid, it shall be lawful for the Council to require the

Buildings projecting beyond general line when taken down to be set back.

E

same building or structure, or any new building or structure proposed to be erected on the site or any part of the site thereof, to be set back to such a line and in such a manner as the Council shall direct.

2. The Council shall make compensation to the owner of such building for any damage and expenses which he may sustain and incur thereby, and the amount of such compensation, if not agreed between the Council and the parties concerned, shall be recovered in a summary manner, except where the amount of compensation claimed exceeds fifty pounds, in which case the amount thereof shall be settled by arbitration according to the provisions contained in the Lands Clauses Acts, which are applicable where questions of disputed compensation are authorised or required to be settled by arbitration, and for that purpose those Acts so far as applicable shall be deemed to be incorporated with this Act. For the purpose of this section the expression "owner" has the same meaning as in the Lands Clauses Acts.

Notices of certification of general line.

24—The superintending architect shall, within fourteen days after the issue of the certificate defining the general line of buildings in any street or part of a street, place or row of houses, cause a notice of his certificate to be served on the local authority, and on the owner of the building or land to which the certificate relates, and on the owner of the houses in the same block or row within a distance not exceeding fifty yards on either side of the building or land to which the certificate relates, or, where there is no such block or row, upon the owner of the adjoining land on either side of the building or land to which the certificate relates. Certificates made by the superintending architect under this Part of this Act shall be preserved by the Council, and be open to inspection at all reasonable times by all persons desiring to inspect the same.

Appeal against certificate of architect as to general line.

25—The local authority, or any person deeming to be aggrieved by the certificate of the superintending architect, may appeal to the tribunal of appeal.

Conditions may be attached to consent to erection of building beyond general line.

26—In giving their consent for the erection of any building or structure beyond the general line of buildings, in any street or part of a street, place, or row of houses, the Council may attach any conditions to such consent,

and such conditions may include any or all of the conditions following, viz. :—
1. That land in front of the building or structure to such an extent as the Council may think proper shall be dedicated to and left open for the use of the public.
2. That the building or structure shall be used only for such purposes as may be specified in the consent, or shall not be used for any particular purposes specified in the consent, unless with the further consent of the Council, obtained when a change of purpose is desired.

And generally any other condition which the Council may deem it expedient to impose in the public interest.

27—The consent by the Council to the erection of any building or structure beyond the general line of buildings in any part of a street, or the erection of such building or structure, shall not be deemed to affect or alter in that or any other part of the street the general line of buildings as existing at the time of such consent. Consent not to affect rest of general line.

28—The Council shall keep a register of all conditional consents given by them under this part of this Act, and shall keep the same open for inspection by all persons interested at all reasonable times. Register of conditional consents to be kept and open for inspection.

29—The superintending architect shall, if required by the Council, the local authority, or any person interested for the purposes of this Part of this Act, determine in any case in what street or streets a building or structure is situate, such determination to be evidenced by his certificate. Any person aggrieved by such certificate may appeal to the tribunal of appeal. Defining in what street a building or structure is situate.

30—This Part of this Act shall not apply within the City. Part of Act not to apply in City.

31—Nothing in this Part of this Act shall affect the exercise of any powers conferred upon any railway company by any special Act of Parliament for railway purposes. Certain powers of railway companies not affected by this Part of Act.

Part IV.
NAMING AND NUMBERING OF STREETS.

Notice of new name of street.

32—Before any name is given to any street, notice of the intended name shall be given to the Council, and the Council may by notice in writing, given to the person by whom notice of such intended name has been given to them, at any time within one month after receipt of such notice, object to such intended name; and it shall not be lawful to set up any name to any street in London until the expiration of one month after notice thereof has been given as aforesaid to the Council, or to set up any name objected to as aforesaid.

Affixing names of streets by local authority.

33—The local authority shall and may cause the name of every street to be painted or affixed on a conspicuous part of some house or building at or near each end or entrance to such street, or some other convenient part of the street, and shall renew such name whenever it may be obliterated or defaced.

Altering names of streets.

34—The Council may by order alter the name of any street to any other name which to the Council may seem fit.

Notice of altering names of streets.

35—One month before making an order altering the name of a street, the Council shall notify their intention of making such alteration to the local authority, and shall also cause notice of their intention to be posted at each end of the street, or in some conspicuous position in the street, or, at the option of the Council, to be notified by circular delivered at every house in the street.

Every such notice shall state that the order altering the name of the street may be issued on or after a day to be therein named, if no objection in writing to the proposed alteration be given to the Council.

Numbering houses.

36—1. The Council may order that any houses or buildings in any street, or way, or any part thereof, shall for the purpose of distinguishing the same, be marked with such numbers as they shall deem convenient for that purpose, and which they shall specify in their order in that behalf.

2. Whenever the Council have made any such order they shall transmit a copy thereof to the local authority, and it shall be the duty of the local authority to perform all necessary acts, and to take all requisite proceedings for carrying the order of the Council into execution.

3. The local authority shall give notice to the owners or occupiers of the houses and buildings in such street or way to mark their several houses and buildings with such numbers as the Council shall have ordered, and to renew the numbers of such houses or buildings as often as they are obliterated or defaced.

4. If any occupier of any such house or building neglect for one week after notice from the local authority to mark such house or building with such number as shall be mentioned and required in such notice, the local authority may and shall cause such number to be so marked or renewed, and recover the expenses thereof from the owner or occupier of such house or building in a summary manner.

37—Whenever the Council have transmitted a copy of any order made by them in pursuance of the provisions of this Part of this Act to any local authority, and such local authority have for the space of three months after the receipt of such order failed to perform all or any of the necessary acts, or to take all or any of the requisite proceedings for carrying such order into execution, then, and in every such case the Council may perform all or any of such necessary acts, or take all or any of such necessary proceedings which the local authority have failed to perform or take, and the Council may exercise all the rights, powers, authorities and jurisdiction of a local authority with respect thereto, including the recovery of expenses from owners of houses and buildings. *Power to Council to name and number streets in default of local authority complying with order.*

38—The Council shall keep a register of all alterations made by them in the names of streets and in the numbers of the houses therein, and such register shall be kept in such form as to show the date of every such alteration, and the name of the street previous to such alteration as well as the new name thereof. It shall be lawful for any person to inspect such register, and to take a copy of any portion thereof, upon payment of such reasonable fee as the Council may from time to time determine. *Register to be kept of alterations in names of streets.*

Part V.
OPEN SPACES ABOUT BUILDINGS AND HEIGHT OF BUILDINGS.

Meaning of "domestic building" in this Part of Act.

39—For the purposes of this Part of this Act the expression "domestic building," shall not include any buildings used or constructed, or adapted to be used wholly or principally as offices or counting-houses.

Light and ventilation of habitable basements.

40—In the case of domestic buildings erected after the commencement of this Act which shall have a habitable basement, there shall for the purpose of giving light and air to such basement be provided in the rear of the building and exclusively belonging thereto, an open space of an aggregate extent of not less than one hundred square feet free from any erection thereon above the level of the adjoining pavement, which open space, notwithstanding anything hereinafter contained, need not necessarily adjoin the rear boundary of the premises.

Space at rear of domestic buildings.

41—1. With respect to domestic buildings erected after the commencement of this Act, and abutting upon a street formed or laid out after the commencement of this Act, the following provisions shall have effect:—

(i.) There shall be provided in the rear of every such building an open space exclusively belonging to such building, and of an aggregate extent of not less than one hundred and fifty square feet;

Where there is a basement storey directly and sufficiently lighted and ventilated by the open space provided under the preceding section, irrespective of any use to which the ground storey is appropriated, or where there is no such basement storey, but where the ground storey is not constructed or adapted to be inhabited, the open space required by this section may be provided above the level of the ceiling of the ground storey, or a level of sixteen feet, exclusive of lantern lights, measured from the level of the adjoining pavement;

In all other cases the open space shall be free

ILLUSTRATION AS TO SEC. 41. BACK YARDS.

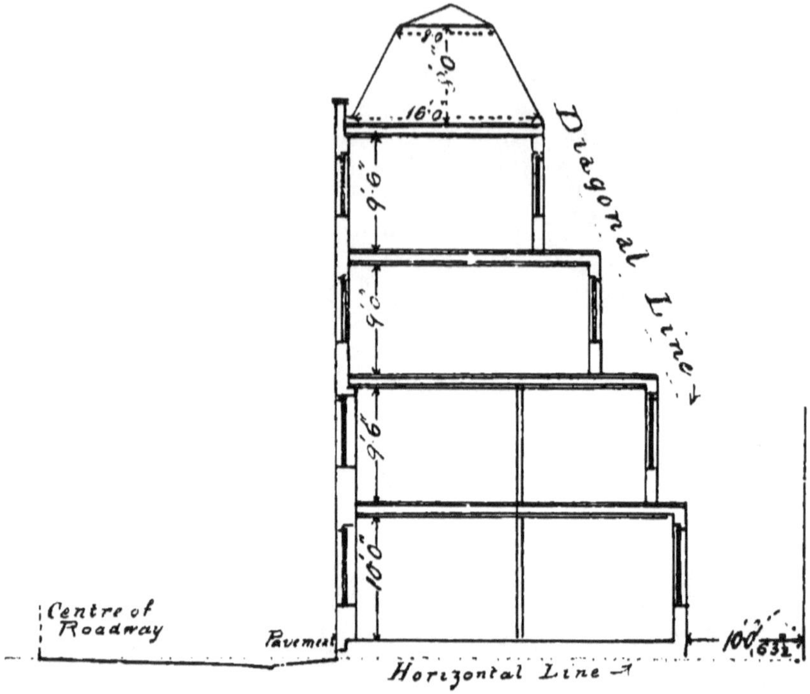

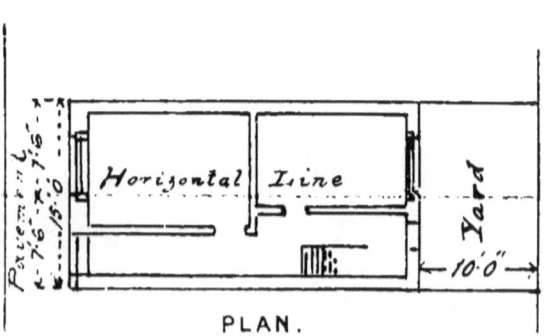

SECTION.

PLAN.

This diagram is in illustration of the angle where Domestic Buildings are erected abutting on Streets laid out after January 1895 & the stringency is relaxed where the Domestic Building abuts on Streets laid out before the commencement of from any erection thereon above the level of the adjoining pavement, except a water-closet, earth-closet or privy, and a receptacle for ashes, and enclosing walls, none of which erections shall exceed nine feet in height;

(ii.) Such open space shall extend throughout the entire width of such building, and to a depth in every part of at least ten feet from such building;

(iii.) The height of any such building in relation to the space required in the rear thereof shall be fixed and ascertained as follows:—

    (*a*) An imaginary line (hereafter referred to as " the horizontal line,") shall be drawn at right angles to the roadway formed, or to be formed in front of the building, and through or directly over a point in front of the centre of the face of the building;

    (*b*) The horizontal line shall be produced to intersect the boundary of the open space furthest from the said roadway;

    (*c*) The horizontal line shall be drawn throughout at the level of the pavement formed or to be formed in front of the centre of the building, unless the site of the building incline towards the roadway or site of the roadway, in which case the horizontal line shall be drawn directly over the said point in front of the centre of the face of the building at the level throughout of the ground, at the boundary of the space furthest from such roadway where such boundary is intersected by the horizontal line;

    (*d*) A second imaginary line (in this Part of this Act called "the diagonal line") shall be drawn in the direction of the building above and in the same vertical plane with the horizontal line, and inclined thereto at an angle of sixty-three and a half degrees, and meeting the horizontal line where it intersects the boundary of the space furthest removed from such roadway;

(e) No part of such building shall extend above the diagonal line except chimneys, dormers, gables, turrets or other architectural ornaments, aggregating in all to not more than one-third of the width of the rear elevation of such building, and except any building which under the provisions of this section is permitted on the open space;

(f) When the pavement in front of a building is not all on one level, then for the purpose of compliance with this section the mean level of such pavement shall be deemed to be the level thereof. And where the boundary of the space at the rear of such building is not parallel with the rear wall of the building, then for the purpose of this section the horizontal line shall be drawn to a point distant from such rear wall, the mean distance from such wall of the boundary of the space at the rear of such building, whether such point be beyond the said boundary or not;

(g) When the boundary of the space at the rear of any such building shall be so irregular in shape that a doubt arises as to how the measurement shall be taken, application shall be made to the Council, and the applicant if dissatisfied with the determination of the Council may appeal to the tribunal of appeal.

(h) When the land at the rear of any such building and exclusively belonging thereto abuts immediately upon a street, or upon an open space which is dedicated to the public, or the maintenance of which as an open space is secured permanently or to the satisfaction of the Council by covenant or otherwise, the horizontal line shall be produced and the diagonal line may be drawn from the horizontal line at the centre of the roadway of such street at the level of the surface thereof, or at the further boundary of such open space, and it shall not be necessary to provide any open space at the rear of such building :

(iv.) The Council may—
  (a) In the case of a building at a corner abutting upon two streets ;
  (b) In the case of a building at a corner abutting on one side upon a street, and on another side upon an open space not less than forty feet wide at any part, the maintenance of which as an open space is secured permanently, or to the satisfaction of the Council by covenant or otherwise ;

permit the erection of buildings not exceeding thirty feet in height, upon such part of the space in the rear as they may think fit, provided that the Council be satisfied that such buildings shall be so placed as not to interfere unduly with the access of light and air to neighbouring buildings ;

When the Council refuse any application under this sub-section for permission to erect a building not exceeding thirty feet in height upon the space at the rear, the applicant if dissatisfied with the determination of the Council may appeal to the tribunal of appeal :

(v.) In the case of buildings at a corner as hereinbefore described, nothing in this Part as to the determination of height by the diagonal line shall prevent the return front of such buildings being carried up to the full height of the front elevation for a distance of forty feet, or for such less distance as the requirements for open space at the rear may demand :

(vi.) In exceptional cases where, owing to the irregular shape of the land, any of the preceding provisions of this section cannot be applied, the Council may allow such modifications as they may think fit, provided the Council be satisfied that such modifications shall not interfere with the due access of light or air ; and all persons interested, dissatisfied with any determination of the Council under this sub-section, may appeal to the tribunal of appeal.

2. With respect to domestic buildings, erected after the commencement of this Act, abutting upon a street formed or laid out before the commencement of this Act, the provisions of this section shall apply with this modification, that the horizontal line shall be drawn throughout at a level of sixteen feet above the level of the adjoining pavement, and that in any such case (except in the case of dwelling houses to be inhabited or adapted to be inhabited by persons of the working class) the open space to be provided in accordance with paragraphs (i.) and (ii.) of sub-section 1 of this section may be provided above the level of the ceiling of the ground storey, or above a level of sixteen feet (exclusive of lantern-lights) above the level of the adjoining pavement.

Provided always that notwithstanding the preceding provisions of this Part of this Act, any part of any domestic building may extend above the diagonal line, provided that the Council or tribunal of appeal shall be satisfied that an open cubic space of air will be provided at the rear of such building equivalent to the open cubic space which would have been provided at the rear of such building if such diagonal line had been drawn from the ground level in manner provided in sub-section 1 (iii.) of this section, and if no part of such building (except as permitted under the preceding provisions of this section) had extended above such diagonal line. The applicant if dissatisfied with the determination of the Council may appeal to the tribunal of appeal.

Nothing in this section shall apply to houses abutting in the rear on the River Thames, or on a public park, or on an open space of not less than eighty feet in depth which is dedicated to the public, or the maintenance of which as an open space is secured permanently or to the satisfaction of the Council by covenant or otherwise.

Open space to be provided about certain buildings not on the public way.

42—The following provisions shall have effect with respect to dwelling-houses to be inhabited or adapted to be inhabited by persons of the working class, erected after the commencement of this Act, not abutting upon a street :—

(i.) At least one month before commencing to erect any such dwelling-house, the person intending to erect the same shall deliver at the county hall a sufficient plan or plans exhibiting the extent and height of the intended dwelling-house in its several parts, and also its position in relation to every other building, either already existing or in course of erection, which is adjacent thereto:

(ii.) In any case where the Council are satisfied, taking all the circumstances of the case into consideration, that there will not be provided about such dwelling-house a sufficient open space or spaces for the admission of light and air thereto, it shall be lawful for the Council at any time before the expiration of one month from the delivery of the said plan or plans, by order to refuse to sanction such plan or plans, or to sanction the same subject to such conditions as they may by such order prescribe. Provided always that nothing in this sub-section shall authorise the Council to refuse to sanction such plan or plans, or to prescribe any conditions when sanctioning the same, in any case where the open space or spaces for the admission of light and air proposed to be provided about such dwelling-house is, or are, equivalent to the open space or spaces which would have been provided about such dwelling-house under the provisions of this Act, in case the same had been erected after the commencement of this Act, abutting upon a street or way formed or laid out before the commencement of this Act:

(iii.) No person shall commence to erect any such dwelling-house without having obtained the sanction of the Council to the plans delivered by him:

(iv.) Unless the Council shall, within one month after the delivery of the said plan or plans to them, give notice to the person delivering the same of their disapproval thereof, the Council shall be deemed to have given their sanction thereto:

(v.) In case any person intending to erect any such dwelling-house considers that the refusal of the Council to sanction the plans delivered by him, or any of the conditions prescribed by the Council is or are unreasonable, he may appeal to the tribunal of appeal.

Saving for certain domestic buildings on old sites.

43—When any person intends to erect a domestic building (not being a dwelling-house to be inhabited or adapted to be inhabited by persons of the working class) abutting upon a street on the site of domestic buildings existing at the commencement of this Act, or on a site vacant at the commencement of this Act, but which has been occupied by a domestic building at any time within seven years previous to the commencement of this Act, the following provisions shall have effect:—

(i.) It shall be lawful for such person, before commencing to erect the intended domestic building, to cause to be prepared plans showing the extent of the previously existing domestic building in its several parts (or in the event of such building having been taken down before the commencement of this Act, or having been accidentally destroyed, the best plans available under all the circumstances of the case), and to cause such plans to be submitted to the district surveyor, who shall (if reasonably satisfied with the evidence of their accuracy) certify the same under his hand, and such certificate shall be taken to be conclusive evidence of the correctness of the plans;

Such person may then erect the intended domestic building, but so that no more land shall be occupied by the newly erected building than was occupied by the previously existing domestic building as so certified. If such person fail to submit such plans to the district surveyor, or the district surveyor or the tribunal of appeal refuse to certify the accuracy of the same, such person shall in rebuilding be bound by the preceding provisions of this Part of this Act relating to domestic buildings erected after the commencement of this Act, abutting upon a street formed or laid out before that date:

(ii.) If a person erecting the intended domestic building shall desire to deviate in any respect from the plan or plans certified by the district surveyor, it shall be lawful for him to apply to the Council, who shall sanction such deviations on such conditions as they may think fit, provided that such conditions shall not in any case be more onerous than the conditions prescribed for domestic buildings erected after the commencement of this Act, abutting on a street formed or laid out before that date:

(iii.) A person dissatisfied with any decision of the Council or of a district surveyor under this section may appeal to the tribunal of appeal.

44—When any person desires to re-arrange a cleared area previously occupied in whole or in part by buildings, by forming or laying out a new street or streets, or widening a street or streets, he may make application to the Council with such plans and sections as may be required by the Council, and the Council may, if under all the circumstances of the case they think it desirable, modify or relax any of the foregoing provisions of this Part of this Act, subject to such conditions as the Council may impose. *Laying out of new streets on cleared area.*

Within two months after the receipt of the application, the Council shall either sanction the plans and sections or give notice to the applicant of their disapproval thereof, stating fully all their reasons for such disapproval.

Provided that if within the said period of two months the Council fail to give notice of their disapproval of any such plan or section, they shall be deemed to have given their sanction thereto.

Any applicant dissatisfied with the determination of the Council may appeal to the tribunal of appeal.

45—Where a court wholly or in part open at the top but enclosed on every side, and constructed or used for admitting light or air to a domestic building, is constructed in connection with such domestic building, and the depth of such court from the eaves or top of the parapet to the ceiling of the ground storey exceeds the length or breadth of such court, adequate provision for the ventilation of such court shall be made and maintained by the owner of the building by means of a communication between the lower end of the court and the outer air. *Courts within a building.*

No habitable room not having a window directly opening into the external air, otherwise than into a court enclosed on every side, shall be constructed in any building, unless the width of such court measured from such window to the opposite wall shall be equal to half the height, measured from the sill of such window to the eaves or top of the parapet of the opposite wall.

Provided that a court, of which the greater dimension does not exceed twice the less dimension, shall be held to comply with this section if a court of the same area but square in shape would comply therewith.

No habitable room above the level of the ground storey, not having a window directly opening into the external air otherwise than into a court open on one side, the depth whereof, measured from the open side, exceeds twice the width, shall be constructed in any building unless every window of such room be placed not nearer to the opposite wall of such court or to any other building than one-half the height of the top of such wall or building above the level of the sill of such window.

Superintending architect may define front or rear of buildings.

46—In any case when it may be necessary the superintending architect shall determine which is the front and which is the rear of a building, such determination to be evidenced by his certificate. Any person dissatisfied with such certificate may appeal to the tribunal of appeal.

Height of buildings limited.

47—A building (not being a church or chapel) shall not be erected of, or be subsequently increased to a greater height than eighty feet (exclusive of two storeys in the roof and of ornamental towers, turrets, or other architectural features or decorations) without the consent of the Council.

Provided that where a contract shall have been lawfully made previously to the passing of this Act for the erection or increase of a building to a greater height than eighty feet, nothing in this section shall prevent the erection or increase of such building to any height to which it might have been lawfully erected or increased immediately before the passing of this Act.

This section shall not apply to the rebuilding to the same height as at present of any building existing at the passing of this Act of a greater height than eighty feet.

Provided also that where any existing buildings forming part of a continuous block or row of buildings exceed the height prescribed by this section, nothing in this section shall prevent any other building in the same block or row, belonging at the date of the passing of this Act to the same owner, from being carried to a height equal to but not exceeding that of the existing buildings.

Nothing in this section shall affect the exercise of any powers conferred upon any railway company by any special Act of Parliament for railway purposes.

48—1. Whenever the Council consent to the erection of any building of a greater height than that prescribed by this Act, notice of such consent shall, within one week after such consent has been given, be published and served in such manner as the Council may direct, and the consent shall not be acted on until twenty-one days after such publication or service, or in the event of any appeal against such consent, until after the determination of such appeal. *Procedure where greater height allowed.*

2. (*a*) The owner or lessee of any building or land within one hundred yards of the site of any intended building who may deem himself aggrieved by the grant of such consent in respect of the last-mentioned building; or

(*b*) Any applicant for consent which has been refused;

may respectively within twenty-one days after the publication of notice of the consent, or after the date of the refusal (as the case may be), appeal to the tribunal of appeal.

3. Whenever such consent has been refused and the applicant to whom it has been refused intends to appeal against such refusal, such applicant shall give notice within twenty-one days of such refusal, in such manner as the Council may direct, to the owner or lessee of any building or land within one hundred yards of the site of the building to which such refusal relates, that he intends to appeal from such refusal.

4. In the case of an appeal against the refusal of consent, any owner or lessee of any building or land within one hundred yards of the site of the intended building may appear and be heard before the tribunal of appeal against any application to reverse or vary the refusal.

49—After the commencement of this Act no existing building (other than a church or chapel), on the side of a *Heights of buildings in certain cases.*

RECESSES IN EXTERNAL & PARTY WALLS & CHASES IN PARTY WALLS.

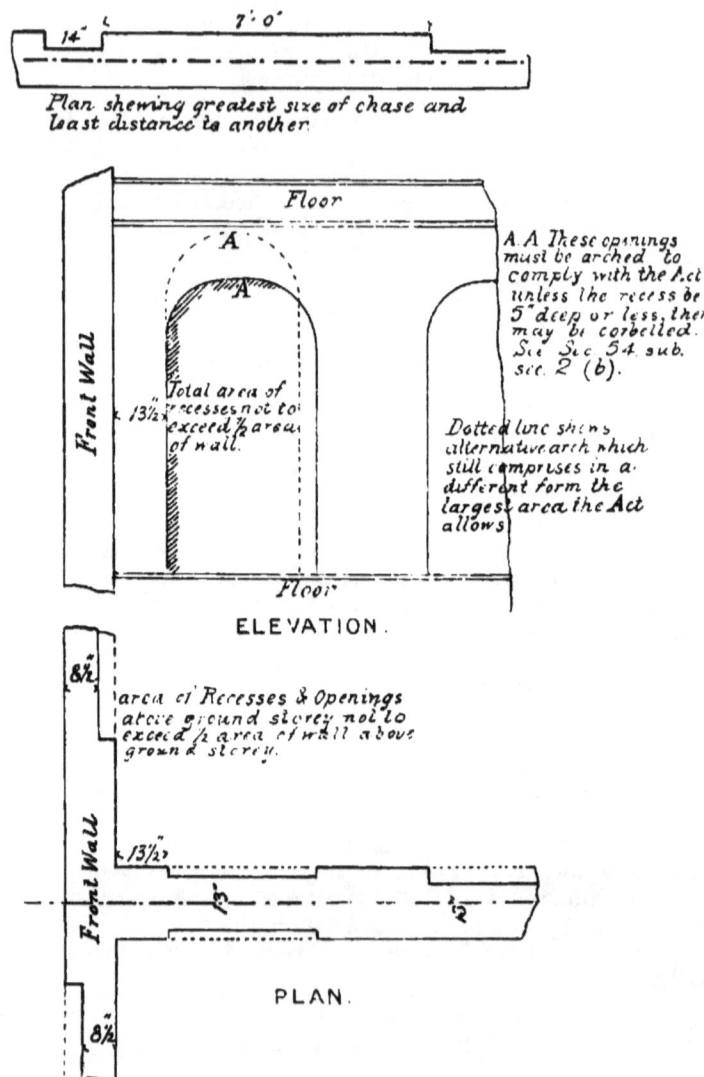

the following provisions shall in certain cases have effect:—

If the stable buildings be limited to a depth of fifty feet, measured from the mews frontage, and to a height of twenty-five feet, measured from the level of the mews, and if the open space required for the domestic building under section 41 of this Act be provided between, the domestic building and the stable building may for all other purposes of the said section, whether in one occupation or not, be deemed to be one domestic building with the rear abutting upon a street.

Part VI.

CONSTRUCTION OF BUILDINGS.

53—Subject to any bye-laws of the Council made in pursuance of this Act, walls shall be constructed of the substances and in the manner and of not less than the thickness prescribed by this Act or mentioned in the First Schedule to this Act.

Structure and thickness of walls.

54—1. Recesses and openings may be made in external walls provided—

Rules as to recesses and openings.

   (a) That the backs of such recesses are not of less thickness than eight and a half inches; and

   (b) That the area of such recesses and openings above the ground storey do not, taken together, exceed one-half of the whole area of the wall above the ground storey in which they are made.

2. Recesses may be made in party walls provided—

   (a) That the backs of such recesses are not of less thickness than thirteen inches; and

   (b) That over every recess so formed an arch of at least two rings of brickwork of the full depth of the recess be turned on every storey, except in the case of recesses formed for lifts; but where such recess does not exceed five inches in depth, corbelling in brick or stone may be substituted for the arching; and

   (c) That the areas of such recesses do not, taken together, exceed one-half of the whole area of the wall of the story in which they are made; and

(d) That such recesses do not come within thirteen and a half inches of the inner face of the external walls.

3. An opening shall not be made in any party wall except in accordance with the provisions of this Act in relation thereto.

Provided that it shall be lawful for the superintending architect, on application made to him in accordance with any rules made in that behalf by the Council, to give consent in writing to any modification or relaxation of the requirements of this section with respect to the area of recesses and openings in any special cases where he may think proper. The word area as used in this section shall mean the area of the vertical face or elevation of the wall or recess to which it refers.

55—All woodwork fixed in any external wall, except bressummers and storey-posts under the same, and frames of doors and windows of shops on the ground storey of any building, shall be set back four inches at the least from the external face of such wall; but loophole frames and frames of doors and windows may be fixed flush with the face of any external wall:

Provided that it shall be lawful for the Council, by byelaw or otherwise, to exempt from the provisions of this section, oak, teak or other wood, provided the work be constructed to the satisfaction of the district surveyor.

56—1. Every bressummer, whether of wood or metal, shall have a bearing in the direction of its length of four inches at least at each end upon a sufficient pier of brick or stone, or upon a timber or iron storey-post fixed on a solid foundation, in addition to its bearing upon any party wall or external wall, and the district surveyor shall have power in his discretion to require that every bressummer shall have such other storey-posts, iron columns, stanchions, or piers of brick or stone, or corbels, as may be sufficient to carry the superstructure, and the ends of such bressummer, if of wood, shall not be placed nearer to the centre line of the party walls than four inches.

2. At each end of every metallic bressummer a space shall be left equal to one-quarter of an inch for every ten feet, and also for any fractional part of ten feet of the length of such bressummer to allow for expansion.

3. A bond timber or wood plate shall not be built into any party wall, and the ends of any wooden beam or joist bearing on such walls shall be at least four inches distant from the centre line of the party walls.

4. Every bressummer bearing upon a party wall shall be borne by a templet or corbel of stone or iron tailed through at least half the thickness of the wall, and of the full breadth of the bressummer.

5. The end of any timber not permitted to be placed in or to have a bearing on a party wall, may be carried on a corbel or templet of stone or iron, or vitrified stoneware, tailed into the wall to a distance of at least eight and a half inches, or otherwise supported to the satisfaction of the district surveyor.

57—If any gutter, any part of which is formed of combustible materials, adjoin an external wall, such wall shall be carried up so as to form a parapet one foot at the least above the highest part of the gutter, and the thickness of the parapet so carried up shall be at least eight and a half inches throughout. Height and thickness of parapets to external walls.

58—In either of the following cases:— Cases in which a wa to be deem a party wal
(a) When a wall is, after the commencement of this Act, built as a party wall in any part; or
(b) Where a wall built before or after the commencement of this Act becomes after the commencement of this Act a party wall in any part;
the wall shall be deemed a party wall for such part of its length as is so used.

59.—1. Every party wall shall be carried up of a thickness in a building of the warehouse class equal to the thickness of such wall in the topmost storey, and in any other building of eight and a half inches above the roof, flat or gutter of the highest building adjoining thereto, to such a height as will give a distance (in a building of the warehouse class exceeding thirty feet in height) of at least three feet, and (in any other building) of fifteen inches, measured at right angles to the slope of the roof, Height of party walls above roof.

or fifteen inches above the highest part of any flat or gutter, as the case may be.

2. Every party wall shall be carried up of the thickness aforesaid above any turret, dormer, lantern light or other erection of combustible materials fixed upon the roof or flat of any building within four feet from such party wall, and shall extend at the least twelve inches higher and wider on each side than such erection, and every party wall shall be carried up above any part of any roof opposite thereto, and within four feet therefrom.

Rules as to chases in party walls.

60—In a party wall a chase shall not be made wider than fourteen inches, nor more than four and a half inches deep from the face of the wall, nor so as to leave less than eight and a half inches in thickness at the back or opposite side thereof, and a chase shall not be made within a distance of seven feet from any other chase on the same side of the wall, or within thirteen inches from an external wall. No chase shall be made in a wall of less thickness than thirteen inches.

Rules as to construction of roofs.

61—1. The flat, gutter and roof of every building, and every turret, dormer, lantern light, skylight or other erection placed on the flat or roof thereof shall be externally covered with slates, tiles, metal or other incombustible materials, except wooden cornices and barge boards to dormers not exceeding twelve inches in depth, and the doors, door frames, windows, and window frames of such dormers, turrets, lantern lights, skylights or other erections.

2. Every building exceeding thirty feet in height, used wholly or in part as a dwelling house or factory, and having a parapet, shall be provided either—

    (*a*) with a dormer window, or a door opening on to the roof; or

    (*b*) with a trap door furnished with a fixed or hinged step ladder leading to the roof; or

    (*c*) with other proper means of access to the roof.

3. The plane of the surface of the roof of a building of the warehouse class shall not incline from the external or party walls upwards at a greater angle than forty-seven degrees with the horizon. Provided that this sub-section shall not apply to towers, turrets or spires.

4. The plane of the surface of the roof of any other

LANTERN LIGHT SHEWING NEAREST POSITION TO PARTY WALL.

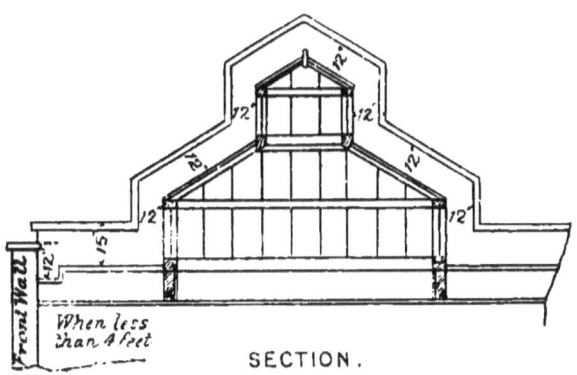

SECTION.

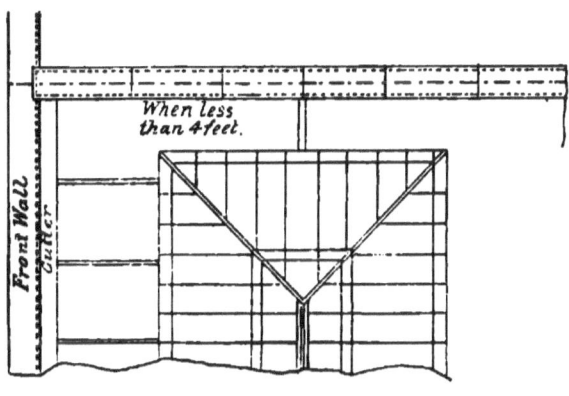

PLAN.

building shall not incline from the external or party walls upwards at a greater angle than seventy-five degrees with the horizon. Provided that this subsection shall not apply to towers, turrets or spires.

62—1. Not more than two storeys shall be constructed in the roof of any domestic building. *Storeys in roofs.*

2. Any storey constructed in the roof of any domestic building, the upper surface of the floor of which storey is at a height of above sixty feet from the street level, shall be constructed of fire-resisting materials throughout.

63—Every new building exceeding sixty feet in height shall be provided on the storeys, the upper surface of the floor whereof is above sixty feet from the street level, with such means of escape in the case of fire for the persons dwelling or employed therein as can be reasonably required under the circumstances of the case, and no such storeys of such building shall be occupied until the Council shall have issued a certificate that the provisions of this section have been complied with in relation thereto. *Means of escape at top of high buildings.*

64—1. Chimneys built on corbels of brick, stone or other incombustible materials may be erected if the work so corbelled out do not project from the wall more than the thickness of the wall, measured immediately below the corbel, but all other chimneys shall be built on solid foundations, and with footings similar to the footings of the wall against which they are built, unless they are carried upon iron girders with direct bearings upon party external or cross walls, to the satisfaction of the district surveyor. *Rules as to chimneys and flues.*

2. Chimneys and flues having proper soot doors of not less than forty square inches may be constructed at any angle, but in no other case shall any flue be inclined at a less angle than forty-five degrees to the horizon, and every angle shall be properly rounded.

All soot doors shall be at least fifteen inches distant from any woodwork.

3. An arch of brick or stone, or a bar of wrought iron of sufficient strength, shall be built over the opening of every chimney to support the breast thereof, and if the breast project more than four inches from the face of the

wall, and the jamb on either side be of less width than seventeen and a half inches, the abutments shall be tied in by an iron bar or bars of sufficient strength, turned up and down at the ends, and built into the jambs for at least eight and a half inches on each side.

4. A flue shall not be adapted to or used for any new oven, furnace, cockle, steam boiler, or close fire, used for any purpose of trade or business, or to or for the range or cooking apparatus of any hotel, tavern, or eating-house, unless the flue be surrounded with brickwork at least eight and a half inches thick from the floor on which such oven, furnace, cockle, steam boiler or close fire is situate to the level of the ceiling of the room next above the same.

5. A flue shall not be used in connection with a steam boiler or hot-air engine unless the flue is at least twenty feet in height, measured from the level of the floor on which such engine is placed.

6. The inside of every flue, and also the outside where passing through any floor or roof or behind or against any woodwork, shall be rendered, pargeted or lined with fire-resisting piping of stoneware.

7. The position and course of every flue shall be distinguished on the outside of the work as it is carried up by outline marks in some durable manner, except when the exterior face of the flue forms part of the outer face of an external wall not likely to be built against.

8. The jambs of every fireplace opening shall be at least eight and a half inches wide on each side of the opening thereof.

9. The breast of every chimney and the brickwork surrounding every smoke flue shall be at least four inches in thickness.

10. The back of every fireplace opening in a party wall, from the hearth up to the height of twelve inches above the mantel, shall be at least eight and a half inches thick.

11. The thickness of the upper side of every flue, when its course makes with the horizon an angle of less than forty-five degrees, shall be at least eight and a half inches.

12. Every chimney shaft or smoke flue shall be carried up in brick or stone work at least four inches thick throughout, to a height of not less than three feet above the roof, flat or gutter adjoining thereto, measured at the

CHIMNEYS & FLUES IN EXTERNAL & PARTY WALLS.

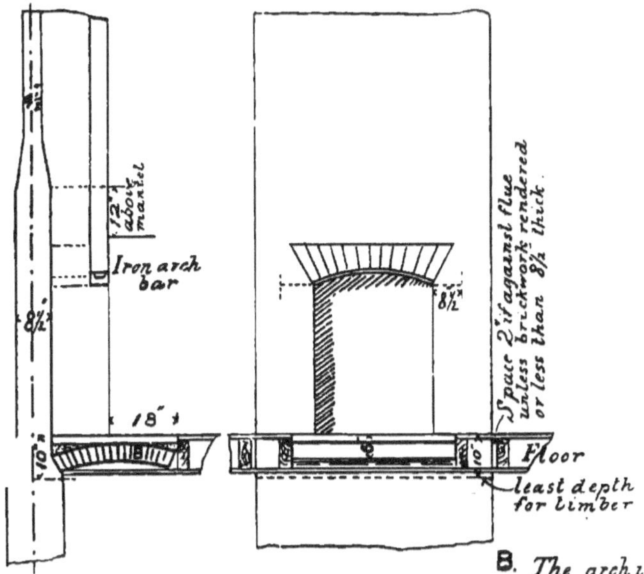

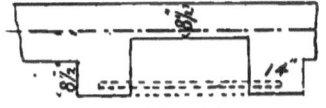

12" above mantel
Iron arch bar
8½"
18"
10"
8½"
Space 2" if against flue unless brickwork rendered or less than 8½ thick.
10"
Floor
least depth for timber

SECTION FRONT

B. The arch is the usual form of construction but the Act does not insist on this, see Sec. 64, sub. Sec. 17.

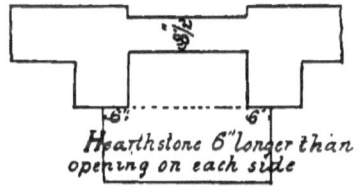

8½
8½
14"

PLAN
Shewing thickness & projection of Jambs requiring arch bar

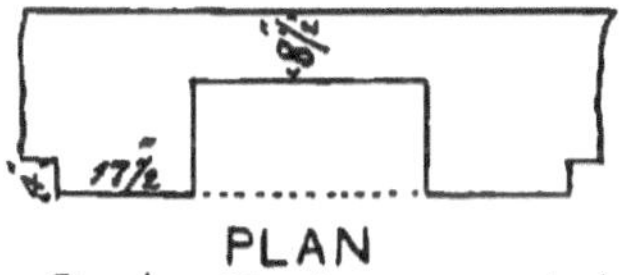

8½
17½

PLAN
Shewing thickness & projection of Jambs that require no arch bar

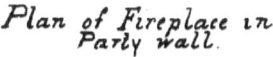

8½
6"
6"
Hearthstone 6" longer than opening on each side

Plan of Fireplace in Party wall.

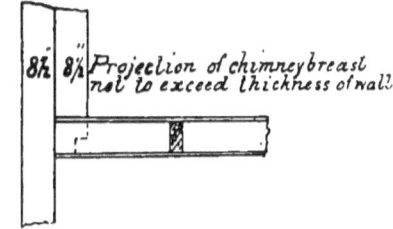

8½
8½"
Projection of chimneybreast not to exceed thickness of wall.

highest point in the line of junction with such roof, flat or gutter.

13. The highest six courses of every chimney stack or shaft shall be built in cement.

14. The brickwork or stonework of any chimney shaft, except that of the furnace of any steam engine, brewery, distillery or manufactory, shall not be built higher above the roof, flat or gutter adjoining thereto than a height equal to six times the least width of such chimney shaft at the level of such highest point in the line of junction, unless such chimney shaft is built with and bonded to another chimney shaft not in the same line with the first, or otherwise rendered secure.

15. There shall be laid level with the floor of every storey before the opening of every chimney, a slab of stone, slate or other incombustible substance, at the least six inches longer on each side than the width of such opening, and at the least eighteen inches wide in front of the breast thereof.

16. On every floor, except the lowest floor, such slab shall be laid wholly upon stone or iron bearers, or upon brick trimmers or other incombustible materials, but on the lowest floor it may be bedded on concrete covering the site, or on solid materials placed on such concrete.

17. The hearth or slab of every chimney shall be bedded wholly on brick, stone or other incombustible substance, and shall, together with such substance, be solid for a thickness of six inches at least beneath the upper surface of such hearth or slab.

18. A flue shall not be built in or against any party structure unless it be surrounded with new brickwork at least four inches in thickness, properly bonded.

19. A chimney breast or shaft built with or in any party wall shall not be cut away, unless the district surveyor certifies that it can be done without injuriously affecting the stability of any building.

20. A chimney shaft, jamb, breast or flue shall not be cut into except for the purpose of repair or during some one or more of the following things:—

(*a*) Letting in or removing or altering flues, pipes or funnels for the conveyance of smoke, hot air or steam, or letting in, removing or altering smoke jacks;

(b) Forming openings for soot doors, such openings to be fitted with a close iron door and frame;

(c) Making openings for the insertion of ventilating valves subject to the following restriction, that an opening shall not be made nearer than twelve inches to any timber or combustible substance.

21. Timber or woodwork shall not be placed—
(a) In any wall or chimney breast nearer than twelve inches to the inside of any flue or chimney opening;
(b) Under any chimney opening within ten inches from the upper surface of the hearth of such chimney opening;
(c) Within two inches from the face of the brickwork or stonework about any chimney or flue where the substance of such brickwork or stonework is less than eight and a half inches thick, unless the face of such brickwork or stonework is rendered.

22. Wooden plugs shall not be driven nearer than six inches to the inside of any flue or chimney opening, nor any iron holdfast or other iron fastening nearer than two inches thereto.

Furnace chimney shafts.

65—Unless the Council otherwise permit, every chimney shaft for the furnace of a steam engine, brewery, distillery or manufactory shall be constructed in conformity with the following rules:—

1. Every shaft shall be carried up throughout in brickwork and mortar of the best quality, and if detached shall taper gradually from the base to top of the shaft at the rate of at least two inches and a half in ten feet of height:

2. The thickness of brickwork at the top of the shaft, and for twenty feet below the top, shall be at least eight and a half inches, and shall be increased at least one-half brick for every additional twenty feet measured downwards:

3. Every cap, cornice, pedestal, plinth, string course, or other variation from plain brickwork shall be

provided as additional to the thickness of brickwork required under this Act, and every cap shall be constructed and secured to the satisfaction of the district surveyor:

4. The foundation of the shaft shall always be made to the satisfaction of the district surveyor on concrete or other sufficient foundation:
5. The footings shall spread all round the base by regular offsets to a projection equal to the thickness of the enclosing brickwork at the base of the shaft, and the space enclosed by the footings shall be filled in solid as the work progresses:
6. The width of the base of the shaft if square shall be at least one-tenth of the proposed height of the shaft, or if the same is round or of any other shape then one-twelfth of the height:
7. Any firebricks built inside the lower portion of the shaft shall be provided as additional to and independent of the thickness of brickwork prescribed by these rules, and shall not be bonded therewith.

66—1. The floor under every oven, copper, steam boiler or stove which is not heated by gas, and the floor around the same shall for a space of eighteen inches be formed of materials of an incombustible and non-conducting nature not less than six inches thick.

2. A pipe for conveying smoke or other products of combustion, heated air, steam or hot water shall not be fixed against any building on the face adjoining to any street or public way.

3. A pipe for conveying smoke or other products of combustion shall not be fixed nearer than nine inches to any combustible materials.

4. A pipe for conveying heated air or steam shall not be fixed nearer than six inches to any combustible materials.

5. A pipe for conveying hot water shall not be placed nearer than three inches to any combustible materials.

Provided that the restrictions imposed by this section with respect to the distance at which pipes for conveying hot water or steam may be placed from any combustible materials, shall not apply in the case of pipes for conveying hot water or steam at low pressure.

Rules as to close fires and pipes for conveying vapour, &c.

For the purposes of this section, hot water or steam shall be deemed to be at low pressure when provided with a free blow-off.

Floors above furnaces and ovens.

67—The floor over any room or enclosed space in which a furnace is fixed, and any floor within eighteen inches from the crown of an oven, shall be constructed of fire-resisting materials.

Rules as to accesses and stairs in certain buildings.

68—In every public building and in any other building of more than one hundred and twenty-five thousand feet in cubical extent, and which is constructed or adapted to be used as a dwelling-house for separate families, the floors of the lobbies, corridors, passages and landings, and also the flights of stairs shall be of fire-resisting material and carried by supports of a fire-resisting material.

Ventilation of staircases.

69—1. In every building constructed or adapted to be occupied in separate tenements by more than two families, the principal staircase used by the several families in common shall be ventilated upon every storey above the ground storey by means of windows or skylights opening directly into the external air, or shall be otherwise adequately ventilated.

2. The principal staircase in every building being a dwelling house and not subject to the provisions of sub-section 1 of this section, shall be ventilated by means of a window or skylight opening directly into the external air.

Rules as to habitable rooms.

70—1. (*a*) Every habitable room except rooms wholly or partly in the roof shall be in every part at least eight feet six inches in height from the floor to the ceiling;

(*b*) Every habitable room wholly or partly in the roof of any building shall be at least eight feet in height from the floor to the ceiling throughout not less than one-half the area of such room;

(*c*) Every habitable room shall have one or more windows opening directly into the external air or into a conservatory, with a total superficies clear of the sash frames free from any obstruction to the light equal to at least one-tenth of the floor area of the room, and so constructed that a portion equal to at least one-twentieth of such floor area can be opened, and the opening in each

SHEWS THE LEAST HEIGHT PERMITTED BY THE ACT FOR HABITABLE ROOMS WHOLLY OR PARTLY IN THE ROOF.

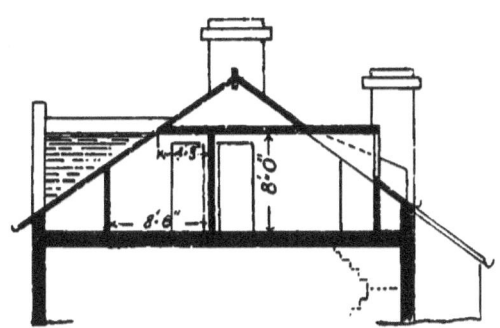

SECTION A.B.

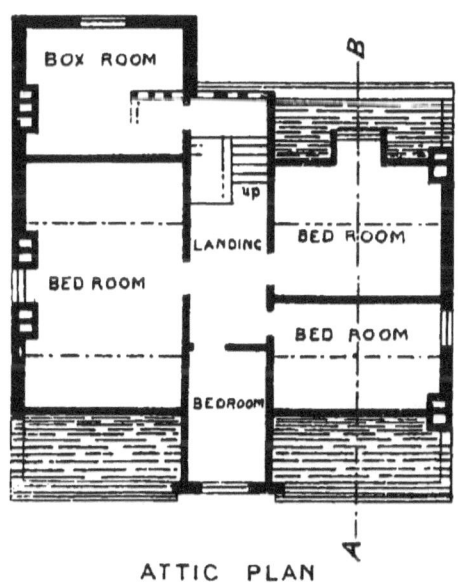

ATTIC PLAN

case shall extend to at least seven feet above the floor level ; but a room having no external wall, or a room constructed wholly or partially in the roof, may be lighted through the roof by a dormer window, with a total superficies clear of the sash frames free from any obstruction to the light equal to at least one-twelfth of the floor area of the room, and so constructed that a portion of such window equal to at least one-twenty-fourth of such floor area can be opened, and the opening in each case shall extend to at least five feet above the floor level, or such room may be lighted by a lantern light, of which a portion equal to at least one-twentieth of the floor area can be opened ;

(d) In a building being a dwelling-house, every basement room having a wooden floor, other than a floor constructed of solid wood bedded on concrete, shall have a sufficient space between the ground and the floor surfaces to admit of ventilation by means of air-bricks or otherwise ;

(e) Every habitable room constructed over a stable shall be separated from the stable by a floor which shall have, in every part not occupied by a joist or girder, a layer of concrete pugging of good quality or of other solid construction three inches in thickness, finished smooth upon the upper surface and properly supported, and the underside of such floor shall be ceiled with lath and plaster of good quality or of other solid construction ;

Any staircase or gallery or structure by which such rooms shall be approached shall be separated from any stable to which it may adjoin by a brick wall not less than nine inches in thickness ;

(f) Nothing in this Act shall affect, alter or repeal any of the provisions of the Public Health (London) Act, 1891, relating to underground rooms.

2. If any person knowingly suffer any room constructed after the commencement of this Act that is not constructed in conformity with this section to be inhabited, he shall, in addition to any other liabilities to which he may be subject, be liable to a penalty for every day during which such room is inhabited.

71—1. Every party arch or party floor and every arch or floor over any public way, or any passage leading through or under a building or part of a building to

<small>Rules as to party arches over public ways.</small>

premises in other occupation, shall be formed of brick, stone or other incombustible materials.

2. If an arch of brick or stone be used it shall be of the thickness of eight and a half inches at least, and the centre of such arch shall be higher than the springing at the rate of one inch at least for every foot, and also for any fractional part of a foot of span.

3. If an arch or floor of other incombustible material be used, it shall be constructed in such manner as may be approved by the district surveyor.

Rules as to arches under public ways. **72**—1. Every arch or other construction under any passage leading to premises in other occupation, or under any public way or intended public way, shall be formed of brick, stone or other incombustible materials.

2. If an arch of brick or stone be used, it shall—
   (a) Where its span does not exceed ten feet, be of the thickness of eight and a half inches at least;
   (b) Where its span exceeds ten, but does not exceed fifteen feet, be of the thickness of thirteen inches at least; and
   (c) Where its span exceeds fifteen feet, be of such thickness as may be approved by the district surveyor.

3. If an arch or other construction of other incombustible material be used, it shall be constructed in such manner as may be approved by the district surveyor.

Rules as to projections. **73**—The following provisions shall (except with the consent of the Council) apply to projections from buildings:—

1. Every coping, cornice, string course, facia, window-dressing, portico, porch, balcony, verandah, balustrade, outside landing, outside stairs and outside steps, and architectural projection or decoration whatsoever, and also the eaves, barge boards and cornices to any overhanging roof, except the cornices and dressings to the window fronts of shops, and except the eaves, barge boards and cornices to detached and semi-detached dwelling-houses, and to other dwelling-houses in which the party walls are corbelled out so as to project four inches beyond such

GREATEST PROJECTIONS OF SHOP FRONTS AND CORNICES IN FRONT OF EXTERNAL WALL OF THE BUILDING TO WHICH IT BELONGS.

If street or way less than 30'-0" wide

13"
5"

Public way

If street or way more than 30'-0" wide

18"
10"

Public way

NOTE. *No part of the above projection may go on or over the public way or on any land given up to public way save only for cornice.*

eaves, barge boards or cornices, shall be of brick, tile, stone, artificial stone, slate, cement or other fireproof material :

For the purpose of this sub-section a pair of semi-detached houses shall be deemed to be one building :

2. Every balcony, cornice or other projection shall be tailed into the wall of the building and weighted or tied down to the satisfaction of the district surveyor, and no cornice shall exceed in projection two feet six inches over the public way :

3. In a street or way of a width not greater than thirty feet, any shop front may project beyond the external wall of the building to which it belongs to any extent not exceeding five inches, and any cornice of any such shop front may project to any extent not exceeding thirteen inches ; and in any street or way of a width greater than thirty feet, any shop front may project to any extent not exceeding ten inches, and any cornice of any such shop front may project to any extent not exceeding eighteen inches beyond the external wall of the building to which it belongs, over the ground of the owner of the building, provided that this provision shall not authorise in any such street the projection of any part of any such shop front other than the cornice on or over the public way or any land to be given up to the public way :

4. No part of the woodwork of any shop front shall be fixed higher than twenty-five feet above the level of the pavement of the public footpath in front of the shop. No part of the woodwork of any shop front shall be fixed nearer than four inches to the centre of the party wall where the adjoining premises are separated by a party wall, or nearer than four inches to the face of the wall of the adjoining premises, where the adjoining premises have a separate wall, unless a pier or corbel of stone, brick or other incombustible material, four inches wide at the least, be placed as high as such woodwork, and projecting throughout an inch at the least in front

thereof between such woodwork and the centre of the party wall or the separate wall, as the case may be:

5. In a street of a width not less than forty feet, or to a building the front wall of which is not at a less distance than forty feet from the opposite boundary of the street, bay windows to dwelling-houses may be erected on land belonging to the owner of the building, notwithstanding the provisions of this Act relating to buildings beyond the general line of buildings in streets, provided that such bay windows—

    (a) Do not exceed three storeys in height above the level of the footway;
    (b) Do not project more than three feet from the main wall of the building to which they are attached;
    (c) Do not project in any part within the prescribed distance of the centre of the roadway;
    (d) Are in no part nearer to the centre of the nearest party wall than the extreme amount of their projection from the main wall of the building to which they are attached;
    (e) Do not taken together exceed in width three-fifths of the frontage of the building towards the street to which such bays face;
    (f) Are not constructed upon any part of the public way or upon any land agreed to be given up to the public way; and
    (g) Shall not be used for trade purposes:

    Bay windows to which the foregoing rules do not apply shall not be erected without the consent of the Council after consulting the local authority.

6. In a street of a width not less than forty feet, or to a building the front wall of which is not at a less distance than forty feet from the opposite boundary of the street, projecting oriel windows or turrets may be constructed. Provided that—

    (a) No part of any such projection extend more than three feet from the face of the front wall of the building, or more than twelve inches over the public way;

(b) No part of any such projection be less than ten feet above the level of the footway of the street;

(c) No part of any such projection (where it overhangs the public way) be within a distance of four feet of the centre of the nearest party wall;

(d) On no floor shall the total width of any such projections taken together exceed three-fifths of the length of the wall of the building on the level of that floor;

(e) Every such projection be constructed to the satisfaction of the district surveyor, or in the event of disagreement, to the satisfaction of the superintending architect, whose determination shall be final:

Oriel windows or turrets to which the foregoing rules do not apply, shall not be erected without the consent of the Council after consulting the local authority:

7. The roof, flat or gutter of every building and every balcony, verandah, shop front or other similar projection or projecting window shall be so arranged and constructed, and so supplied with gutters and pipes as to prevent the water therefrom from dropping upon or running over any public way:

8. Except in so far as is permitted by this section in the case of shop fronts and projecting windows, and with the exception of water pipes and their appurtenances, copings, string courses, cornices, facias, window dressings and other like architectural decorations, no projection from any building shall extend beyond the general line of buildings in any street except with the permission of the Council after consulting the local authority.

74—1. Every building shall be separated either by an external wall or by a party wall or other proper party structure from the adjoining building (if any), and from each of the adjoining buildings (if more than one). *Separation of buildings.*

2. In every building exceeding ten squares in area,

used in part for purposes of trade or manufacture, and in part as a dwelling-house, the part used for the purposes of trade or manufacture shall be separated from the part used as a dwelling-house by walls and floors constructed of fire-resisting materials, and all passages, staircases and other means of approach to the part used as a dwelling house shall be constructed throughout of fire-resisting materials. The part used for purposes of trade or manufacture shall (if extending to more than two hundred and fifty thousand cubic feet) be subject to the provisions of this Act relating to the cubical extent of buildings of the warehouse class:

Provided that there may be constructed in the walls of such staircases and passages, such doorways as are necessary for communicating between the different parts of the building, and there may be formed in any walls of such building openings fitted with fire-resisting doors.

3. In every building exceeding twenty-five squares in area, containing separate sets of chambers or offices, or rooms tenanted or constructed or adapted to be tenanted by different persons, the floors and principal staircases shall be of fire-resisting materials:

But this provision shall not entitle the district surveyor to charge for the inspection of each set of chambers as a separate building.

Cubical extent of buildings.

75—Except as in this section provided, no building of the warehouse class shall extend to more than two hundred and fifty thousand cubic feet, unless divided by party walls in such manner that no division thereof extend to more than two hundred and fifty thousand cubic feet.

No addition shall be made to any building of the warehouse class, or to any division thereof, so that the cubical extent of any such building or division shall exceed two hundred and fifty thousand cubic feet.

The restriction contained in this section upon the cubical extent of a building shall not apply to any building which, being at a greater distance than two miles from Saint Paul's Cathedral, is used wholly for the manufacture of the machinery and boilers of steam vessels, or for a retort-house for the manufacture of gas, or for generating electricity, provided that such building consist of one floor only, and be constructed of brick, stone, iron or other incombustible material throughout, and shall not be used for any purpose other than such as hereinbefore specified. Every such building shall, for the purpose of the provisions of this Act with respect to special buildings, be deemed to be a building to which the general rules of this Act are inapplicable.

76—Where the Council are satisfied on the report of the superintending architect and of the chief officer of the fire brigade that additional cubical extent is necessary for any building to be used for any trade or manufacture, and are satisfied that proper arrangements have been or will be made and maintained for lessening so far as reasonably practicable danger from fire, the Council may consent to such building containing additional cubical extent. <small>Consent to larger dimensions.</small>

Provided that such building shall not—
- (i.) Extend to a number of cubic feet exceeding four hundred and fifty thousand, or any less number allowed by the Council, without being divided by party walls in such manner that the cubical extent of each division do not exceed that number;
- (ii.) Exceed sixty feet in height;
- (iii.) Be used for purpose of any trade or manufacture involving the use of explosive or inflammable materials.

Such consent shall continue in force only while the said building is actually used for the purposes of the trade or manufacture in respect of which the consent was granted.

77—1. Buildings shall not be united except where they are wholly in one occupation, or are constructed or adapted to be so. <small>Rules as uniting buildings.</small>

2. Buildings shall not be united if when so united and considered as one building only they would not be in conformity with this Act.

3. An opening shall not be made in any party wall or in two external walls dividing buildings, which if taken together would extend to more than two hundred and fifty thousand cubic feet, except under the following conditions:—

(a) Such opening shall not exceed in width seven feet, or in height eight feet, and such opening or openings taken together shall not exceed one-half the length of such party wall on each floor of the building in which they occur;

(b) Such opening shall have the floor, jambs and head formed of brick, stone or iron, and be closed by two wrought-iron doors, each one-fourth of an inch thick in the panel, at a distance from each other of the full thickness of the wall, fitted to rebated frames without woodwork of any kind, or by wrought-iron sliding doors or shutters, properly constructed, fitted into grooved or rebated iron frames;

(c) If the thickness of the wall be not less than twenty-four inches, or the doors be placed at a distance from each other of not less than twenty-four inches, such opening may be nine feet six inches in height.

4. Whenever any buildings which have been united cease to be in one occupation, all openings made for the purpose of uniting the same in any party wall between the buildings or in any external wall shall be stopped up with brick or stone work not less than thirteen inches in thickness (except in the case of a wall eight and a half inches in thickness, in which case eight and a half inches shall be sufficient) and properly bonded with such wall, and any timber not in conformity with this Act placed in the wall shall be removed.

5. Whenever any buildings which have been united cease to be in one occupation, the owner thereof shall forthwith give notice to the district surveyor, and shall cause any openings made in the party wall to be stopped up and bonded as aforesaid.

78—Notwithstanding anything in this Act, every public building, including the walls, roofs, floors, galleries and staircases, and every structure and work constructed or done in connection with or for the purposes of the same, shall be constructed in such manner as may be approved by the district surveyor, or in the event of such disagreement may be determined by the tribunal of appeal, and save so far as respects the rules of construction every public building shall throughout this Act be deemed to be included in the term building, and be subject to all the provisions of this Act in the same manner as if it were a building erected for a purpose other than a public purpose.

No public building shall be used as such until the district surveyor or the tribunal of appeal shall have declared his or their approval of the construction thereof.

After the district surveyor shall have so declared his approval, or shall certify that it has been constructed as directed by the tribunal of appeal, any work affecting or likely to affect the building shall not be done to, in or on the building without the approval of the district surveyor or such certificate as aforesaid.

79—Where it is proposed to convert or alter any building erected for a purpose other than a public purpose into a public building, such conversion or alteration shall be carried into effect, and the public building thereby formed, including the walls, roofs, floors, galleries and staircases thereof shall be constructed in such manner as may be approved by the district surveyor, or in the event of disagreement may be determined by the tribunal of appeal, and the provisions of this Act shall apply to such alteration or conversion as though it were the construction of a public building. *Conversion of houses, &c., into public buildings.*

80—The following rules shall be observed with respect to new churches, chapels, meeting-houses, public halls, public lecture-rooms, public exhibition-rooms and public places of assembly, or additions or alterations by which increased accommodation is to be provided to existing churches, chapels and meeting-houses, public halls, public lecture-rooms, public exhibition-rooms or public places of assembly :— *Staircases in churches and chapels.*

(a) Every staircase for the use of the public shall be supported and enclosed by brick walls not less than nine inches thick. The treads of each flight of stairs shall be of uniform width :

(b) No staircase, internal corridor or passage-way for the use of the public shall be less than four feet six inches wide. Provided that where not more than two hundred persons are to be accommodated in such church, chapel, meeting-house, hall, lecture-room, exhibition-room or place of assembly,

G 2

such staircase, internal corridor or passage-way may be of the width of three feet six inches:

(c) Every staircase, corridor or passage-way for the use of the public, and which communicates with any portion of the building intended for the accommodation of a larger number of the public than four hundred, shall be increased in width by six inches for every additional one hundred persons, until a maximum width of nine feet be obtained. Provided always that in every case where the staircases are six feet wide and upwards, they shall be divided by a hand-rail. Provided also that in lieu of a single staircase, corridor or passage-way of the width in this sub-section prescribed, it shall be lawful to substitute two staircases, corridors or passage-ways, each being of a width at least equal to two-thirds of the width in this sub-section prescribed for the single staircase, corridor or passage-way, but so that neither of such two substituted corridors, staircases or passage-ways shall be less than three feet six inches wide:

(d) In all cases where a portion of the public is to be accommodated over or at a higher level than others of the public, a separate means of exit of the width above prescribed for staircases, internal corridors or passage-ways, and communicating directly with the street or open space shall be provided from each floor or level:

(e) All doors and barriers shall be made to open outwards, and no outside locks or bolts are to be affixed thereto.

Application of Act to buildings under railway arches.

81—Where a building erected after the commencement of this Act under, or in, or by inclosure of a railway arch or abutting thereon, is constructed or adapted to be used for human habitation, this Act shall apply to the building and to every work done to, in or on the same in like manner, and to the like extent as far as may be, as if the building were built in any other position.

Part VII.

SPECIAL AND TEMPORARY BUILDINGS AND WOODEN STRUCTURES.

82—1. Where a builder is desirous of erecting an iron building or structure, or any other building or structure to which the general provisions of Part VI. of this Act are inapplicable, or in the opinion of the Council inappropriate, having regard to the special purpose for which the building or structure is designed and actually used, he shall make an application to the Council, accompanied by a plan of the proposed building, with such particulars as to the construction thereof as may be required by the Council. *[Application to Council for buildings to which rules of Act are inapplicable.]*

2. The Council, if satisfied with such plan and particulars, shall signify their approval of the same in writing, and thereupon the building may be constructed according to such plan and particulars, but the Council shall not authorise any building of the warehouse class to be erected of greater cubical extent than two hundred and fifty thousand cubic feet except in accordance with the foregoing provisions of this Act.

3. The Council may, for the purpose of regulating the procedure in relation to such applications, issue such general rules as they think fit as to the time and manner of making applications, and as to the plans to be presented, the expenses to be incurred, and any other matter or thing connected therewith.

4. All expenses incurred in and about the obtaining the approval of the Council shall be paid by the builder to the superintending architect, or to such other person as the Council may appoint, and in default of payment may be recovered in a summary manner.

5. A copy of any plans and particulars approved by the Council shall be furnished to the district surveyor within whose district the building to which such plans and particulars relate is situate, and it shall be his duty to ascertain that the same is built in accordance with the said plans and particulars.

Control by Council of certain temporary buildings.

83—Where an application is made to the Council by any person stating his desire to erect in any place an iron or other building, or structure of a temporary character, to which the general provisions of Part VI. of this Act are inapplicable, the Council may, if they approve of the plan and particulars of the building or structure, limit the period during which it shall be allowed to remain in that place, and may make their approval subject to such conditions as to the removal of the building or structure, or otherwise as they think fit; and if at the expiration of that period, the building or structure be not removed in accordance with those conditions, the Council may serve a notice on the occupier or owner of such building or structure, requiring him to remove it within a reasonable time specified in the notice, and if the occupier or owner fail to remove such building or structure within the time named, the Council may, notwithstanding the imposition and recovery of any penalty, cause complaint thereof to be made before a petty sessional court, who shall thereupon issue a summons requiring such occupier or owner to appear to answer such complaint, and if the said complaint is proved to the satisfaction of the Court, the Court may make an order in writing authorising the Council to enter upon the land upon which such building is situated, and to remove or take down the same and do whatever may be necessary for such purpose, and also to remove the materials of which the same is composed to a convenient place, and (unless the expenses of the Council be paid to them within fourteen days after such removal) sell the same as they think proper.

Wooden structures not to be erected without license of Council

84—1. No person shall set up in any place any wooden structure (unless it be exempt from the operation of this Part of this Act) except hoardings enclosing vacant land and not exceeding in any part twelve feet in height, without having first obtained for that purpose a license from the Council, and the license may contain such conditions with respect to the structure and the time for which it is to be permitted to continue in the said place as the Council think expedient.

2. Provided that a license shall not be required in the case of any wooden structure of a movable or temporary character erected by a builder for his use during the con-

struction, alteration or repair of any building, unless the same is not taken down or removed immediately after such construction, alteration or repair.

Provided that this section shall not extend to or apply within the City, or to any hoarding duly licensed by the local authority under any statutory powers in that behalf.

85—This Part of this Act shall not apply in the case of a pile, stack or store of timber not being a structure affixed or fastened to the ground.

Piles of loose timber not regarded as structures.

86—Structures or erections erected or set up upon the premises of any railway company, and used for the purposes of or in connection with the traffic of such railway company, shall be exempt from the operation of this Part of this Act.

As to structures of railway companies.

PART VIII.

RIGHTS OF BUILDING AND ADJOINING OWNERS.

87—Where lands of different owners adjoin and are unbuilt on at the line of junction, and either owner is about to build on any part of the line of junction, the following provisions shall have effect:—

Rights of owners of adjoining lands respecting walls on line of junction.

1. If the building owner desire to build a party wall on the line of junction he may serve notice thereof on the adjoining owner, describing the intended wall:
2. If the adjoining owner consent to the building of a party wall, the wall shall be built half on the land of each of the two owners, or in such other position as may be agreed between the two owners:
3. The expense of the building of the party wall shall be from time to time defrayed by the two owners in due proportion, regard being had to the use made and which may be made of the wall by the two owners respectively :
4. If the adjoining owner do not consent to the building of a party wall, the building owner shall not build the wall otherwise than as an external wall placed wholly on his own land:

5. If the building owner do not desire to build a party wall on the line of junction, but desires to build an external wall placed wholly on his own land, he may serve notice thereof on the adjoining owner describing the intended wall:

6. Where in either of the cases aforesaid the building owner proceeds to build an external wall on his own land, he shall have a right at his own expense, at any time after the expiration of one month from the service of the notice, to place on the land of the adjoining owner, below the level of the lowest floor, the projecting footings of the external wall, with concrete or other solid substructure thereunder, making compensation to the adjoining owner or occupier for any damage occasioned thereby, the amount of such compensation, if any difference arise, to be determined in the manner in which differences between building owners and adjoining owners are hereinafter directed to be determined.

Where an external wall is built against another external wall or against a party wall, it shall be lawful for the district surveyor to allow the footing of the side next such other external or party wall to be omitted.

88—The building owner shall have the following rights in relation to party structures (that is to say):—
1. A right to make good, underpin or repair any party structure which is defective or out of repair:
2. A right to pull down and rebuild any party structure which is so far defective or out of repair as to make it necessary or desirable to pull it down:
3. A right to pull down any timber or other partition which divides any buildings and is not conformable with the regulations of this Act, and to build instead a party wall conformable thereto:
4. In the case of buildings having rooms or storeys, the property of different owners intermixed, a right to pull down such of the said rooms or storeys, or any part thereof as are not built in conformity with this Act, and to rebuild the same in conformity with this Act:
5. In the case of buildings connected by arches or com-

munications over public ways, or over passages belonging to other persons, a right to pull down such of the said buildings, arches or communications, or such parts thereof, as are not built in conformity with this Act, and to rebuild the same in conformity with this Act :

6. A right to raise and underpin any party structure permitted by this Act to be raised or underpinned, or any external wall built against such party structure, upon condition of making good all damage occasioned thereby to the adjoining premises, or to the internal finishings and decorations thereof, and of carrying up to the requisite height all flues and chimney stacks belonging to the adjoining owner, on or against such party structure or external wall :

7. A right to pull down any party structure which is of insufficient strength for any building intended to be built, and to rebuild the same of sufficient strength for the above purpose upon condition of making good all damage occasioned thereby to the adjoining premises or to the internal finishings and decorations thereof :

8. A right to cut into any party structure upon condition of making good all damage occasioned to the adjoining premises by such operation :

9. A right to cut away any footing or any chimney breasts, jambs or flues projecting, or other projections from any party wall or external walls in order to erect an external wall against such party wall, or for any other purpose, upon condition of making good all damage occasioned to the adjoining premises by such operation :

10. A right to cut away or take down such parts of any wall or building of an adjoining owner as may be necessary in consequence of such wall or building overhanging the ground of the building owner, in order to erect an upright wall against the same, on condition of making good any damage sustained by the wall or building by reason of such cutting away or taking down :

11. A right to perform any other necessary works incident to the connection of a party structure

with the premises adjoining thereto. But the above rights shall be subject to this qualification, that any building which has been erected previously to the date of the commencement of this Act shall be deemed to be conformable with the provisions of this Act if it be conformable with the provisions of the Acts of Parliament regulating buildings in London before the commencement of this Act:

12. A right to raise a party fence wall, or to pull the same down and rebuild it as a party wall.

<small>Rights of adjoining owner.</small>

89—1. Where a building owner proposes to exercise any of the foregoing rights with respect to party structures, the adjoining owner may, by notice, require the building owner to build on any such party structure such chimney copings, jambs, or breasts, or flues, or such piers or recesses, or any other like works as may fairly be required for the convenience of such adjoining owner, and may be specified in the notice, and it shall be the duty of the building owner to comply with such requisition in all cases where the execution of the required works will not be injurious to the building owner, or cause to him unnecessary inconvenience or unnecessary delay in the exercise of his right.

2. Any difference that arises between a building owner and adjoining owner in respect of the execution of any such works shall be determined in manner in which differences between building owners and adjoining owners are hereinafter directed to be determined.

<small>Rules as to exercise of rights by building and adjoining owners.</small>

90—1. A building owner shall not, except with the consent in writing of the adjoining owner and of the adjoining occupiers, or in cases where any wall or party structure is dangerous (in which cases the provisions of Part IX. of this Act shall apply), exercise any of his rights under this Act in respect of any party fence wall, unless at least one month, or exercise any of his rights under this Act in relation to any party wall or party structure other than a party fence wall, unless at least two months before doing so he has served on the adjoining owner a party wall or party structure notice, stating the nature and particulars of the proposed work, and the time at which the work is proposed to be commenced.

LONDON BUILDING ACT, 1894. 91

2. When a building owner in the exercise of any of his rights under this Part of the Act lays open any part of the adjoining land or building, he shall at his own expense make and maintain for a proper time a proper hoarding and shoring or temporary construction for protection of the adjoining land or building and the security of the adjoining occupier.

3. A building owner shall not exercise any right by this Act given to him in such manner or at such time as to cause unnecessary inconvenience to the adjoining owner or to the adjoining occupier.

4. A party wall or structure notice shall not be available for the exercise of any right unless the work to which the notice relates is begun within six months after the service thereof and is prosecuted with due diligence.

5. Within one month after receipt of such notice the adjoining owner may serve on the building owner a notice requiring him to build on any such party structure any works to the construction of which he is hereinbefore declared to be entitled.

6. The last-mentioned notice shall specify the works required by the adjoining owner for his convenience, and shall, if necessary, be accompanied by explanatory plans and drawings.

7. If either owner do not within fourteen days after the service on him of any notice express his consent thereto he shall be considered as having dissented therefrom, and thereupon a difference shall be deemed to have arisen between the building owner and the adjoining owner.

91—1. In all cases not specially provided for by this Act where a difference arises between a building owner and adjoining owner in respect of any matter arising with reference to any work to which any notice given under this Part of this Act relates, unless both parties concur in the appointment of one surveyor they shall each appoint a surveyor, and the two surveyors so appointed shall select a third surveyor, and such one surveyor or three surveyors or any two of them shall settle any matter from time to time during the continuance of any work to which the notice relates in dispute between such building and adjoining owner, with power by his or their award to determine the right to do and the time and manner of

Settlement of difference between building and adjoining owners.

doing any work, and generally any other matter arising out of or incidental to such difference, but any time so appointed for doing any work shall not, unless otherwise agreed, commence until after the expiration of the period by this Part of this Act prescribed for the notice in the particular case.

2. Any award given by such one surveyor or by such three surveyors, or by any two of them shall be conclusive, and shall not be questioned in any court with this exception, that either of the parties to the difference may appeal therefrom to the county court within fourteen days from the date of the delivery of the award, and the county court may, subject as hereafter in this section mentioned, rescind the award or modify it in such manner as it thinks just.

3. If either party to the difference make default in appointing a surveyor for ten days after notice has been served on him by the other party to make such appointment, the party giving the notice may make the appointment in the place of the party so making default.

4. The costs incurred in making or obtaining the award shall be paid by such party as the surveyor or surveyors determine.

5. If the appellant from any such award on appearing before the county court declare his unwillingness to have the matter decided by that court, and prove to the satisfaction of the judge of that court that in the event of the matter being decided against him he will be liable to pay a sum exclusive of costs exceeding fifty pounds, and gives security to be approved by the judge duly to prosecute his appeal and to abide the event thereof, all proceedings in the county court shall thereupon be stayed, and the appellant may bring an action in the High Court against the other party to the difference.

6. The plaintiff in such action shall deliver to the defendants an issue whereby the matters in difference between them may be tried, and the form of such issue in case of dispute or in case of the non-appearance of the defendant shall be settled by the High Court, and such action shall be prosecuted and issue tried in the same manner and subject to the same incidents in and subject to which actions are prosecuted and issues tried in other cases within the jurisdiction of the High Court, or as near thereto as circumstances admit.

7. If the parties to any such action agree as to the facts, a special case may be stated for the opinion of the High Court, and any case so stated may be brought before the court in like manner and subject to the same incidents in, and subject to which other special cases are brought before such court, or as near thereto as circumstances admit, and any costs that may have been incurred in the county court by the parties to such action as is mentioned in this section shall be deemed to be costs incurred in such action, and be payable accordingly.

8. Where both parties to the difference have concurred in the appointment of one surveyor for the settlement of such difference, then if such surveyor refuse or for seven days neglect to act, or die, or become incapable to act before he has made his award, the matters in dispute shall be determined in the same manner as if such single surveyor had not been appointed.

9. Where each party to the difference has appointed a surveyor for the settlement of the difference, and a third surveyor has been selected, then if such third surveyor refuse, or for for seven days neglect to act, or before such difference is settled die, or become incapable to act, the two surveyors shall forthwith select another third surveyor in his place, and every third surveyor so selected as last aforesaid, shall have the same powers and authorities as were vested in his predecessor.

10. Where each party to the difference has appointed a surveyor for the settlement of the difference, then if the two surveyors so appointed refuse or for seven days after request of either party neglect to select a third surveyor, or another third surveyor in the event of the refusal or neglect to act, death or incapacity of the third surveyor, for the time being, a Secretary of State may on the application of either party select some fit person to act as third surveyor, and every surveyor so selected shall have the same powers and authorities as if he had been selected by the two surveyors appointed by the parties.

11. Where each party to the difference has appointed a surveyor for the settlement of the difference, then if before such difference is settled either surveyor so appointed die or become incapable to act, the party by whom such surveyor was appointed may appoint in writing some other surveyor to act in his place, and if for the space of seven

days after notice served on him by the other party for that purpose he fail to do so the other surveyor may proceed *ex parte*, and the decision of such other surveyor shall be as effectual as if he had been a single surveyor in whose appointment both parties had concurred, and every surveyor so to be substituted as aforesaid shall have the same powers and authorities as were vested in the former surveyor at the time of his death or disability as aforesaid.

12. Where each party to the difference has appointed a surveyor for the settlement of the difference, then if either of the surveyors refuse or for seven days neglect to act, the other surveyor may proceed *ex parte* and the decision of such other surveyor shall be as effectual as if he had been a single surveyor in whose appointment both parties had concurred.

<small>Power for building owner to enter premises.</small>

92—A building owner, his servants, agents and workmen at all usual times of working may enter and remain on any premises for the purpose of executing, and may execute, any work which he has become entitled or is required in pursuance of this Act to execute, removing any furniture or doing any other thing which may be necessary, and if the premises are closed he and they may, accompanied by a constable or other officer of the peace, break open any fences or doors in order to effect such entry:

Provided that before entering on any premises for the purposes of this section the building owner shall, except in the case of emergency, give fourteen days' notice of his intention so to do to the owner and occupier, and in case of emergency shall give such notice as may be reasonably practicable.

<small>Building owner to underpin adjoining owner's building.</small>

93—Where a building owner intends to erect within ten feet of a building belonging to an adjoining owner a building or structure, any part of which within such ten feet extends to a lower level than the foundations of the building belonging to the adjoining owner, he may, and if required by the adjoining owner, shall (subject as hereinafter provided) underpin or otherwise strengthen the foundations of the said building so far as may be necessary, and the following provisions shall have effect:—

1. At least two months' notice in writing shall be given

by the building owner to the adjoining owner, stating his intention to build and whether he proposes to underpin or otherwise strengthen the foundations of the said building, and such notice shall be accompanied by a plan and sections showing the site of the proposed building and the depth to which he proposes to excavate:

2. If the adjoining owner shall, within fourteen days after being served with such notice, give a counter-notice in writing that he disputes the necessity of or require such underpinning or strengthening, a difference shall be deemed to have arisen between the building owner and the adjoining owner:

3. The building owner shall be liable to compensate the adjoining owner and occupier for any inconvenience, loss or damage which may result to them by reason of the exercise of the powers conferred by this section:

4. Nothing in this section contained shall relieve the building owner from any liability to which he would otherwise be subject in case of injury caused by his building operations to the adjoining owner.

94—An adjoining owner may if he think fit by notice in writing require the building owner (before commencing any work which he may be authorised by this Part of this Act to execute) to give such security as may be agreed upon or in case of difference may be settled by the Judge of the County Court for the payment of all such expenses, costs and compensation in respect of the work as may be payable by the building owner. {Security to be given by building owner and adjoining owner.}

The building owner may if he think fit, at any time after service on him of a party wall or party structure requisition by the adjoining owner, and before beginning a work to which the requisition relates, but not afterwards, serve a counter-requisition on the adjoining owner requiring him to give such security for payment of the expenses, costs and compensation for which he is or will be liable as may be agreed upon or in case of difference may be settled as aforesaid.

If the adjoining owner do not within one month after service of that counter-requisition give security accordingly, he shall at the end of that month be deemed to have ceased to be entitled to compliance with his party wall or party structure requisition, and the building owner may proceed as if no party wall or party structure requisition had been served on him by the adjoining owner.

Rules as to expenses in respect of party structures.

95—1. As to expenses to be borne jointly by the building owner and adjoining owner:—

(a) If any party structure be defective or out of repair the expense of making good, underpinning or repairing the same shall be borne by the building owner and adjoining owner in due proportion, regard being had to the use that each owner makes or may make of the structure;

(b) If any party structure be pulled down and rebuilt by reason of its being so far defective or out of repair as to make it necessary or desirable to pull it down, the expense of such pulling down and rebuilding shall be borne by the building owner and adjoining owner in due proportion, regard being had to the use that each owner may make of the structure;

(c) If any timber or other partition dividing a building be pulled down in exercise of the right by this Part of this Act vested in a building owner, and a party structure be built instead thereof, the expense of building such party structure, and also of building any additional party structures that may be required by reason of the partition having been pulled down, shall be borne by the building owner and adjoining owner in due proportion, regard being had to the use that each owner may make of the party structure and to the thickness required for support of the respective buildings parted thereby;

(d) If any rooms or storeys or any parts thereof, the property of different owners and intermixed in any building, be pulled down in pursuance of the right by this Part of this Act vested in a building owner and be rebuilt in conformity with this Act, the expense of such pulling down and rebuilding shall be borne by the building owner and adjoining owner in due proportion, regard being had to the use that each owner may make of such rooms or storeys;

(e) If any arches or communications over public ways, or over passages belonging to other persons than the owners of the buildings connected by such arches or communications or any parts thereof, be pulled down in pursuance of the right by this Part of this Act vested in a building owner and be rebuilt in conformity with this Act, the expense of such pulling down and rebuilding shall be borne by the building owner and adjoining owner in due proportion, regard being had to the use that each owner may make of such arches or communications.

2. As to expenses to be borne by the building owner :—

(a) If any party structure or any external wall built against another external wall be raised or underpinned, in pursuance of the power by this Part of this Act vested in a building owner, the expense of raising or underpinning the same, and of making good all damage occasioned thereby, and of carrying up to the requisite height all such flues and chimney-stacks belonging to the adjoining owner on or against any such party structure or external wall as are by this Part of this Act required to be made good and carried up, shall be borne by the building owner;

(b) If any party structure which is of proper materials and sound, or not so far defective or out of repair as to make it necessary or desirable to pull it down, be pulled down and rebuilt by the building owner, the expense of pulling down and rebuilding the same and of making good any damage by this Part of this Act required to be made good, and a fair allowance in respect of the disturbance and inconvenience caused to the adjoining owner, shall be borne by the building owner;

(c) If any party structure be cut into by the building owner, the expense of cutting into the same and of making good any damage by this Part of this Act required to be made good shall be borne by such building owner;

(d) If any footing, chimney-breast, jambs or floor be cut away in pursuance of the powers by this Part of this Act vested in a building owner, the expense of such cutting away and of making good any damage by this Part of this Act required to be made good shall be borne by the building owner;

(e) If any party fence wall be raised for a building, the expense of raising such wall shall be borne by the building owner;

(f) If any party fence wall be pulled down and built as a party wall, the expense of pulling down such party fence wall and building the same as a party wall shall be borne by the building owner.

If at any time the adjoining owner make use of any party structure or external wall (or any part thereof) raised or underpinned as aforesaid, or of any party fence wall pulled down and built as a party wall (or any part thereof), beyond the use thereof made by him before the alteration, there shall be borne by the adjoining owner from time to time a due proportion of the expenses (having regard to the use that the adjoining owner may make thereof):—

(i.) Of raising or underpinning such party structure or external wall, and of making good all such damage occasioned thereby to the adjoining owner, and of carrying up to the requisite height all such flues and chimney-stacks belonging to the adjoining owner on or against any such party structure or external wall as are by this Part of this Act required to be made good and carried up;

(ii.) Of pulling down and building such party fence wall as a party wall.

96—Within one month after the completion of any work which a building owner is by this Part of this Act authorised and required to execute, and the expense of which is in whole or in part to be borne by an adjoining owner, the building owner shall deliver to the adjoining owner an account in writing of the particulars and expense of the work, specifying any deduction to which such adjoining owner or other person may be entitled in respect of old materials or in other respects, and every such work shall be estimated and valued at fair average rates and prices, according to the nature of the work and the locality and the market price of materials and labour at the time.

Account of expenses to be delivered to adjoining owner.

97—At any time within one month after the delivery of the said account, the adjoining owner, if dissatisfied therewith, may declare his dissatisfaction to the building owner by notice in writing, served by himself or his agent, and specifying his objection thereto, and thereupon a difference shall be deemed to have arisen between the parties, and shall be determined in manner herein-before in this Part of this Act provided for the settlement of differences between building and adjoining owners.

Adjoining owner may object to account.

98—If within the said period of one month the adjoining owner do not declare in the said manner his dissatisfaction with the account, he shall be deemed to have accepted the same, and shall pay the same on demand to the party delivering the account, and if he fail to do so the amount so due may be recovered as a debt.

Building owner may recover if no appeal made.

99—Where the adjoining owner is liable to contribute to the expenses of building any party structure, then until such contribution is paid the building owner at whose expense the same was built shall stand possessed of the sole property in the structure.

Structure to belong to building owner until contribution paid.

100—The adjoining owner shall be liable for all expenses incurred on his requisition by the building owner, and in default payment of the same may be recovered from him as a debt.

Adjoining owner liable to expenses incurred on his requisition.

101—Nothing in this Act shall authorise any interference with an easement of light or other easements in or

Saving for rights in party walls, &c.

relating to a party wall, or take away, abridge or prejudicially affect any right of any person to preserve or restore any light or other thing in or connected with a party wall, in case of the party wall being pulled down or rebuilt.

Part IX.
DANGEROUS AND NEGLECTED STRUCTURES.
Dangerous Structures.

Meaning of structure.

102—In this Part of this Act the expression "structure" includes any building, wall or other structure, and anything affixed to or projecting from any building, wall or other structure.

Survey to be made of dangerous structures.

103—1. Where it is made known to the Council that any structure is in a dangerous state, the Council shall require a survey of such structure to be made by the district surveyor or by some other competent surveyor.

2. For the purposes of this Part of this Act the expression "district surveyor" shall be deemed to include any surveyor so appointed.

3. The district surveyor shall make known to the Council any information which he may receive with respect to any structure being in a dangerous state.

4. It shall be lawful for the district surveyor to enter into any structure, or upon any land upon which any structure is situate, for the purpose of making a survey of such structure.

Effect of this Part of Act within the City.

104—In cases where any such structure is situate within the City, this Part of this Act relating to dangerous structures shall be read as if the Commissioners of Sewers were named therein instead of the Council, and all costs and expenses of, and all payments hereby directed to be made by or to such Commissioners, shall be made by or to the Chamberlain of the City out of or to the consolidated rate made by such Commissioners, in the same manner as payments are made by or to such Chamberlain in the ordinary course of his business.

Surveyor to give certificate.

105—Upon the completion of his survey the district

surveyor employed shall certify to the Council his opinion as to the state of the structure.

106—If the certificate is to the effect that the structure is not in a dangerous state no further proceeding shall be had in respect thereof, but if it is to the effect that the same is in a dangerous state the Council may cause the same to be shored up or otherwise secured, and a proper hoard or fence to be put up for the protection of passengers, and shall cause notice to be served on the owner or occupier of the structure requiring him forthwith to take down, secure or repair the same as the case requires.

<small>Notice to be given to owner in respect of certificate.</small>

107—1. If the owner or occupier on whom the notice is served fail to comply as speedily as the nature of the case permits with the notice, a petty sessional court, on complaint by the Council, may order the owner to take down, repair or otherwise secure, to the satisfaction of the district surveyor, the structure, or such part thereof as appears to the court to be in a dangerous state, within a time to be fixed by the order, and if the same be not taken down, repaired or otherwise secured within the time so limited, the Council may with all convenient speed cause all or so much of the structure as is in a dangerous condition to be taken down, repaired or otherwise secured in such manner as may be requisite :

<small>Proceedings to enforce compliance with notice.</small>

Provided that if the owner of the structure dispute the necessity of any of the requisitions comprised in the notice, he may by notice in writing to the Council, within seven days from the service of the notice upon himself, require that the subject shall be referred to arbitration.

2. In case the owner require arbitration, he may at the time of giving such notice appoint an independent surveyor to report on the condition of the structure in conjunction with the district surveyor, within seven days of the receipt by the Council of the notice of appointment of the owner's surveyor, and all questions of fact or matters in dispute which cannot be agreed between the owner's surveyor and the district surveyor shall be referred for final decision to a third surveyor, who shall (before the owner's surveyor and the district surveyor enter upon the discussion of the question in dispute) have been appointed to act as arbitrator by such two surveyors,

or, in the event of their disagreeing, by a petty sessional court on the application of either of them:

Such arbitrator shall make his award within fourteen days.

3. The notice served by the Council shall be discharged, amended or confirmed in accordance with the decision of the two surveyors, or the arbitrator, as the case may be.

4. Unless the arbitrator otherwise direct, the costs of and incident to the determination by the two surveyors or the arbitrator of the question in dispute shall be borne and paid, in the event of such determination being adverse to the contention of the district surveyor, by the Council, or, in the event of such determination being adverse to the contention of the owner's surveyor, by the owner.

Court may make order notwithstanding arbitration.

108—Notwithstanding any such notice requiring arbitration as aforesaid, a petty sessional court on application by the Council may, if of opinion that the structure is in such a dangerous condition as to require immediate treatment, make any order which such court may think fit with respect to the taking down, repairing or otherwise securing the structure.

Expenses.

109—1. All expenses incurred by the Council in relation to the obtaining of any order as to a dangerous structure, and carrying the same into effect under this Part of this Act, shall be paid by the owner of the structure, but without prejudice to his right to recover the same from any person liable to the expenses of repairs.

2. If the owner cannot be found, or if on demand he refuse or neglect to pay the said expenses, the Council, after serving on him three months' notice of their intention to do so, may, if in their discretion they think fit, sell the structure, but they shall, after deducting from the proceeds of the sale the amount of all expenses incurred by them, pay the surplus (if any) to the owner on demand.

Provisions respecting sale of dangerous structure.

110—Where under this Part of this Act any dangerous structure is sold for payment of expenses incurred in respect thereof by the Council, the purchaser, his agents and servants, may enter upon the land whereon the structure is standing for the purpose of taking down the same, and of removing the materials of which it is constructed.

111—Where the proceeds of the sale of any such structure are insufficient to repay to the Council the amount of the expenses incurred by them in respect of such structure, no part of the land whereon the structure stands or stood shall be built upon until after the balance due to the Council in respect of the structure has been paid.

If proceeds insufficient, land not to be built on till balance paid.

112—If the materials are not sold by the Council, or if the proceeds of the sale are insufficient to defray the said expenses, the Council may recover the expenses or the balance thereof from the owner of the building, together with all costs in respect thereof, in a summary manner.

Recovery of expenses.

113—1. There shall be paid to the district surveyor in respect of his services under this Part of this Act in relation to any dangerous structures, the fees specified in Part II. of the Third Schedule to this Act.

2. Provided that if any special service is required to be performed by the district surveyor under this Part of this Act for which no fee is specified in the said schedule, the Council may order such fee to be paid for that service as they think fit.

3. All fees paid to any surveyor by virtue of this section shall be deemed to be expenses incurred by the Council in the matter of the dangerous structure in respect of which such fees are paid, and shall be recoverable by them from the owner accordingly.

Fees to surveyor.

114—Where a structure has been certified by a district surveyor to be dangerous to its inmates, a petty sessional court may, if satisfied of the correctness of the certificate, upon the application of the Council, by order direct that any inmates of such structure be removed therefrom by a constable or other peace officer, and if they have no other abode he may require that they be received into the workhouse for the place in which the structure is situate.

Power to remove inmates from dangerous structure.

Neglected Structures.

115—1. Where a structure is ruinous, or so far dilapidated as thereby to have become and to be unfit for use or occupation, or is from neglect or otherwise in a structural condition prejudicial to the property in or the inhabitants of the neighbourhood, a petty sessional court, on

Removal of dilapidated and neglected buildings.

complaint by the Council, may order the owner to take down or repair or rebuild such structure (in this Act referred to as a neglected structure), or any part thereof, or to fence in the ground upon which it stands or any part thereof, or otherwise to put the same or any part thereof into a state of repair and good condition to the satisfaction of the Council within a reasonable time to be fixed by the order, and may also make an order for the costs incurred up to the time of the hearing.

2. If the order is not obeyed, the Council may with all convenient speed enter upon the neglected structure or such ground as aforesaid and execute the order.

3. Where the order directs the taking down of a neglected structure or any part thereof, the Council in executing the order may remove the materials to a convenient place, and (unless the expenses of the Council under this section in relation to such structure are paid to them within fourteen days after such removal) sell the same if and as they in their discretion think fit.

4. All expenses incurred by the Council under this section in relation to a neglected structure may be deducted by the Council out of the proceeds of the sale, and the surplus (if any) shall be paid by the Council on demand to the owner of the structure, and if such neglected structure or some part thereof is not taken down and such materials are not sold by the Council, or if the proceeds of the sale are insufficient to defray the said expenses, the Council may recover such expenses or such insufficiency from the owner of the structure, together with all costs in respect thereof, in a summary manner, but without prejudice to his right to recover the same from any lessee or other person liable to the expenses of repairs.

Supplemental as to Dangerous and Neglected Structures.

116 —1. Where the Council have incurred any expenses in respect of any dangerous or neglected structure, and have not been paid or have not recovered the same, a petty sessional court, on complaint by the Council, may make an order fixing the amount of such expenses and the costs of the proceedings before such petty sessional court, and directing that no part of the land upon which such dangerous or neglected structure stands or stood shall be built upon, or that no part of such dangerous or neglected structure if repaired or rebuilt shall be let for occupation until after payment to the Council of the said amount, and thereupon, and until payment to the Council of the said amount, no part of such land shall be built upon, and no part of such dangerous or neglected structure so repaired or rebuilt shall be let for occupation.

2. Every such order shall be made in duplicate, and one copy of such order shall be retained by the proper officer of the court, and the other copy shall be kept at the county hall.

3. The Council shall keep at the county hall a register of all orders made under this section, and shall keep the same open for inspection by all persons at all reasonable times, and any such order not entered in such register within ten days after the making thereof shall cease to be of any force. No property shall be affected by any such order unless and until such order is entered in such register.

117—The fees specified in Part IV. of the Third Schedule to this Act as payable to the Council shall be payable to and may be recovered in a summary way by the Council.

<small>Fees on dangerous or neglected structures to Council.</small>

Part X.

DANGEROUS AND NOXIOUS BUSINESSES.

118—1. No person shall erect any building nearer than fifty feet to a building used for any dangerous business to which this section applies.

<small>Regulations for building near dangerous business.</small>

2. Provided that where a building erected before the ninth day of August, one thousand eight hundred and forty-four, within fifty feet from any building for the time being used for any such dangerous business, is pulled down, burnt or destroyed by tempest, such building may be rebuilt.

3. No person shall establish or carry on a dangerous business to which this section applies in any building or vault, or in the open air, at a less distance than forty feet from any public way, or than fifty feet from any other

building or any vacant ground belonging to any person other than his landlord.

4. The following businesses shall be deemed to be dangerous businesses within the meaning of this section (that is to say): The business of the manufacture of matches, ignitable by friction or otherwise, or of other substances liable to sudden explosion, inflammation or ignition, or of turpentine, naphtha, varnish, tar, resin or Brunswick black, and any other manufacture dangerous on account of the liability of the materials or substances employed therein to cause sudden fire or explosion.

Regulations for building near noxious business.

119—1. No person shall erect any dwelling-house nearer than fifty feet to a building used for any noxious business to which this section applies.

2. Provided that where a dwelling-house erected before the ninth day of August, one thousand eight hundred and forty-four, within fifty feet from any building for the time being used for any such noxious business, is pulled down, burnt or destroyed by tempest, such dwelling-house may be rebuilt.

3. Subject to the provisions of the next following section, no person shall establish or carry on a noxious business to which this section applies in any building or vault, or in the open air, at a less distance than forty feet from any public way or than fifty feet from any dwelling-house.

4. The following businesses shall be deemed to be noxious businesses within the meaning of this section (that is to say): The business of a blood boiler or bone boiler, and any other like business which is offensive or noxious, but nothing in this section shall apply to any of the following businesses, namely, the businesses of a soap boiler, tallow melter, knacker, fellmonger, tripe boiler and slaughterer of cattle and horses.

Provisions as to certain old noxious businesses.

120—The following provisions shall apply to any noxious business existing before the ninth day of August, one thousand eight hundred and forty-four :—

1. If any party charged with carrying on such business show that in carrying on such business all the means known to be available for mitigating the effect of such business have been adopted, then it shall be lawful for the petty sessional court to remit or mitigate the penalty. Provided further,

that if it shall appear to the said court or to the court of quarter sessions, whether on appeal or on trial by jury as hereinafter provided, that the person carrying on any such business shall have made due endeavours to carry on the same with a view to mitigate so far as possible the effects of such business, then, although he have not adopted all or the best means available for the purpose, yet it shall be lawful for the court to suspend the execution of their order, upon condition that within a reasonable time to be named the party convicted do adopt such other or better means as to the court shall seem fit, or before passing final sentence, and without consulting the prosecutor, to make such other order touching the carrying on of such business as the court shall think fit for preventing the nuisance in future. Provided always, that if the matter come before any superior court it shall be lawful for such court to exercise such power of mitigating, or remitting such penalty, or of suspending the execution of any judgment, order or determination in the matter, or to make such order touching the carrying on of such business as to the court shall seem fit:

2. Any person dissatisfied with the decision of the petty sessional court may appeal to the court of quarter sessions in manner provided by the Summary Jurisdiction Acts:

3. If before conviction by the petty sessional court the person complained against desire to have the matter tried by a jury, and enter into a recognisance to try such matter without delay, and to pay all costs of trial if a verdict be found against him, then such matter shall be tried at the next practicable court of quarter sessions, or whensoever that court shall appoint, and if that court shall think fit, it shall be lawful for them to authorise the jury to view the place in question in such manner as they shall direct, and the jury shall inquire and try and determine by their verdict whether the business in question be offensive or noxious, and whether the party in question have

done any act whereby the penalty imposed by this Act in respect thereof has been incurred, and, subject to the power hereinbefore conferred of mitigating such penalty or suspending their judgment, order or determination thereon, or making such order touching the carrying on of the business, the said court shall give judgment according to such verdict, and shall award the penalty (if any) incurred by the defendant, and shall and may (if they see fit) award to either of the parties such costs as they may deem reasonable, which verdict, and the judgment, award, order or determination thereon shall be binding and conclusive.

<small>Saving for gasworks and distilleries.</small> **121**—The provisions of this Part of this Act relating to dangerous and noxious businesses shall not apply to any public gasworks nor to any premises used for the purpose of distillation or the rectification of spirits under the survey of the Commissioners of Inland Revenue or their officers.

Part XI.
DWELLING-HOUSES ON LOW-LYING LAND.

<small>Dwelling-houses on low-lying land.</small> **122**—It shall not be lawful for any person upon land of which the surface is below the level of Trinity high-water mark, and which is so situate as not to admit of being drained by gravitation into an existing sewer of the Council, to erect any building to be used wholly or in part as a dwelling-house, or to adapt any building to be used wholly or in part as a dwelling-house, except with the permission of the Council, and subject to and in accordance with such regulations as the Council may from time to time prescribe with reference to the erection of buildings on such land:

And the Council may by such regulations (subject to appeal as hereinafter provided)—

(i.) Prohibit the erection of dwelling-houses, or the adaptation of any buildings for use as dwelling-houses, on such land or any defined area or areas of such land;

(ii.) Regulate the erection of dwelling-houses, or the adaptation of buildings for use as dwelling-houses, on such land or any defined area or areas of such land;

(iii.) Prescribe the level at which the under side of the lowest floor of any permitted building shall be placed on such land, or any defined area or areas of such land, and as to the provision to be made and maintained by the owner for securing efficient and proper drainage of the buildings, either directly or by means of a local sewer into a main sewer of the Council:

Any person seeking to erect any dwelling-house, or any building, any part of which is to be used as a dwelling-house, or to adapt any building or any part of a building for use as a dwelling-house, on any of such land, shall make application to the Council for a licence to erect the same, and the matter shall thereupon be referred to the chief engineer of the Council, who shall decide whether, and if so upon what conditions, such erection or adaptation may be permitted, and any such decision shall be given by the said engineer by a certificate in writing under his hand. Any person objecting to the refusal of the Council to permit on such land, or any defined area or areas of such land, the erection of any dwelling-house, or the adaptation for use as a dwelling-house, of any building, or to any regulation made by the Council under this Part of this Act, or to any decision of the said engineer, or as to the reasonableness of any requirement or condition made by him, may appeal to the tribunal of appeal.

123—The Council may, with the concurrence of the tribunal of appeal, from time to time make regulations prescribing the procedure to be followed by persons making applications under this Part of this Act. *Power to make regulations.*

124—1. Regulations made by the Council under this Part of this Act shall have no force until a copy thereof shall have been published in the 'London Gazette,' and it shall be the duty of the Council to give notice of every such regulation by publishing a copy thereof in two or more London daily newspapers, and if there be a local newspaper circulating in the parish or district to which such regulation applies, then also in such local newspaper. *Publication and copies of regulations.*

2. Printed copies of every regulation from time to time

in force under this Part of this Act shall be kept at the county hall, and shall be supplied free of charge to any person concerned who may apply for the same.

Part XII.

SKY SIGNS.

Sky signs.

125—In this Part of this Act the expression "sky sign" means any word, letter, model, sign, device or representation, in the nature of an advertisement, announcement or direction, supported on or attached to any post, pole, standard, framework or other support, wholly or in part upon, over or above any building or structure, which, or any part of which sky sign, shall be visible against the sky from any point in any street or public way, and includes all and every part of any such post, pole, standard, framework or other support. The expression "sky sign" shall also include any balloon, parachute or similar device, employed wholly or in part for the purposes of any advertisement or announcement on, over or above any building, structure or erection of any kind, or on or over any street or public way, but shall not be deemed to include—

(i.) Any flagstaff, pole, vane or weathercock, unless adapted or used wholly or in part for the purposes of any advertisement or announcement;

(ii.) Any sign on any board, frame or other contrivance securely fixed to or on the top of the wall or parapet of any building, on the cornice or blocking course of any wall, or to the ridge of a roof, provided that such board, frame or other contrivance be of one continuous face and not open work, and do not extend in height more than three feet above any part of the wall or parapet or ridge to, against or on which it is fixed or supported; or

(iii.) Any such word, letter, model, sign, device or representation as aforesaid which relates exclusively to the business of a railway company, and which is placed or may be placed wholly upon or over any railway, railway station, yard, platform or station approach, or premises belonging to a railway company, and which is also so placed that it could not fall into any street or public place.

126—For the purpose of giving effect to the provisions of this Part of this Act, the district surveyor of each district acting under this Act shall inspect and survey sky signs in his district, and report from time to time to the Council. *[District surveyor to act for purposes of this of Act.]*

The expression "the surveyor" in this Part of this Act means the district surveyor so acting within his district.

127—From and after the commencement of this Act it shall be unlawful to erect any sky sign as defined in this Act. *[Prohibition of future sky signs.]*

128—From and after the commencement of this Act it shall be unlawful to retain any sky sign as defined in this Act which previously to the passing of this Act shall have been erected, except in pursuance of and in accordance with the terms of a license granted or renewed before the passing of this Act by the Council, or by the Commissioners of Sewers as the case may be, under the provisions of the London Sky Signs Act, 1891, as amended by section 17 of the London County Council (General Powers) Act, 1893, or renewed after the passing of this Act as hereinafter provided. *[Regulation of existing sky signs.]*

129—1. A license granted under the provisions of the London Sky Signs Act, 1891, and renewed under the same Act, may, on the expiration of the period for which such renewal was granted, be renewed for one further period of two years, but not longer. *[Renewal of license.]*

2. A license granted under the provisions of the London Sky Signs Act, 1891, as amended by section 17 of the London County Council (General Powers) Act, 1893, after the twenty-fourth day of August, one thousand eight hundred and ninety-three, may be renewed from the expiration of a period of two years from the date of issue of such license for a further period of two years, and, on the expiration of that period, for one other period of two years, making, with the original term of the license, six years in all, but not longer.

3. Every person desirous of obtaining a renewal of a license to retain a sky sign for any such period as aforesaid, may make application to the surveyor for an inspec-

tion and survey of such sky sign, and such application shall be dealt with as hereinafter provided; and any person who shall have obtained a certificate from the surveyor, after any such inspection and survey in accordance with the provisions hereinafter contained, may at any time within fourteen days from the issue thereof forward the same to the Council, with an application for a license from the Council to retain the same sky sign, and every such application for a license shall be accompanied by a fee of five shillings, which shall be paid to the Council for and in respect of the registration of the license; and the Council shall thereupon grant to such person a license for the retention of such sky sign for a period of two years from the date of the issue of such license.

4. Every such application to the surveyor for the inspection and survey of a sky sign shall be accompanied by a payment of two guineas to such surveyor, which shall be his fee for the inspection and survey and for the grant or refusal of the certificate, as the case may be, and it shall not be lawful for the surveyor to demand or receive any further fee or payment in respect thereof.

5. The surveyor shall either grant a certificate that in his opinion the sky sign is so placed, constructed and supported as not to be likely to involve danger to the public, or he shall refuse to grant such certificate, in which case he shall state the grounds of such refusal, and such certificate or refusal shall be in the form set out in this section, with such modifications, if any, as the circumstances may require:—

Form of Certificate.

LONDON BUILDING ACT, 1894.

District of .

Whereas A.B., of   , has made application to me, pursuant to the London Building Act, 1894, to inspect and survey a sky sign erected at   , I hereby certify that I have inspected and surveyed the same, and in my opinion the said sky sign may be retained as now constructed for two years from the date hereof without being likely to cause danger to the public.

Dated this   day of   . 189 .

(Signed)   *C.D.*
Surveyor.

Form of Refusal of Certificate.

LONDON BUILDING ACT, 1894.

District of

Whereas A.B., of , has made application to me, pursuant to the London Building Act, 1894, to inspect and survey a sky sign erected at , I hereby certify that I have inspected and surveyed the same, and I refuse to certify that the said sky sign is so constructed as not to be likely to cause danger to the public for the following reasons—

Dated this day of , 189 .

(Signed) C.D.
Surveyor.

130—1. Where the surveyor refuses to grant a certificate applied for under this Act the applicant may, if he think fit and can lawfully do so, execute such repairs to or alterations in or modifications of the sky sign as shall meet the objections thereto as stated in the form of refusal, and may thereupon make a further application to the surveyor to inspect and survey the sky sign.

2. If the surveyor on re-inspection and re-survey be of opinion that the sky sign has been so repaired, altered or modified that it is not likely to involve danger to the public, he shall grant a certificate under this Act with respect to such sky sign, and an application for license thereof may be made as in this Act provided.

3. Every such application to the surveyor to re-inspect and re-survey a sky sign, and for a certificate in respect thereof, shall be accompanied by a payment of one guinea to such surveyor, which shall be his fee for such re-inspection and re-survey, and for the grant or refusal of a certificate thereupon as the case may be, and it shall not be lawful for the surveyor to demand or receive any further fee or payment in respect thereof.

Alteration of sky signs to meet surveyor's requirements.

131—Where the surveyor refuses to grant a certificate applied for under this Act, it shall be the duty of the surveyor forthwith to forward a copy of his refusal to the Council.

Notice of refusal of certificate to be sent to the Council.

Appeal against refusal of certificate.

132—Where the surveyor refuses to grant a certificate under this Act it shall be lawful for the applicant, at any time within fourteen days after the date of such refusal, to make application to the tribunal of appeal by way of appeal against such refusal, and such appeal shall be accompanied by a copy of the form of refusal by the surveyor.

Forfeiture of license.

133—In any of the following cases a license under this Act shall become void, viz.:—
(i.) If any addition to any sky sign be made except for the purpose of making it secure under the direction of the surveyor;
(ii.) If any change be made in the sky sign or any part thereof;
(iii.) If the sky sign or any part thereof fall either through accident, decay or any other cause;
(iv.) If any addition or alteration be made to or in the house, building or structure, on, over or to which any sky sign is placed or attached, if such addition or alteration involves the disturbance of the sky sign or any part thereof;
(v.) If the house, building or structure, over, on or to which the sky sign is placed or attached, become unoccupied or be demolished or destroyed.

Removal of sky signs.

134—If any sky sign be erected or retained contrary to the provisions of this Act, or after the license for the maintenance or retention thereof for any period shall have become void, it shall be lawful for the Council to take proceedings for the taking down and removal of the sky sign in the same manner in all respects as if it were a structure certified to be in a dangerous state under Part IX. of this Act, except that the provisions of the said Part with respect to arbitration shall not apply, and it shall be lawful for the Council or any officers, servants or workmen appointed by them for that purpose (after obtaining the order of a petty sessional court for the taking down of the sky sign, and after the expiration of the period (if any) fixed by such order for taking down the same) to enter upon the land, building or premises, on or over which the sky sign is erected, and to take down and remove the sky sign, and to execute and do any works which may be necessary for that purpose, and for leaving any building to which the same was attached in a condition of safety ; and all the expenses of and incidental to any such work shall be repaid and be recoverable as though the same were a penalty imposed by this Act.

For the purpose of any such proceeding the expression "the owner" in the said Part of this Act shall mean the occupier of the house, building or structure on or to which the sky sign is erected or attached, or if the house, building or structure is unoccupied then the person who would be the owner thereof within the meaning of this Act.

135—As regards the City, this Part of this Act shall be read and have effect as if the Commissioners of Sewers were named therein instead of the Council, and all costs and expenses of such Commissioners in the execution of this Part of this Act shall be paid out of their consolidated rate as part of the expenses of such Commissioners. <small>Application of this Part of Act within the City.</small>

Part XIII.
SUPERINTENDING ARCHITECT AND DISTRICT SURVEYORS.

136—1. The Council may, for the purpose of aiding in the execution of this Act, appoint some fit person to be called "the superintending architect of metropolitan buildings," together with such number of clerks as they think fit. <small>Power for Council to appoint superintending architect.</small>

2. Such architect and clerks shall be removable by the Council, and perform such duties as the Council direct.

3. The superintending architect shall not practise as an architect, or follow any other occupation.

4. There shall be paid to the superintending architect and clerks such salaries as the Council may direct.

5. Subject to the foregoing provisions of this section, the person who at the commencement of this Act is the superintending architect of metropolitan buildings shall continue to be the superintending architect under this Act.

137—If the superintending architect is prevented by illness, infirmity or any other unavoidable cause from <small>Power of superintending</small>

architect to appoint deputy.

attending to the duties of his office he may, with the consent of the Council, appoint some other person as his deputy to perform all his duties for such time as he may be temporarily prevented from executing them.

Buildings to be supervised by district surveyors.

138—Subject to the provisions of this Act and to the exemptions in this Act mentioned, every building or structure, and every work done to, in or upon any building or structure, and all matters relating to the width and direction of streets, the general line of buildings in streets, the provision of open spaces about buildings, and the height of buildings, shall be subject to the supervision of the district surveyor appointed to the district in which the building or structure is situate.

Powers of Council as to surveyors and districts.

139—1. The Council shall have the following powers with regard to the district surveyors and their districts (that is to say):—

(a) They may alter the limits of the district of any district surveyor, or unite any two or more such districts, and place any such altered district under the supervision of any district surveyor, and do all such matters and things as are necessary for carrying into effect the power hereby given;

(b) They may dismiss or suspend any district surveyor, and in case of any suspension or during any vacancy may appoint a temporary substitute, provided that their dismissal of a district surveyor who held such office before the fourteenth day of August, one thousand eight hundred and fifty-five, shall be subject to the consent of a Secretary of State;

(c) On a vacancy occurring in the office of a district surveyor they may appoint another qualified person in his place;

(d) They may pay such amount of compensation as they think fit, or as in case of disagreement shall be determined by the tribunal of appeal, to any district surveyor who is deprived of his office in pursuance of the power hereby given of altering the limits of districts.

2. Subject to the foregoing provisions of this section

the districts existing at the commencement of this Act shall continue to be districts for the purposes of this Act, and the several persons who at the commencement of this Act are district surveyors shall continue to be district surveyors under this Act.

140—The Royal Institute of British Architects may cause to be examined, by such persons and in such manner as they think fit, all candidates presenting themselves for the purpose of being examined as to their competency to perform the duties of district surveyor, and shall grant certificates of competency to the candidates found deserving of the same; and a person who has not already filled the office of district surveyor shall not be qualified to be appointed to that office unless he has received a certificate of competency from the said institute, or has been examined in such other manner as the Council may direct and been found competent in such examination. Examination of candidates for office of surveyor.

141—Every district surveyor shall have and maintain an office at his own expense in such part of his district as may be approved by the Council, and the Council shall forthwith communicate to the local authority any change in the office of such district surveyor. Surveyor to have an office.

142—If any district surveyor is prevented by illness, infirmity or any other unavoidable circumstances from attending to the duties of his office he may, with the consent of the Council, appoint some other person as his deputy to perform all his duties for such time as he may be prevented from executing them. Power of surveyor to appoint deputy.

143—Where it appears to the Council that, on account of the pressure of business in any district, or on any other account, the surveyor of that district cannot discharge his duties promptly and efficiently, the Council may direct any other district surveyor to assist the surveyor of that district in the performance of his duties, or appoint some other person to give such assistance, and the assistant shall be entitled to receive all fees payable in respect of the services performed by him. Power to appoint assistant surveyor.

144—If any building or structure be executed or any work done to, in or upon any building or structure by or Surveyor not to act in case of

118   LONDON BUILDING ACT, 1894.

works under his professional superintendence.

under the superintendence of any district surveyor, acting professionally or on his own private account, that surveyor shall not survey such building or structure for the purpose of this Act, or act as district surveyor in respect thereof or in any matter connected therewith, but it shall be his duty to give notice to the Council, who shall then appoint some other district surveyor to act in respect of the matter.

Notices to be given to surveyor by builder.

145—In the following cases and at the following times (that is to say):—

(a) Where a building or structure or work is about to be begun, then two clear days before it is begun; and

(b) Where a building or structure or work is after the commencement thereof suspended for any period exceeding three months, then two clear days before it is resumed; and

(c) Where during the progress of a building or structure or work the builder employed thereon is changed, then two clear days before a new builder enters upon the continuance thereof;

the builder or other person causing or directing the work to be executed shall serve on the district surveyor a building notice respecting the building or structure or work. Every building notice shall state the situation, area, height, number of storeys and intended use of the building or structure, and the number of buildings or structures if more than one, and the particulars of the proposed work, and the name and address of the person giving the notice and those of the owner then in possession of and the occupier of the building or structure, or of its site or intended site. All works in progress at the same time to, in or on the same building or structure may be included in one building notice.

Surveyor to enforce execution of Act.

146—Every district surveyor shall, upon the receipt of any such notice as aforesaid, and also upon any work being observed by or made known to him which is affected by the provisions of this Act or byelaws made thereunder, but in respect of which no notice has been given, and also from time to time during the progress of any work affected by such provisions and byelaws, as often as may be necessary for securing the due observance of such provisions and byelaws, survey any building or work hereby placed under his supervision and cause all such provisions and byelaws to be duly observed.

147—Every notice served in pursuance of this Act shall be deemed in any question relative to any building, structure or work to be *primâ facie* evidence as against the builder of the nature of the building, structure or work proposed to be built or done.

<small>Notice to be evidence of intended works.</small>

148—1. The district surveyor of any district at all reasonable times during the progress and during fourteen days next after the completion of any building, structure or work in such district affected by any of the provisions of this Act, or by any byelaws made thereunder, or by any terms or conditions on which the observance of any such provisions or byelaws may have been dispensed with, may enter and inspect such building, structure or work.

<small>Power of entry to inspect buildings.</small>

2. The district surveyor may, for the purpose of ascertaining whether any buildings erected in those premises are in such a situation or possess such characteristics as are required in order to exempt them from the operation of this Part of this Act, at all reasonable times and after reasonable notice enter any premises except buildings exempt from the operations of Parts VI. and VII. of this Act, and he may do therein all such things as are reasonably necessary for the above purpose.

149—Where by reason of any emergency any act or work is required to be done immediately or before notice can be given as aforesaid, such act or work may be done on condition that before the expiration of twenty-four hours after it has been begun notice thereof is served on the district surveyor.

<small>In case of emergency works to be commenced without notice.</small>

150—Where it appears from the building notice served on the district surveyor under this Act that it is proposed to erect any building or structure or to do any work to, in or upon any building which will be in contravention of this Act, or that anything required by this Act is proposed to be omitted, the district surveyor shall serve upon the builder or building owner a notice of objection to such proposed erection, and in the event of the builder or the

<small>As to service of notice of objection on builder or building owner.</small>

building owner being dissatisfied with the decision of the surveyor, he may within fourteen days of the date of the notice of objection appeal to a petty sessional court, who may make an order either affirming the objection or otherwise.

Notice by surveyor in case of irregularity

151—In any of the following cases (that is to say):—

(*a*) Where in erecting any building or structure or in doing any work to, in or upon any building anything is done in contravention of this Act, or anything required by this Act is omitted to be done; or

(*b*) Where the district surveyor on surveying or inspecting any building or work in respect of which notice has not been served as required by this Part of this Act, finds that the same is so far advanced that he cannot ascertain whether anything has been done in contravention of this Act, or whether anything required by this Act has been omitted to be done;

the district surveyor shall serve on the builder engaged in erecting such building or structure or in doing such work a notice (hereinafter referred to as a notice of irregularity) requiring him within forty-eight hours from the date of the notice to cause anything done in contravention of this Act to be amended, or to do anything required to be done by this Act which has been omitted to be done, or to cause so much of any building, structure or work as prevents such district surveyor from ascertaining whether anything has been done or omitted to be done as aforesaid, to be to a sufficient extent cut into, laid open or pulled down.

Notice of irregularity after completion of building.

152—1. In order to provide for the service of a notice of irregularity after and notwithstanding that the building or structure has ceased to be in charge of or under the control of the builder, the following provisions shall have effect:—

(*a*) If notice in writing shall have been served upon the district surveyor by the builder or owner of the date at which such building has ceased to be in the charge of or under the control of the builder, then at any time before the expiration

of fourteen days after the service of such notice
a notice of irregularity may, if the district surveyor think fit, be served on the owner or occupier of the building or structure, or other, the
person causing or directing, or who has caused or
directed the work instead of or in addition to
the builder (if any);

(b) Where no such notice shall have been served upon
the district surveyor a notice of irregularity
may, at any time within twenty-one days after
completion of the building or structure, be served
on the owner or occupier of the building or
structure, or other, the person causing or directing, or who has caused or directed the work
instead of or in addition to the builder (if any).

2. When the owner of the building or structure does
not allow the builder to comply with the requisition of a
notice of irregularity served on the builder, and the
builder serves notice on the district surveyor to that effect,
a notice of irregularity may, at any time within fourteen
days after service of the notice by the builder on the
district surveyor, be served on the owner or occupier of
the building or structure, or other, the person causing or
directing or who has caused or directed the work instead
of or in addition to the builder (if any).

3. When a notice of irregularity is served under this
section the provisions of this Act as to the consequences
of such a notice, so far as they relate to the builder, shall
apply to the owner, occupier or other person served.

4. Nothing in this section shall prejudice any remedy
of an owner, occupier or other person against the builder.

153—1. If the person on whom the notice of irregularity is served make default in complying with that notice within the period named therein, a petty sessional court, on complaint made in a summary manner, as provided by the Summary Jurisdiction Acts, by the district surveyor, may make an order on such person requiring him to comply with the notice or with any requisitions therein which may, in the opinion of the court, be authorised by this Act within a time to be named in the order. *Summary proceedings on non-compliance with notice.*

2. If the order be not complied with the Council may,
if they think fit, after giving seven days' notice to such

person, enter with a sufficient number of workmen upon the premises and do all such things as may be necessary for enforcing the requisitions of the notice and for bringing any building or work into conformity with the provisions of this Act, and all expenses incurred by the Council in so doing may be recovered in a summary way either from the person on whom the order was made or from the owner of the premises.

Payments to surveyors for ordinary and special services.

154—1. There shall be paid by the builder, or in his default by the owner or occupier, as the case may be, of the building or structure in respect whereof the same are chargeable to every district surveyor in respect of the several matters mentioned in Parts I. and III. of the Third Schedule to this Act, the fees therein specified or such other fees not exceeding the amounts therein specified as may be directed by the Council.

2. If in consequence of any reduction being made by the Council in the amount of the said fees the income of any existing district surveyor is diminished, the Council shall grant to him compensation in respect of such diminution.

Council to pay district surveyor in relation to formation of streets, &c.

155—The Council shall pay to the district surveyor such fees as the Council shall from time to time determine in respect of any service required to be performed by the district surveyor in relation to the formation or laying out of streets, lines of building frontage and any like service which the district surveyor may be required to perform under this Act.

Fees in relation to evidence before tribunal.

156—The Council shall pay to the district surveyor such fees as may be from time to time appointed by the tribunal of appeal in respect of any work done by the district surveyor in relation to the preparation of evidence and giving the same before the tribunal of appeal.

Periods when surveyors entitled to fees.

157—1. At the expiration of the following periods (that is to say):—

(*a*) Of fourteen days after the roof of any building surveyed by a district surveyor under this Act has been covered in; and

(*b*) Of fourteen days after the completion of any work

by this Act placed under the supervision of a district surveyor; and

(c) Of fourteen days after any special service in respect of any building, structure or land has been performed by a district surveyor;

the district surveyor shall be entitled to receive the fees due to him from the builder employed in erecting such building or structure, or in doing such work, or in doing any matter in respect of which any special service has been performed by the surveyor, or from the owner or occupier of the building or structure so erected, or in respect of which such work has been done or service performed, or of the land in, upon or in respect of which such work has been done or service performed.

2. If any such builder, owner or occupier refuses to pay the said fees they may be recovered in a summary manner on its being shown to the satisfaction of the court that a proper bill specifying the amount of the fees was delivered to him or sent to him in a registered letter addressed to his last known residence.

158—1. The Council may at any time, by order, cause such fixed salary as they may determine to be paid to any district surveyor by way of remuneration instead of fees, so that the amount of such remuneration be not less than the amount of the average of the fees for the last seven completed years preceding such determination, and thereupon the fees which would have been payable to such district surveyor in pursuance of this Act shall be paid to the Council and carried to the credit of the county fund. *Power of Council to pay salaries to surveyors.*

2. The Council may at any time provide either wholly or partially for the payment of salaries to the district surveyors, or to any of them, out of the county fund, and may thereupon abolish or reduce any fees by this Act made payable to the district surveyors.

159—The Council may in any case, where they shall think fit so to do, undertake on behalf of a district surveyor any proceedings which would otherwise be undertaken by such district surveyor, or may pay the costs incurred by any district surveyor in any proceedings taken by him under this Act. *Council may proceed on behalf of district surveyor.*

Returns by District Surveyors.

Monthly returns by district surveyor to Council.

160—Every district surveyor shall, within seven days after the first day of every month, make a return to the Council, in such manner as they may appoint, of all notices and complaints received by him relative to the business of his district, and the results thereof and of all matters brought by him before any petty sessional court, and of all the several works supervised and special services performed by him in the exercise of his office within the previous month, and of all fees charged or received in respect thereof, and shall specify in such return the description and locality of every building which has been built, rebuilt, enlarged or altered, or on which any work has been done under his supervision, with the particular nature of every work in respect of which any fee has been charged or received.

Return to be a certificate that works are in accordance with Act.

161—Every such return shall be signed by the district surveyor, and shall be deemed to be a certificate that all the works enumerated therein as completed have been done in all respects in accordance with this Act to the best of his knowledge and belief, and that they have been duly surveyed by him.

Audit of accounts of fees charged by district surveyor.

162—The superintending architect, or such other officer as the Council appoint, shall examine the monthly returns of the district surveyors, and if any fees therein specified appear to him to be unauthorised by this Act, or to exceed in amount the fees so authorised, or if any such account appears to be in any respect fraudulent or incorrect, he shall make his report in writing to that effect to the Council, who shall thereupon take such steps in the matter as they deem expedient.

District surveyor to notify certain irregularities to the Council.

163—Every district surveyor shall forthwith notify to the Council any actual or probable contravention of the provisions of this Act in relation to any matter or thing with which it is not within his competency to deal, of which notice or information has been given to him or which he has discovered.

PART XIV.

BYELAWS.

164—1. Subject to the provisions of this Act the Council may make such byelaws, not repugnant or contrary to the provisions of this Act, as they may think expedient for the better carrying into effect the objects and powers of this Act with respect to the following matters (that is to say):— Power to Council to make byelaws.

    The regulation of the plans, level, width, surface and inclination of new streets, and for regulating the plans and level of sites for new buildings;

    The forms of notice and other documents to be used for the purposes of this Act and other like matters of procedure;

    Foundations and sites of buildings and other erections;

    The mode in which and the materials with which such foundations and sites are to be made, excavated, filled up, prepared and completed for securing stability and for purposes of health;

    The thickness and the description and quality of the substances of which walls may be constructed for securing stability, the prevention of fires and for purposes of health;

    The dimensions of wooden bressummers;

    The dimensions of joists of floors;

    The protection of ironwork used in the construction of buildings from the action of fire;

    Woodwork in external walls;

    The description and quality of the substances of which plastering may be made;

    The mode in which, and the materials with which, any excavation made within a line drawn outside the external walls of a house, building or other erection, and at a uniform distance therefrom of three feet, shall be filled up;

    The regulation of lamps, signs or other structures overhanging the public way not being within the City;

        Provided that any such byelaws as to the regulation of lamps, signs and other overhanging structures shall be administered by the local authority;

The means of escape from fire in buildings exceeding sixty feet in height;

The duties of district surveyors in relation to any byelaws made in pursuance of this section;

The deposit with district surveyors of any plans of buildings submitted for their certificate;

The regulations of the amounts of the fees to be paid to district surveyors in respect of their duties under any such byelaws;

The imposition for every offence committed against any byelaws made under this Act of a penalty not exceeding five pounds, and a daily penalty not exceeding two pounds for every day during which such offence continues after conviction. Such penalties to be recovered by summary proceedings.

2. The Council may provide by any byelaw that in any case in which the Council think it expedient they may dispense with the observance of any byelaw made under this section on such terms and conditions (if any) as they think proper.

3. No byelaw shall have any force or effect unless or until it shall have been submitted to and confirmed at a meeting of the Council subsequent to that at which the byelaw shall have been made, nor shall any byelaw have any force or effect until the same shall have been allowed by the Local Government Board.

4. Not less than two months before applying to the Local Government Board for the allowance of any such byelaws, the Council shall give notice of their intended application by advertisement in the London Gazette, and otherwise as the Local Government Board shall direct, and the Council shall send a copy of the proposed byelaws as approved by them to the local authority, the Ecclesiastical Commissioners, the Royal Institute of British Architects, the Surveyors' Institution, the London Chamber of Commerce (Incorporated) and to the Institute of Builders, and to such other societies and persons as the Local Government Board may direct, and for one month at least before any such application a copy of the proposed bye-

laws shall be kept at the county hall and shall be open during office hours thereat to inspection without charge.

5. All byelaws made and confirmed and allowed as aforesaid in pursuance of this Act shall be published in the London Gazette, and printed and hung up at the county hall and be open to public inspection without payment, and copies thereof shall be delivered to any person applying for the same on payment of such sum, not exceeding two pence, as the Council shall direct, and such byelaws when so published shall come into operation upon a date to be fixed by the Local Government Board in allowing the byelaws, and the production of a printed copy of such byelaws, authenticated by the seal of the Council, shall be evidence of the existence and of the due making, allowance and publication of such byelaws in all prosecutions or other proceedings under the same without adducing proof of such seal or of the fact of such making, confirmation, allowance or publication of such byelaws.

165—No byelaw in respect of any matter from which the City is exempted by this Act or by any Act hereby repealed shall have any force or effect within the City. <small>Saving for the City of London.</small>

Part XV.
LEGAL PROCEEDINGS.

166—All offences, penalties, costs and expenses under this Act, or any byelaw made under this Act directed to be prosecuted or recovered in a summary manner, or the prosecution or recovery of which is not otherwise provided for, may be prosecuted and recovered in manner directed by the Summary Jurisdiction Acts. <small>Summary proceedings for offences, &c., and recovery of penalties.</small>

167—Any proceedings taken by a district surveyor may be continued by his duly appointed deputy or successor in the office. <small>Proceedings by surveyor.</small>

168—Where jurisdiction is by this Act given to a county court, that court may settle the time and manner of executing any work or of doing any other thing, and may put the parties to the case upon such terms as respects the execution of the work as the court thinks fit: <small>Powers of and appeal from county court.</small>

Provided that any person shall have the same right of appeal from any decision of a county court in any matter in which jurisdiction is given to such court by this Act as he would have under the County Courts Act, 1888, from any decision of such court in any matter.

<small>Application of penalties.</small> **169**—Notwithstanding anything in any other Act one-half of all penalties recovered by the Council under this Act shall be paid to the Council. Provided that it shall be lawful for any court by whom any penalty is imposed under this Act to direct that the whole or part thereof shall be applied in or towards payment of the costs of the proceedings.

<small>Council may demolish buildings and sell materials, and recover expenses.</small> **170**—Where any person has been convicted of an offence against any of the provisions of any Part of this Act, or any byelaw made thereunder, by constructing, erecting, adapting, extending, raising, altering, uniting, or separating any building or structure, or any part of any building or structure, in contravention of any provisions of any Part of this Act, it shall be lawful for the Council, after giving fourteen days' notice to such person to bring such building or structure into conformity with the said provisions, and after default shall have been made in complying with such notice, and notwithstanding the imposition and recovery of any penalty, to cause complaint thereof to be made before a petty sessional court, who may thereupon issue a summons requiring the person making such default as aforesaid to appear to answer such complaint, and if the said complaint is proved to the satisfaction of the court, the court may make an order in writing authorising the Council, and it shall thereupon be lawful for the Council to enter upon such building or structure with a sufficient number of workmen and to demolish or alter such building or structure, or any part thereof, so far as the same shall have been adjudged to be in contravention of this Act, or any byelaw under this Act, and to do whatever other acts may be necessary for such purpose, and to remove the materials to some convenient place, and if in their discretion they think fit, sell the same in such manner as they may think fit, and all expenses incurred by the Council in demolishing or altering such building

or structure, or any part thereof, and in doing such other acts as aforesaid, or the balance of such expenses, after deducting the proceeds of sale of the aforesaid materials (if the Council thinks fit to sell the same), may be recovered from the person committing the offence aforesaid in a summary manner.

If the proceeds of such sale shall be more than sufficient to defray such expenses the Council shall restore the surplus of such proceeds, after deducting the amount of all such expenses, to the owner of the building or structure on demand.

171—The powers conferred by this Part of this Act upon the Council with respect to any building or structure, in case such building or structure has been erected, extended or raised contrary to the provisions of this Act beyond the general line of buildings in the street, place or row of houses in which the same is situate, shall extend and apply to and may be exercised by the local authority in like manner as by the Council.

Procedure by local authorities in case of buildings in advance of general line.

172—Where by any provision of this Act any surplus of the proceeds of the sale of any building, structure or materials is made payable to any owner thereof, and no demand is made by any person entitled thereto within one year of the receipt of the proceeds by the Council, then the same shall be paid into the Bank of England (Law Courts Branch) to the account of the Paymaster-General for the time being, for and on behalf of the Supreme Court of Judicature, to be placed to the credit of "ex parte the London County Council London Building Act 1894, the account of" the owner (describing him so far as reasonably practicable), subject to the control of the High Court, and to be paid out to the owner on his proving his title thereto.

Payment of surplus of proceeds into court.

173—Where it is by any provision of this Act declared that expenses are to be borne by or may be recovered from the owner of any premises (including under the term "owner" the adjoining and building owners respectively), the following rules shall be observed with respect to the payment of those expenses :—

Payment of expenses by owners.

1. The owner immediately entitled in possession to the

K

premises, or the occupier thereof, shall in the first instance pay the expenses with this limitation, that an occupier shall not be liable to pay any sum exceeding in amount the rent due, or that will thereafter accrue due from him in respect of the premises during the period of his occupancy;

2. If there are successive owners each of them shall be liable to contribute to the expenses in proportion to his interest;

3. Any difference arising as to the amount of contribution shall be decided by arbitration;

4. If some of the owners liable to contribution cannot be found, the deficiency so arising shall be divided amongst the owners who can be found;

5. Any occupier of premises who has paid any such expenses may deduct the amount so paid from any rent payable by him to any owner of the same premises, and any owner who has paid more than his due proportion of any such expenses may deduct the amount so overpaid from any rent payable by him to any other owner of the same premises;

6. If default is made by any person in payment of any expenses payable by him in the first instance under this section, the same may be recovered in a summary way, and if default is made by any person in repaying to any other person any money recoverable under this section, such moneys may be recovered in the same manner as if the obligation to pay such moneys were a simple contract debt.

As to periods for giving consents, &c., expiring in vacations.

174—Where the period within which for the purposes of this Act any sanction, consent, approval or allowance in respect of any matters arising under Parts II. or V. of this Act is to be given or refused by the Council, or within which any objection is to be made or other act done by the Council would expire on any day between the eighth day of August and the fourteenth day of September (both inclusive), such period shall be deemed to be extended for twenty-eight days.

Tribunal of Appeal.

175—For the purposes of this Act a tribunal of appeal shall be constituted as follows:— {Constitution of tribunal of appeal.}
One member shall be appointed by a Secretary of State;
One member shall be appointed by the council of the Royal Institute of British Architects;
One member shall be appointed by the council of the Surveyors' Institution:
No member or officer of the Council shall be a member of the tribunal of appeal.

176—Members of the tribunal of appeal shall be appointed for a term of five years, and any such member shall be eligible for re-appointment. {Duration of office.}

177—It shall be lawful for the Lord Chancellor, if he think fit, to remove for inability or misbehaviour, or other good and sufficient cause, any member of the tribunal of appeal. {Removal of members.}

178—Upon the occurrence of any vacancy in the tribunal of appeal, or during the temporary absence through illness or other unavoidable cause of any member thereof, a Secretary of State, the council of the Royal Institute of British Architects, or the council of the Surveyors' Institution (as the case may be), whichever of them shall have appointed the member of the tribunal whose place shall be vacated, shall appoint forthwith a fit person to be a member (either temporary or permanent) of the tribunal in lieu of the member whose place is vacated, or who is temporarily absent as aforesaid. {Vacancies to be supplied.}

179—Each member of the tribunal of appeal shall be entitled to such remuneration, either by way of annual salary or by way of fees, or partly in one way and partly in the other, as a Secretary of State may from time to time fix. {Remuneration of members on tribunal.}

180—It shall be lawful for the tribunal of appeal to appoint such clerks, officers and servants as they may find necessary, who shall be paid such salaries as shall be determined by the Council, and to provide offices, and to obtain such professional advice and assistance as they may find necessary. {Officers, &c., of tribunal.}

Power for Council to support decisions of officers before tribunal.	**181**—It shall be lawful for the Council to defray the expenses of supporting any decision of the Council, or of the superintending architect, or of their engineer, or of a district surveyor, by counsel and witnesses before the tribunal.
Tribunal may state case for opinion of High Court.	**182**—It shall be lawful for the tribunal at any time to state, and the tribunal shall, if ordered by the High Court or a judge thereof on an application in a summary manner made by any party to the appeal, state a case for the opinion of the High Court on any question of law involved in any appeal submitted to them. The High Court shall hear and determine the question or questions of law arising on any case stated by the tribunal of appeal, and shall thereupon reverse, affirm or amend the determination (if any) in respect of which the case has been stated, or remit the matter to the tribunal of appeal with the opinion of the court on the case stated, or may make such other order in relation to the matter as the circumstances of the case require, and may make such order as to the costs of the case and in the High Court as to the court may seem fit.
Procedure of tribunal.	**183**—The tribunal of appeal shall, subject to the provisions of this Act, have jurisdiction and power to hear and determine appeals referred to them under this Act. For all the purposes of and incidental to the hearing and determination of any appeal, the tribunal shall, subject to any rules of procedure duly made, have power to hear the Council and the parties interested, either in person or by counsel, solicitor or agent, as they may think fit, and to administer oaths and to hear and receive evidence, and to require the production of any documents or books, and to confirm or reverse or vary any decision, and make any such order as they may think fit, and the costs of any of the parties to the appeal, including the Council, shall be in the discretion of the tribunal.
Regulations as to procedure and fees.	**184**—The tribunal of appeal may from time to time, subject to the approval of the Lord Chancellor, make regulations consistent with the provisions of this Act as to the procedure to be followed in cases of appeal to the tribunal, including the time and notice of appeal, and as to fees to be paid by appellants and other parties.

185—Any order of the tribunal of appeal may be enforced by the High Court as if it had been an order of that court. *Enforcement of decision of tribunal.*

186—All fees and sums of money paid to the tribunal of appeal shall be paid over to the Council and carried to the county fund, and the salaries or fees payable to members of the tribunal, and the office and establishment expenses of the tribunal, and expenses incurred by the tribunal and the Council in reference thereto, shall be defrayed out of the county fund. *Fees, &c., to be paid to Council. Expenses.*

Notices.

187—1. Notices, orders and other such documents under this Act shall be in writing, and notices and documents other than orders when issued by the Council shall be sufficiently authenticated if signed by their clerk or by the officer by whom the same are given or served. *Notices to be in writing.*

2. Orders shall be under the seal of the Council.

188—1. Any notice, order or other document required or authorised to be served under this Act, the service of which is not provided for by the Summary Jurisdiction Acts, the Lands Clauses Acts, or the Companies Clauses Consolidation Act, 1845, may be served by delivering a copy thereof at, or by sending a copy thereof by post in a registered letter to the usual or last known residence in the United Kingdom of the person to whom it is addressed, or by delivering the same to some person on the premises to which it relates, or if no person be found on the premises, then by fixing a copy thereof on some conspicuous part of the building to which it relates, and in the case of a railway company by delivering a copy thereof to the secretary at the principal office of the said company. *Service of notices.*

2. Any notice, order or other document to be served upon a builder shall be deemed to be sufficiently served if posted in a registered letter addressed to such builder at the place of address stated in his building notice (if any), or in default thereof at his office or any one of his principal offices, or if a copy thereof be fixed on some conspicuous part of the building to which it relates.

3. Any notice by this Act required to be given to or served on the owner or occupier of any premises may be

addressed by the description of the "owner" or "occupier" of the premises (naming the premises) in respect of which the notice is given or served, without further name or description.

4. Any notice required by this Act to be served on a district surveyor may be served on him by post in a registered letter addressed to him at his office, or by leaving the same at his office.

Part XVI.
MISCELLANEOUS.

Expenses, how borne.

189—All expenses incurred by the Council in carrying this Act into execution and not otherwise provided for shall be deemed to be general expenses incurred by the Council and shall be raised and paid accordingly, and the costs, charges and expenses preliminary to and of and incidental to the preparing, applying for and obtaining passing of this Act shall be raised and paid by the Council in like manner.

Power for Council to annex conditions.

190—In any case where the Council are authorised under this Act to refuse their sanction, consent or allowance to the doing or omission of any act or thing, the Council may, if they think fit, instead of refusing such sanction, consent or allowance, give the same subject to such terms and conditions in relation to the subject matter of such sanction, consent or allowance as the Council think fit. Any such term or condition when accepted shall be binding on the owner or occupier of the building or structure or ground to which the sanction, consent or allowance relates, and if at any time any term or condition so accepted is not observed or fulfilled, the owner or occupier in default shall be subject to a penalty as hereinafter provided.

As to buildings of historical interest.

191—In the event of its being necessary to take down any portion of an old building of architectural or historical interest, constructed otherwise than in accordance with the regulations of this Act, or in the event of the destruction of any part of such building, the part so taken down or destroyed may, with the consent of the Council first obtained, be restored in the same material and in the same design as it formerly was.

192—Any owner, builder or other person and his servants, workmen and agents may, for the purpose of complying with any notice or order served or made on him in pursuance of this Act in respect of any building or structure, room or place, after giving seven days' notice to the occupier thereof, and on production of the first-mentioned notice or order, enter and from time to time without further notice re-enter such building or structure, room or place and do all necessary works and things therein, thereto or in connection therewith. *Power of entry to owner, &c., to execute work.*

193—Where any building has been erected or work done without due notice having been given to the district surveyor (in accordance with this Act or a byelaw made under this Act), the district surveyor may, at any time within one month after he has discovered that such building has been erected or work done, enter the premises for the purpose of seeing that the provisions of this Act or any notice served or order made under the same have been complied with, and the time during which the district surveyor may take any proceedings or do anything authorised or required by this Act to be done by him in respect of such building or work, shall begin to run from the date of his discovering that such building has been erected or work done. *Limitation of time for proceedings where notice not given.*

194—Applications, plans and other documents delivered at the office of the Council or to the district surveyor in pursuance of this Act or of any byelaw of the Council thereunder, shall on delivery there become the property of the Council. *Plans and documents to be property of Council.*

195—The approval by the Council of any plans or particulars for the purposes of this Act shall be signified in writing under the hand of the superintending architect. *Mode of giving approval of Council to plans.*

196—Where any consent is required to be given, any notice to be served, or any other thing to be done by, on or to any owner in pursuance of this Act, if there is no owner or if any such owner cannot be found the judge of the county court may give such consent, or do, or cause to be done such thing on such terms and conditions as he may think fit, and may dispense with the service of any notice which would otherwise be required to be served. *Consent, how given on behalf of owners not to be found.*

Storing of wood and timber.

197—1. It shall not be lawful for any person to erect or place a pile, stack or store of cut or uncut timber, lathwood, firewood, casks or barrels, whether on or above the ground, nearer to a street than the buildings forming the general line of buildings therein, except in a position wherein such a pile, stack or store stood on the first day of January, one thousand eight hundred and ninety-four.

2. It shall not be lawful for any person to pile, stack or store cut or uncut timber, lathwood, firewood, casks or barrels in the same yard or ground, or in any part of the same premises with any furnace except in the following cases:—

(a) Where the furnace is enclosed in a building or chamber constructed of fire-resisting materials; or

(b) Where there is a distance of not less than ten feet between the furnace and the pile, stack or store of timber, lathwood, firewood, casks or barrels.

3. No pile, stack or store of timber, lathwood, firewood, casks or barrels shall exceed sixty feet in height from the level of the ground.

4. It shall not be lawful to form in any pile, stack or store of timber, lathwood, firewood, casks or barrels any room or chamber or space (other than a passage) to be used for any purpose whatever.

5. Timber yards existing at the time of the passing of this Act shall comply with these provisions within two years from the date of the passing of the Act, but the Council shall have power in individual cases if they think fit to prolong this time for a term not exceeding seven years, and shall have power to relax any of the provisions of this section.

6. This section shall not apply to railway companies or canal companies so far as regards timber, lathwood, firewood, casks or barrels in transit or piled, stacked or stored on land occupied by them for the purposes of their undertakings, nor to timber, lathwood, firewood, casks or barrels piled, stacked or stored in or on any yard or other premises occupied by any dock company for the purposes of their undertaking, or to any such yard or premises, or to any person piling or stacking or storing timber, lathwood, firewood, casks or barrels in or on any such yard or premises.

198—Proceedings with respect to a building shall not be affected by the removal or falling in of the roof or covering of such building.   *Removal of roof not to affect proceedings.*

199—No person not being properly authorised shall erect or place, or cause to be erected or placed any post, rail, fence, bar, obstruction or encroachment whatsoever, in, upon, over or under any street, and no person not being lawfully authorised shall alter or interfere with any street in such a manner as to impede or hinder the traffic for which such street was formed or laid out from passing over the same.   *Preventing obstruction in streets.*

The Council may, at the expiration of two days after giving notice in writing to such person to demolish or remove any such post, rail, fence, bar, obstruction or encroachment, or to reinstate or restore such street to its former condition (as the case may be), demolish or remove any such post, rail, fence, bar, obstruction or encroachment, and reinstate or restore such street to its former condition, and recover the expenses thereof from such person in a summary manner.

This section shall not apply within the City.

Offences against Act.

200—Subject to the provisions of this Act every person who does any of the things specified in this section shall be deemed to have committed an offence against this Act, and shall be liable upon conviction in a summary manner to a penalty not exceeding the amount hereafter specified in connection with such offence, and to a further penalty not exceeding the amount hereafter stated as the daily penalty in connection with such offence for every day on which the offence is continued after such conviction (that is to say):—   *Offences against Act.*

1. Every person who—
    (a) commences to form or lay out, alter or adapt any street or way, without having first obtained the sanction of the Council under this Act, or otherwise than in accordance with the conditions (if any) prescribed by the Council in giving their sanction or by the tribunal of appeal, as

the case may be, or commences to widen any street or way to a less extent than the prescribed distance without giving to the Council the notice prescribed by this Act; or

(b) unlawfully erects or places in, upon or over any street or way any post, fence, bar, obstruction or encroachment; or

(c) unlawfully permits any such post, rail, fence, bar, obstruction or encroachment in, upon or over any street or way to remain after notice served upon him by the Council to remove the same; or

(d) unlawfully alters or interferes with any street in such a manner as to impede or hinder the traffic for which such street was formed or laid out;

shall be liable to a penalty not exceeding ten pounds for every such offence, and to a daily penalty not exceeding forty shillings.

2. Every person who neglects or refuses for twenty-eight days after the service of any notices empowered to be served under Part II. of this Act, requiring him to set back any building or structure to comply with the requirements of such notice, or after the expiration of such period fails to carry out or complete the works necessary for such compliance within the time (if any) limited in such notice, shall be liable to a penalty of not less than forty shillings and not more than five pounds, and to a daily penalty of not less than ten shillings and not more than forty shillings. Provided always that this sub-section shall not apply to any non-compliance with such notice in the case of an intended highway where the same shall not be opened as a highway.

3. Every person who—

(a) erects or brings forward any building or structure in contravention of any of the provisions of Part III of this Act, or of any conditions attached by the Council to any consent given pursuant to such provisions; or

(b) erects, alters, enlarges, rebuilds or raises, or commences to erect, alter, enlarge, rebuild or raise any building, or commences so to do so as to contravene any of the provisions of Part V. of this Act; or

(c) fails to comply with any of the provisions of Part VI. of this Act; or

(d) fails to comply with the requirements of any notice given to or served upon him under and in accordance with Part VII. of this Act within the time (if any) specified in such notice; or

(e) sets up, erects or adapts any building or structure to which Part VII. of this Act applies without having obtained any license required by that Part of this Act, or makes default in observing any of the conditions contained in such license;

shall be liable to a penalty not exceeding twenty pounds a day during every day of the continuance of the non-compliance with the order of the Court in reference to the matters aforesaid:

4. Every person who hinders or obstructs any persons empowered by this Act to enter and remain on any premises for the purpose of executing and to execute any work authorised or directed to be done under this Act, or wilfully damages or injures any such work, shall be liable for every such offence to a penalty not exceeding ten pounds:

5. Every person who, being a building owner liable under Part VIII. of this Act to make good any damage which he may occasion to the adjoining owners' or adjoining occupiers' property, by any works authorised to be executed by the building owner, or to do any other thing upon condition of doing which his right to execute such works is by Part VIII. of this Act declared to arise, fails within a reasonable time to make good such damage, or to do such thing, shall be liable to a penalty not exceeding twenty pounds, and to a daily penalty not exceeding the like amount:

6. Every person who refuses to admit the purchaser of

any materials sold under this Act, his servants or agents, upon the land on which the same are, at a reasonable hour, or impedes him or them in removing the same therefrom at a reasonable hour, shall be liable to a penalty not exceeding ten pounds, and to a daily penalty of not exceeding five pounds :

7. Every person who erects a building nearer than fifty feet to a building used for any dangerous business, or a dwelling-house nearer than fifty feet to a building used for any noxious business, shall be liable to a penalty not exceeding fifty pounds, and to a daily penalty not exceeding the like amount for every day during which such first-mentioned building or such dwelling-house shall be allowed to so remain near to such dangerous or noxious business :

8. Every person who establishes or carries on a dangerous or noxious business in contravention of any of the provisions of this Act shall be liable to a penalty not exceeding fifty pounds, and to a daily penalty not exceeding the like amount :

9. Every person who erects or adapts, or commences to erect or adapt otherwise than in accordance with the provisions of Part XI. of this Act any building to which Part XI. of this Act relates, shall be liable to a penalty not exceeding one hundred pounds, and to a daily penalty not exceeding fifty pounds for every day after the conviction for the offence on which the building continues so erected or adapted without a license, or on which default is made in observing or complying with any conditions of a license under that Part of this Act :

10. Every person not complying with any term or condition imposed by the Council under the section the marginal note of which is "Power for Council to annex conditions" shall be liable to a penalty not exceeding ten pounds :

11. (*a*) Any person who places, erects or retains, or suffers or permits to be placed, erected or retained any sky sign contrary to the provisions of this Act; or

(b) Being a person who ought to serve a building notice, fails to do so or begins to execute a work respecting which he ought to serve a building notice, before serving such notice, or having served a building notice begins to execute the work to which it relates before the expiration of two clear days after the notice has ceased to operate; or

(c) Refuses to permit any district surveyor at a reasonable time to enter, survey or inspect any building, work or premises which such surveyor is by this Act authorised to enter and inspect, or refuses or neglects to afford him all reasonable assistance in such inspection; or

(d) Fails to comply with any order of the county court made in pursuance of this Act within the time named in such order; or

(e) Refuses to admit at a reasonable time a builder to a building, or otherwise prevents a builder from complying with any order of the county court made in pursuance of this Act; or

(f) (Being a workman, labourer, servant, or other person employed in or about any building) wilfully and without the privity or consent of the person causing the work to be done, does anything in or about such building contrary to the provisions of this Act; or

(g) Refuses to admit at a reasonable time any owner, builder or person, or his servants, workmen or agents into any land, building or structure for the purpose of complying with any notice or order served or made on him in pursuance of this Act in respect of such land, building or structure, or refuses or neglects to afford them all reasonable assistance in complying with such notice or executing such order; or

(h) Acts in any manner in contravention of any of the provisions of this Act relating to the storing of wood and timber; or

(j) Does any other thing prohibited by this Act, or fails, neglects or omits to do any other thing which he is required to do under or in pursuance of this Act;

shall be liable to a penalty not exceeding forty shillings, and to a daily penalty not exceeding the like amount:

12. Every person who without the consent of the Council converts or uses a building contrary to any of the provisions of the section of this Act of which the marginal note is "Rules as to conversion of buildings," shall be liable to a penalty not exceeding ten pounds, and to a daily penalty not exceeding the like amount for every day on which the building remains so converted, or is used contrary to the provisions of the said section.

The liability to these penalties shall be without prejudice to any other proceedings, whether under this Act or any byelaw under this Act or otherwise, but so that no person shall be punished twice for the same offence.

Application of Act.

201—The following buildings and works shall be exempt from the operation of Parts VI. and VII. of this Act :—

1. Bridges, piers, jetties, embankment walls, retaining walls and wharf or quay walls:
2. The Mansion House, Guildhall and Royal Exchange of the City:
3. The offices and buildings of the Bank of England within the City:
4. All buildings erected before or after the passing of this Act, by or with the sanction of the Commissioners for the Exhibition of 1851, on any lands belonging to them and purchased in pursuance of any power vested in them by charter or Act of Parliament, except streets or

blocks of buildings erected by them or with
their sanction as private dwelling-houses :
5. The Sessions House at the Old Bailey, and all other
session houses or other public buildings belonging to or occupied for public purposes by the
justices of the peace of the counties of Middlesex,
London and the City of London, or by the
County Councils of London and Middlesex
respectively :
6. The erections and buildings authorised by an Act
passed in the ninth year of the reign of his late
Majesty King George the Fourth for the purposes of a market in Covent Garden :
7. The buildings of the Metropolitan Cattle Market and
of the Cattle Market at Deptford ; and any building within the market premises inhabited or
adapted to be inhabited by any official or servant
of the Corporation for the purposes of such
markets or either of them :
8. Any building or part of a building belonging to a
canal company, and used exclusively for the
purposes of canal works under any Act of
Parliament ;
Any building or structure situate upon the railway or
within the railway or station premises, and used
for the purposes of or in connection with the
traffic of a railway company ;
Any building or part of a building belonging to a gas
company and used exclusively for gasworks ;
Any building or part of a building belonging to the
Conservators of the River Thames and used by
them as a workshop or store ;
The foundations and walls of buildings belonging to a
railway company situate over any station or
works of a railway company, or immediately adjoining any railway or works of a railway
company, and upon land acquired under the
powers of an Act of Parliament ;
Any building within the station premises of any railway
company inhabited or adapted to be inhabited in
whole or in part by any official or servant of the
railway company.
Provided always that nothing in this sub-section shall

exempt any other buildings used for the purpose of human habitation so far as they are so used:

9. Any building or structure, or part of a building or structure belonging to a dock company constituted by Act of Parliament, and situate within the dock premises:

10. Buildings not exceeding in area thirty square feet, and not exceeding in height five feet in any part, measured from the level of the ground to the underside of the eaves or roof plate, and distant at least five feet from any other building and from any street, and not having therein any stove, flue, fireplace, hot-air pipe, hot-water pipe or other apparatus for warming or ventilating the same, provided that no portion of the building extends beyond the general line of buildings in any street:

11. All the buildings and structures (not exceeding in height thirty feet, as measured from the footings of the walls, and not exceeding in extent one hundred and twenty-five thousand cubic feet, and not being public buildings) wholly in one occupation, and distant at the least eight feet from the nearest street or way, and at the least thirty feet from the nearest buildings and from the land of any adjoining owner. A detached dwelling-house shall not be excluded from this exemption solely by reason of its being within thirty feet of another detached building constructed as stables or offices to be used in connection with such dwelling-house:

12. All buildings not exceeding in extent two hundred and fifty thousand cubic feet, and not being public buildings, and distant at the least thirty feet from the nearest street or way, and at the least sixty feet from the nearest buildings, and from the land of an adjoining owner. A detached dwelling-house shall not be excluded from this exemption, solely by reason of its being within sixty feet of another detached building constructed as stables or offices to be used in connection with such dwelling-house:

13. All party fence walls not exceeding in height seven

EXEMPTED PRIVATE BUILDINGS.

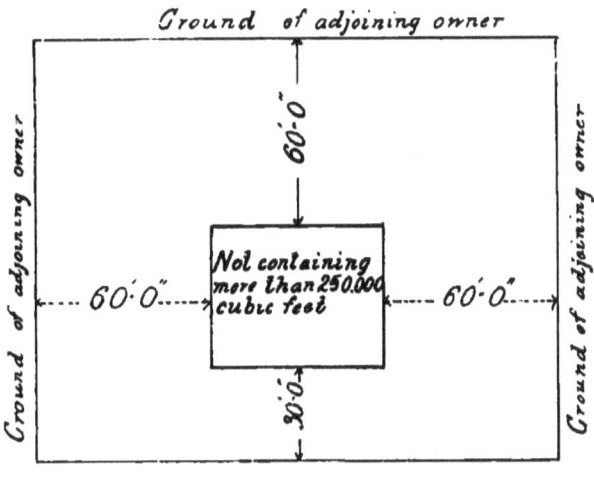

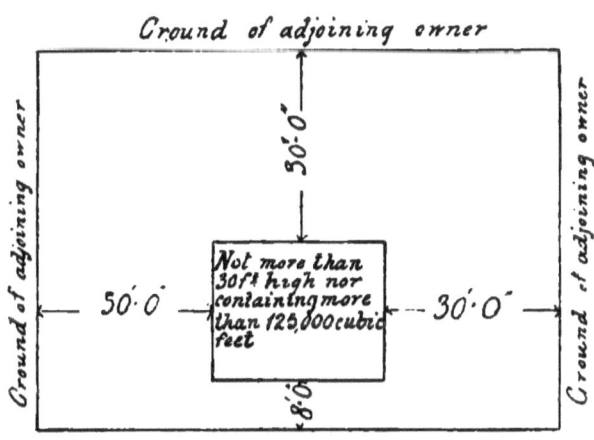

NOTE. These buildings may have Stables or Offices, used in conjunction with detached dwelling houses, within the distance above shewn, provided they are used in connection with such dwelling houses.

feet, measured from the top of the footings of the walls:

14. Greenhouses, if not attached to other buildings:
15. Greenhouses, if attached to other buildings, so far as regards the necessary woodwork of the sashes, doors and frames:
16. Cases of metal and glass used solely for holding plants, fastened to the woodwork of the sill and lower sash of a window, provided that no portion project over the public way, or more than twelve inches beyond the external face of the wall of the building:
17. Openings made into walls, or flues, for the purpose of inserting therein ventilating valves of a superficial extent not greater than forty square inches, if such valves are not nearer than twelve inches to any timber or other combustible material.

If any addition be made to any building or structure specified in sub-sections 10, 11 or 12, whereby any increase is caused in the area, height or extent of any such building or structure beyond the area, height or extent mentioned in the sub-section in which any such building or structure is specified, the Council may give notice to the owner or occupier of such building or structure either to remove such addition or to make the building so increased in height or extent conform with all or any of the provisions of this Act and with any byelaws under this Act relating to the construction of buildings, and upon his failing to do so within fourteen days from the service upon him of such notice, the Council may remove such addition to the building or structure, and may recover the expenses of such removal from the owner or occupier so making default in a summary manner.

202—There shall be exempted from so much of the provisions of this Act as relates to buildings and structures—

Every building, structure or work vested in, and in the occupation of Her Majesty, Her heirs and successors, either beneficially or as part of the hereditary revenues of the Crown, or in trust for the public service or for public services; also

Any building, structure or work vested in and in the occupation of any department of Her Majesty's Government, or of the Metropolitan Police, or of the trustees of the British Museum, for public purposes or for the public service; also

Any building, structure or work vested in and occupied for the service of the Duke of Cornwall for the time being.

As to buildings for the supply of electricity.

203—Where a local authority or a company has statutory powers for the supply of electricity in any metropolitan district, the buildings of such local authority or company used as a generating station, or for works, shall be deemed to be special buildings, to which the general provisions of Parts V., VI. and VII., and the First and Second Schedules of this Act do not apply, and plans thereof shall be submitted to the Council for their approval, and the Council shall have power to authorise the buildings to be erected of greater dimensions than two hundred and fifty thousand cubic feet, and in other respects to exempt such buildings from any of the provisions of this Act if they think fit.

Exempting lands, buildings and property of Inns of Court.

204—The lands, buildings and property of—
1. The Honourable Society of the Inner Temple;
2. The Honorable Society of the Middle Temple;
3. The Honourable Society of Lincoln's Inn;
4. The Honourable Society of Gray's Inn;

herein called "the Inns of Court," shall be exempt from the operation of this Act. Provided that in respect of any building, structure or land which abuts upon any public street, public place or public way, the Inns of Court shall be subject to the provisions of Part III. of this Act (Lines of Building Frontage).

Saving existing rights of gas companies.

205—In addition to any exemption referring to gas companies contained in this Act, nothing in this Act contained shall in any way take away, alter, prejudice or affect any of the powers, rights and privileges conferred upon a gas company by any Act of Parliament, and as existing immediately before the passing of this Act.

206—Any building, structure or work in any respect exempt from the operation of this Act, or in any manner privileged in respect of any provision of this Act, shall remain so exempt or privileged so long only as it is used for the purpose, or retains the character by reason whereof it is so exempt or privileged. Duration of exemption.

207—It shall not be lawful (unless with the consent of the Council) to make any alteration of any building in such manner that when so altered it will by reason of such alteration not be in conformity with the provisions of this Act applicable to new buildings. Buildings not to be altered so as not to conform to Act.

208—Unless in any case the Council otherwise allow, where a party wall or external wall not in conformity with this Act has been taken down, burnt or destroyed to the extent of one-half thereof (measured in superficial feet), every remaining portion of the old wall not in conformity with this Act shall either be made to conform therewith or to be taken down before the rebuilding thereof. When remainder of party wall &c., to be taken down.

209—Every addition to or alteration of a building, and any other work made or done for any purpose in, to or upon a building (except that of necessary repair not affecting the construction of any external or party wall) shall, so far as regards such addition or alteration or other work, be subject to the provisions of this Act and of bye-laws thereunder relating to new buildings. Additions to, and alterations of buildings.

210—A building, structure or work erected or constructed before the commencement of this Act, to which no objection could have been taken under any law then in force, shall (subject to the provisions of this Act as to new buildings or the alteration of buildings) be deemed to be erected or constructed in compliance with the provisions of this Act. Application of Act to buildings erected before commencement of Act.

211—Unless in any case the Council otherwise allow, no person shall— Rules as to conversion of building.
(1) convert into or use as a dwelling-house any building or part of a building not originally constructed for human habitation;

(2) convert into one dwelling-house two or more dwelling-houses constructed originally as separate dwelling-houses;

(3) convert into or use as two or more dwelling-houses any building constructed originally as one dwelling-house;

(4) convert a building which when originally erected was legally exempt from the operation of any building enactments or byelaws in force within London into a building which, had it been originally erected in its converted form, would have been within the operation of these enactments or byelaws;

(5) re-convert into or use as a dwelling-house any building which has been discontinued as or appropriated for any purpose other than a dwelling-house;

(6) convert into or use as a dwelling-room or part of a dwelling-room, any room or part of a room used as a shop; or

(7) convert a dwelling-house or any part of a dwelling-house into a shop;

in such manner that the building or part of a building so converted as aforesaid, when converted will not be in conformity with the provisions of this Act relating to the class of buildings to which the building when so converted will belong.

Buildings in progress.
212—Notwithstanding anything contained in this Act a building, structure or work which has been commenced before, and is in progress at the commencement of this Act, or which is to be carried out under any contract entered into before the passing of this Act, may be completed subject to and in accordance with the provisions of the Acts relating thereto as in force immediately previous to the passing of this Act.

Saving powers of local authorities.
213—Nothing in this Act shall take away or interfere with the powers of the local authorities with respect to the paving of new streets under the Metropolis Management Acts.

Repeal.

214—Section 50 of the Metropolitan Railway (Additional Powers) Act, 1866, is hereby repealed. <small>Repeal of section 50 of Metropolitan Railway Act, 1866.</small>

215—1. The Acts mentioned in the Fourth Schedule to this Act are hereby repealed to the extent specified in the third column of that schedule. <small>Repeal of enactments in schedule.</small>

2. This appeal shall not affect—
 (a) The past operation of any enactment hereby repealed, nor anything duly done or suffered under any enactment hereby repealed; or
 (b) Any right, privilege, obligation or liability acquired, accrued or incurred under or in accordance with any enactment hereby repealed; or
 (c) Any penalty, forfeiture or punishment incurred in respect of any offence committed against any enactment hereby repealed; or
 (d) Any power, investigation, legal proceeding or remedy in respect of any such right, privilege, obligation, liability, penalty, forfeiture or punishment as aforesaid, and any such power, investigation, legal proceeding and remedy may be exercised and carried on as if this Act had not passed; or
 (e) Any of the powers, privileges, exemptions, jurisdictions or authorities given to or vested in the Commissioners of Sewers by or under any Act of Parliament, and existing immediately before the passing of this Act.

216—All byelaws, regulations, orders, consents, conditions and notices duly made, given, imposed or issued under any Act hereby repealed shall, so far as applicable for the purposes of this Act, be of the same validity and effect as if they had been made, given, imposed or issued under this Act. And all such byelaws and regulations shall remain in force until the same shall be revoked, altered or varied by byelaws duly made under the provisions of this Act. <small>Byelaws, &c., under repealed Acts to remain in force.</small>

Saving for existing officers.

217—Officers appointed under any enactment hereby repealed shall continue in office in like manner as if this Act had not been passed.

References in Acts or documents to repealed Acts to be read as referring to this Act.

218—Where in any Act or document, any Act or any provisions of any Act are mentioned or referred to which are repealed by this Act, such Act or document shall with any necessary modifications, and so far only as the circumstances of the case admit, be read as if this Act or the corresponding provisions of this Act were therein mentioned or referred to instead of such repealed provisions.

SCHEDULES.

THE FIRST SCHEDULE.

PRELIMINARY.

Parts I. and II. of this Schedule apply to walls built of bricks not of less than eight and a half inches long, or of stone or other blocks of hard and incombustible substance, the beds or courses being horizontal.

1. Every building, unless otherwise sanctioned in accordance with this Act, shall be enclosed with walls constructed of brick, stone or other hard and incombustible substances, and the footings shall rest on the solid ground or upon concrete, or upon other solid substructure. Provided that open sheds, not exceeding sixteen feet in height and not exceeding four squares in area, may be constructed of any substances and in any manner approved by the district surveyor. Structure of buildings.

2. Every wall constructed of brick, stone or other similar substances shall be properly bonded and solidly put together with mortar or cement, and no part of such wall shall overhang any part underneath it except to the extent of six inches, and provided that the projection be well and solidly corbelled out, and that the side of the wall opposite to the corbelling be carried up vertically in continuation of the inner face thereof. And all return walls shall be properly bonded together. Construction of walls of brick, stone, &c.

3. The thickness of every wall not being built of bricks or stone, or other hard and incombustible substances laid in horizontal beds or courses, shall be one-third greater than the thickness prescribed in Parts I. and II. of this Schedule. Extra thickness of certain walls.

4. The thickness of any wall of a dwelling-house, if built of materials other than those before specified, shall be deemed to be sufficient if made of the thickness required by Parts I. and II. of this Schedule, or of such thickness as may be approved by the Council. Thickness of walls built of materials other than such bricks, &c., as aforesaid.

5. When hollow walls are constructed there shall be a Hollow walls

wall on one side of the hollow space of the full thickness prescribed by this Act.

Height of storey.
6. The heights of storeys shall be measured as follows:—

(a) The height of a topmost storey shall be measured from the level of the underside of its floor joists up to the level of the under surface of the tie of the roof or other covering, or if there is no tie then up to the level of half the vertical height of the rafters or other support of the roof;

(b) The height of every storey other than a topmost storey shall be measured from the level of the underside of the floor joists of the storey up to the level of the underside of the floor joists of the storey next above it.

Height of external and party walls.
7. For the purpose of determining the thickness of a wall the height of such wall shall be measured from the base of the wall to the top of the topmost storey, whether such wall is carried to the full height or not, or in case of a gable when there are no storeys in the roof, to half the height of the gable.

Length of walls.
8. Walls are deemed to be divided into distinct lengths by return walls, and the length of every wall is measured from the centre of one return wall to the centre of another, provided that such return walls are external party or crosswalls of the thickness required under this Schedule, and bonded into the walls so deemed to be divided.

Footings of walls.
9. Unless with the consent of the Council every wall other than a wall carried on a bressummer shall have footings:—

The projection of the bottom of the footing of every wall on each side of the wall shall be at least equal to one-half of the thickness of the wall at its base, unless an adjoining wall interferes, in which case the projection may be omitted where that wall adjoins, and the diminution of the footing of every wall shall be formed in regular offsets, and the height from the bottom of such footing to the base of the wall shall be at the least equal to two-thirds of the thickness of the wall at its base.

Underpinning.
10. The underpinning of walls and chimneys shall be

BUILDINGS NOT PUBLIC & NOT OF THE WAREHOUSE CLASS.

Party & External walls have the same thickness.

Up to 25 feet high

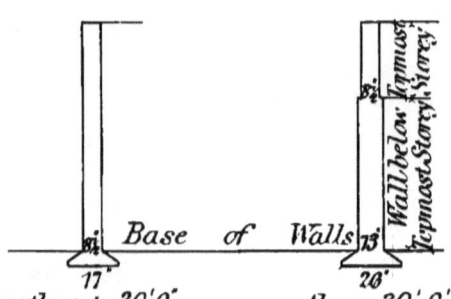

25 to 40 feet high

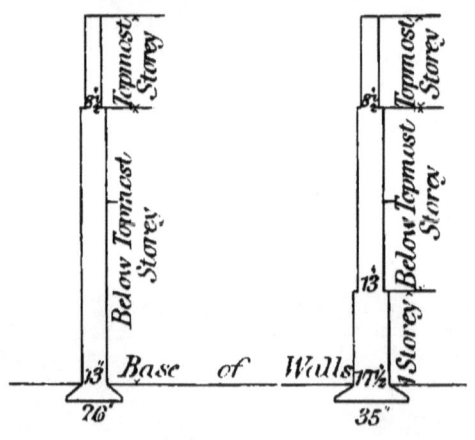

For Rules see Page 153.

built with brick or stone bedded in cement to the full thickness of the old wall or work, and with proper footings, or to an additional thickness if the increased height of the wall so requires, and shall rest on the solid ground or on concrete, or on other solid substructure as a foundation, and the whole shall be executed to the satisfaction of the district surveyor.

11. A wall shall not be thickened except after notice served on the district surveyor of the intention to thicken, and the thickening shall be executed with brick or stone work in cement, properly bonded to the old work to the satisfaction of the district surveyor.

Thickening of walls.

PART I.

BUILDINGS NOT PUBLIC AND NOT OF THE WAREHOUSE CLASS.

External and party walls shall be of not less thickness than the thickness hereinafter specified in each case, viz. :—

1. When the wall does not exceed twenty-five feet in height its thickness shall be as follows :—
    If the wall does not exceed thirty feet in length and does not comprise more than two storeys it shall be eight and a half inches thick for its whole height;
    If the wall exceeds thirty feet in length or comprises more than two storeys it shall be thirteen inches thick below the topmost storey, and eight and a half inches thick for the rest of its height.

2. Where the wall exceeds twenty-five feet but does not exceed forty feet in height its thickness shall be as follows :—
    If the wall does not exceed thirty-five feet in length it shall be thirteen inches thick below the topmost storey, and eight and a half inches thick for the rest of its height;
    If the wall exceeds thirty-five feet in length it shall be seventeen and a half inches thick for the height of one storey, then thirteen inches thick for the rest of its height below the topmost storey, and eight and a half inches thick for the rest of its height.

3. When the wall exceeds forty feet but does not exceed fifty feet in height its thickness shall be as follows:—
> If the wall does not exceed thirty feet in length it shall be seventeen and a half inches thick for the height of one storey, then thirteen inches thick for the rest of its height below the topmost storey, and eight and a half inches thick for the rest of its height;
> If the wall exceeds thirty feet but does not exceed forty-five feet in length it shall be seventeen and a half inches thick for the height of two storeys, then thirteen inches thick for the rest of its height;
> If the wall exceeds forty-five feet in length it shall be twenty-one inches and a half thick for the height of one storey, then seventeen and a half inches thick for the height of the next storey, and then thirteen inches thick for the rest of its height.

4. Where the wall exceeds fifty feet, but does not exceed sixty feet in height, its thickness shall be as follows:—
> If the wall does not exceed forty-five feet in length it shall be seventeen and a half inches thick for the height of two storeys, and thirteen inches thick for the rest of its height;
> If the wall exceeds forty-five feet in length it shall be twenty-one inches and a half thick for the height of one storey, then seventeen and a half inches thick for the height of the next two storeys, and then thirteen inches thick for the rest of its height.

5. Where the wall exceeds sixty feet, but does not exceed seventy feet in height, its thickness shall be as follows:—
> If the wall does not exceed forty-five feet in length it shall be twenty-one inches and a half thick for the height of one storey, then seventeen and a half inches thick for the height of the next two storeys, and then thirteen inches thick for the rest of its height;
> If the wall exceeds forty-five feet in length it shall be increased in thickness in each of the storeys below the uppermost two storeys by four inches

Plate 2

BUILDINGS NOT PUBLIC & NOT OF THE WAREHOUSE CLASS.

Party & External walls have the same thickness.

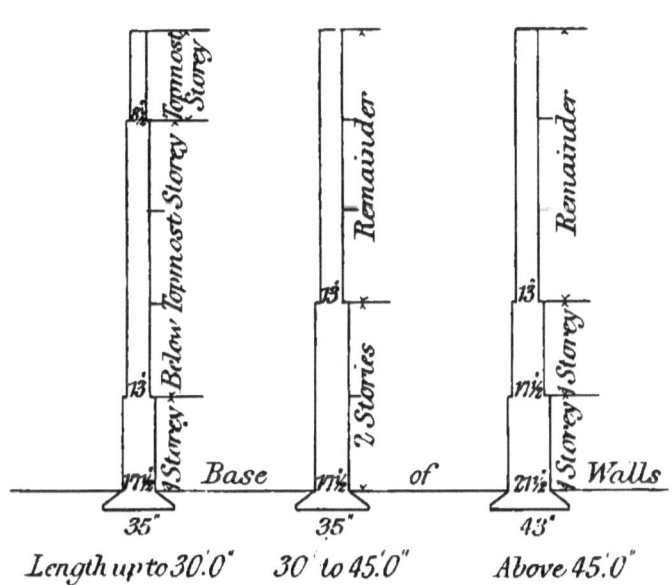

For Rules see Page 154.

BUILDINGS NOT PUBLIC & NOT OF THE WAREHOUSE CLASS.

Party & External walls have the same thickness.

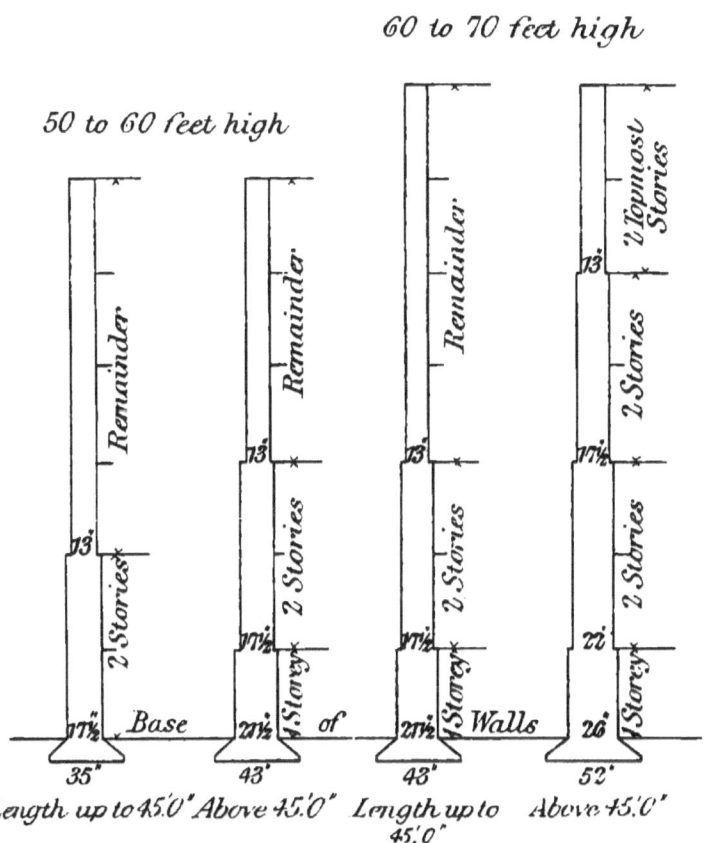

For Rules see Page 154.

BUILDINGS NOT PUBLIC & NOT OF THE WAREHOUSE CLASS.

Party & External walls have the same thickness.

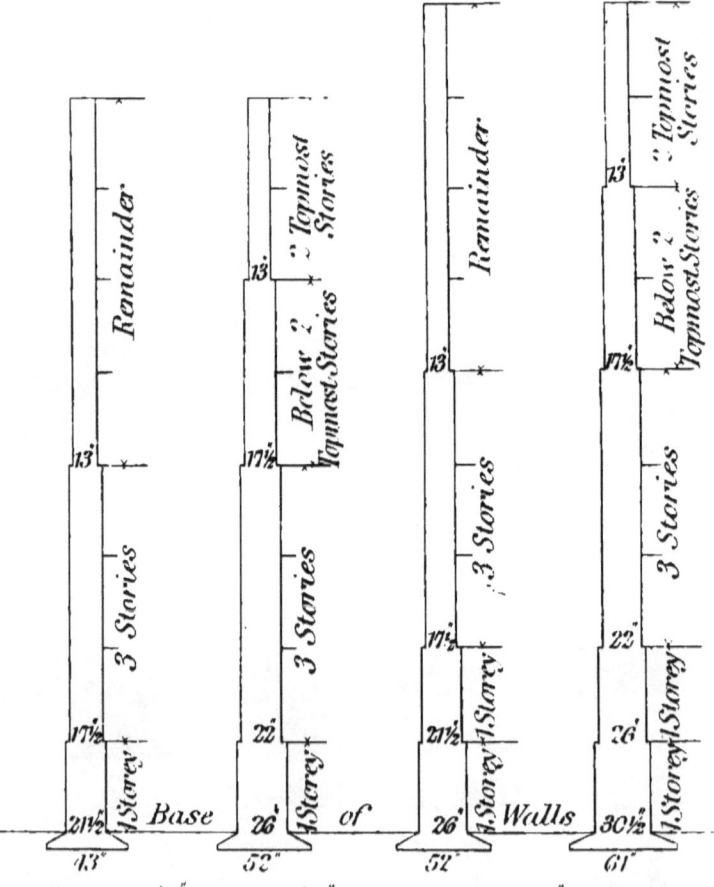

For Rules see Page 155.

Plate 5.

BUILDINGS NOT PUBLIC & NOT OF THE WAREHOUSE CLASS.

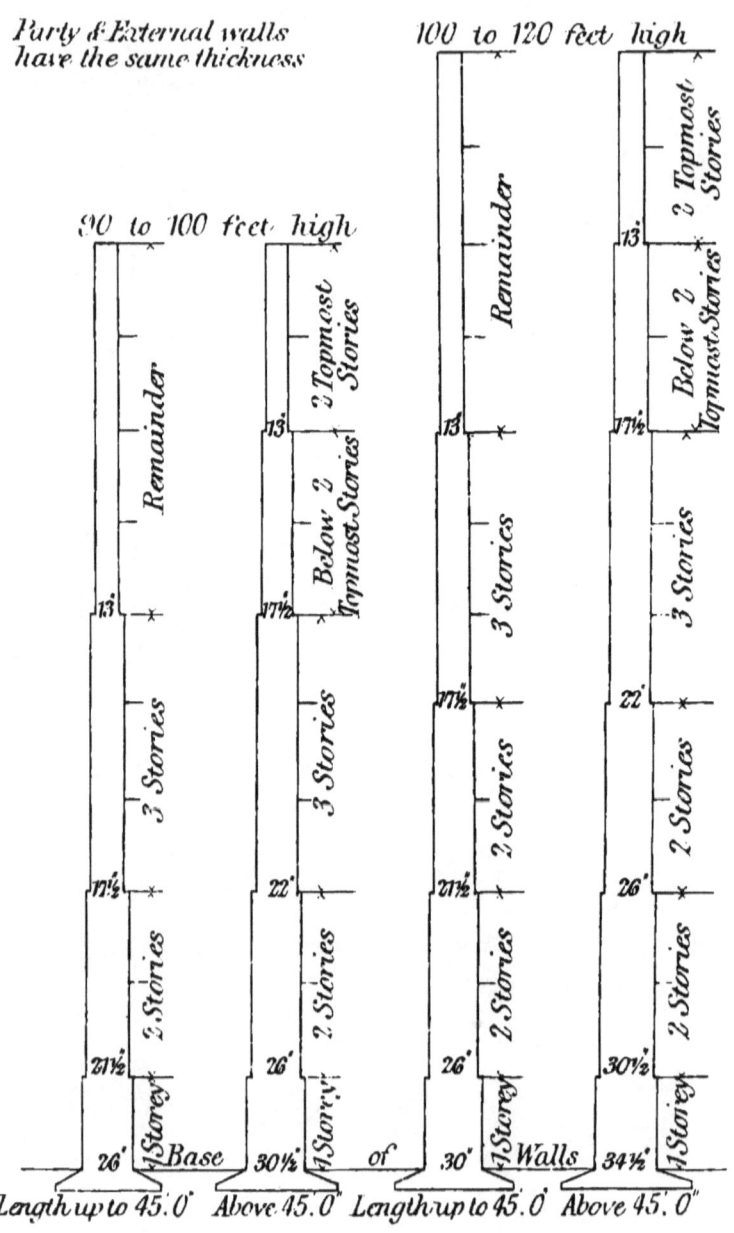

and a half (subject to the provision in this Schedule respecting distribution in piers).

6. Where the wall exceeds seventy feet but does not exceed eighty feet in height its thickness shall be as follows :—

If the wall does not exceed forty-five feet in length it shall be twenty-one inches and a half thick for the height of one storey, then seventeen and a half inches thick for the height of the next three storeys, and thirteen inches thick for the rest of its height;

If the wall exceeds forty-five feet in length it shall be increased in thickness in each of the storeys below the uppermost two storeys by four inches and a half (subject to the provision in this Schedule respecting distribution in piers).

7. Where the wall exceeds eighty feet but does not exceed ninety feet in height its thickness shall be as follows :—

If the wall does not exceed forty-five feet in length it shall be twenty-six inches thick for the height of one storey, then twenty-one inches and a half thick for the height of the next storey, then seventeen and a half inches thick for the height of the next three storeys, and then thirteen inches thick for the rest of its height;

If the wall exceeds forty-five feet in length it shall be increased in thickness in each of the storeys below the uppermost two storeys by four inches and a half (subject to the provision in this Schedule respecting distribution in piers).

8. Where the wall exceeds ninety feet but does not exceed one hundred feet in height its thickness shall be as follows :—

If the wall does not exceed forty-five feet in length it shall be twenty-six inches thick for the height of one storey, then twenty-one inches and a half thick for the height of the next two storeys, then seventeen and a half inches thick for the height of the next three storeys, and then thirteen inches thick for the rest of its height;

If the wall exceeds forty-five feet in length it shall be increased in thickness in each of the storeys below the uppermost two storeys by four inches and a half (subject to the provision in this Schedule respecting distribution in piers).

9. Where the wall exceeds one hundred feet but does not exceed one hundred and twenty feet in height its thickness shall be as follows:—

If the wall does not exceed forty-five feet in length it shall be thirty inches thick for the height of one storey, then twenty-six inches thick for the height of the next two storeys, then twenty-one inches and a half thick for the height of the next two storeys, then seventeen and a half inches thick for the height of the next three storeys, and then thirteen inches thick for the rest of its height;

If the wall exceeds forty-five feet in length it shall be increased in thickness in each of the storeys below the uppermost two storeys by four inches and a half (subject to the provision in this Schedule respecting distribution in piers).

Condition in respect of storeys exceeding certain height.

10. If any storey exceeds in height sixteen times the thickness prescribed under this Schedule for the walls of such storey, the thickness of each external and party wall throughout such storey shall be increased to one-sixteenth part of the height of the storey, and the thickness of each external and party wall below that storey shall be increased to a like extent, but any such additional thickness may be confined to piers properly distributed, of which the collective widths amount to one-fourth part of the length of the wall.

Restriction in case of certain storeys.

11. No storey enclosed with walls less than thirteen inches in thickness shall be more than ten feet in height between the floor and the ceiling thereof or between the floor and the tie of the roof.

Rule as to buildings not being public buildings or buildings of the warehouse class.

12. All buildings excepting public buildings, and such buildings as are in this Act defined to be buildings of the warehouse class, shall, as respects the thickness of their walls, be subject to the provisions contained in this part of this Schedule.

WAREHOUSE WALLS.

Party & External walls have the same thickness.

Up to 25 feet high.   *25 to 30 feet high.*

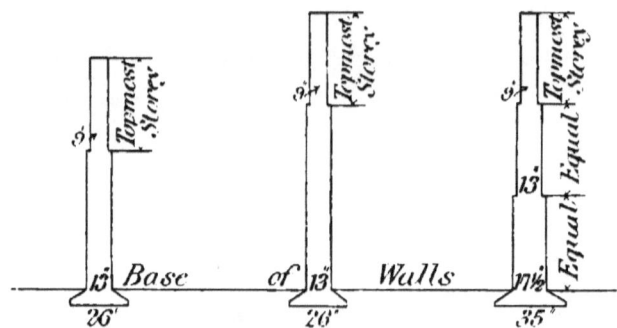

Length unlimited.   Length up to 45.0". Above 45.0".

30 to 40 feet high.

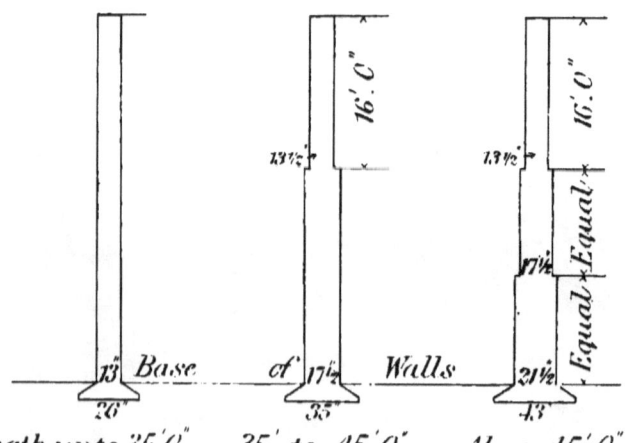

Length up to 35.0".   35' to 45.0".   Above 45.0".

For Rules see Page 157.

WAREHOUSE WALLS.

Party & External walls have the same thickness.

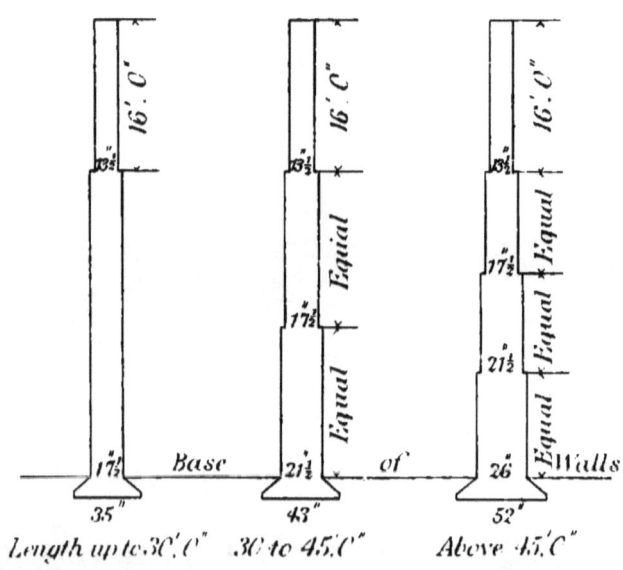

For Rules see Page 157.

PART II.

BUILDINGS OF THE WAREHOUSE CLASS.

The external and party walls of buildings of the ware- Thickness at house class shall at the base be made of not less thickness base. than the thickness hereinafter specified in each case, viz. :—

1. Where the wall does not exceed twenty-five feet in height (whatever is its length) it shall be thirteen inches thick at its base.

2. Where the wall exceeds twenty-five feet but does not exceed thirty feet in height it shall be at its base of the thickness following :—

> If the wall does not exceed forty-five feet in length it shall be thirteen inches thick at its base :
>
> If the wall exceeds forty-five feet in length it shall be seventeen and a half inches thick at its base.

3. Where the wall exceeds thirty feet but does not exceed forty feet in height it shall be at its base of the thickness following :—

> If the wall does not exceed thirty-five feet in length it shall be thirteen inches thick at its base ;
>
> If the wall exceeds thirty-five feet but does not exceed forty-five feet in length, it shall be seventeen and a half inches thick at its base ;
>
> If the wall exceeds forty-five feet in length it shall be twenty-one inches and a half thick at its base.

4. Where the wall exceeds forty feet but does not exceed fifty feet in height it shall be at its base of the thickness following :—

> If the wall does not exceed thirty feet in length it shall be seventeen and a half inches at its base ;
>
> If the wall exceeds thirty feet but does not exceed forty-five feet in length it shall be twenty-one inches and a half thick at its base ;
>
> If the wall exceeds forty-five feet in length it shall be twenty-six inches thick at its base.

5. Where the wall exceeds fifty feet but does not exceed sixty feet in height it shall be at its base of the thickness following :—

> If the wall does not exceed forty-five feet in length

it shall be twenty-one inches and a half thick at its base;

If the wall exceeds forty-five feet in length it shall be twenty-six inches thick at its base.

6. Where the wall exceeds sixty feet but does not exceed seventy feet in height it shall be at its base of the thickness following :—

If the wall does not exceed forty-five feet in length it shall be twenty-one inches and a half thick at its base;

If the wall exceeds forty-five feet in length it shall be increased in thickness from the base up to within sixteen feet from the top of the wall by four inches and a half (subject to the provision in this Schedule respecting distribution in piers).

7. Where the wall exceeds seventy feet but does not exceed eighty feet in height it shall be at its base of the thickness following :—

If the wall does not exceed forty-five feet in length it shall be twenty-one inches and a half thick at its base;

If the wall exceeds forty-five feet in length it shall be increased in thickness from the base up to within sixteen feet from the top of the wall by four inches and a half (subject to the provision in this Schedule respecting distribution in piers).

8. Where the wall exceeds eighty feet but does not exceed ninety feet in height it shall be at its base of the thickness following :—

If the wall does not exceed forty-five feet in length it shall be twenty-six inches thick at its base;

If the wall exceeds forty-five feet in length it shall be increased in thickness from the base up to within sixteen feet from the top of the wall by four inches and a half (subject to the provision in this Schedule respecting distribution in piers).

9. Where the wall exceeds ninety feet but does not exceed one hundred feet in height it shall be at its base of the thickness following :—

If the wall does not exceed forty-five feet in length it shall be twenty-six inches thick at its base;

WAREHOUSE WALLS.

Party & External walls have the same thickness.

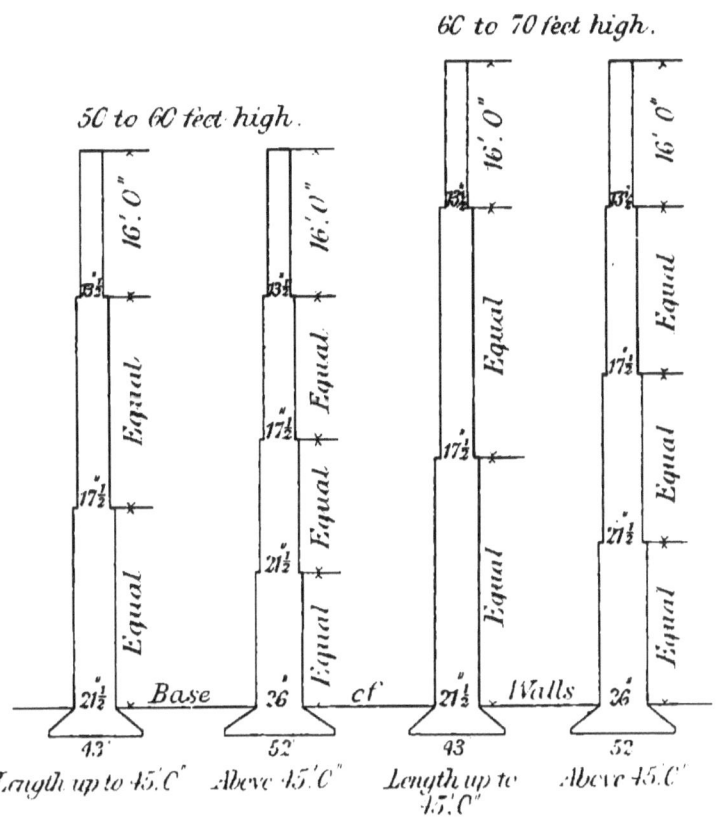

For Rules see Pages 157 & 158

WAREHOUSE WALLS.

Party & External walls have the same thickness.

70 to 80 feet high.

80 to 90 feet high.

- 16′.0″ / 13½″
- 16′.0″ / 13½″
- 16′.0″ / 13½″
- 16′.0″ / 13½″

Equal — 17½″
Equal — 17½″
Equal — 17½″
Equal — 17½″

Equal — 21½″
Equal — 21½″
Equal — 21½″

Equal — 26″

Base: 21½″ | 26″ | 26″ | 30½″
of Walls

48′ | 52′ | 52′ | 61′

Length up to 45′.0″ Above 45′.0″   Length up to 45′.0″ Above 45′.0″

For Rules see Page 158

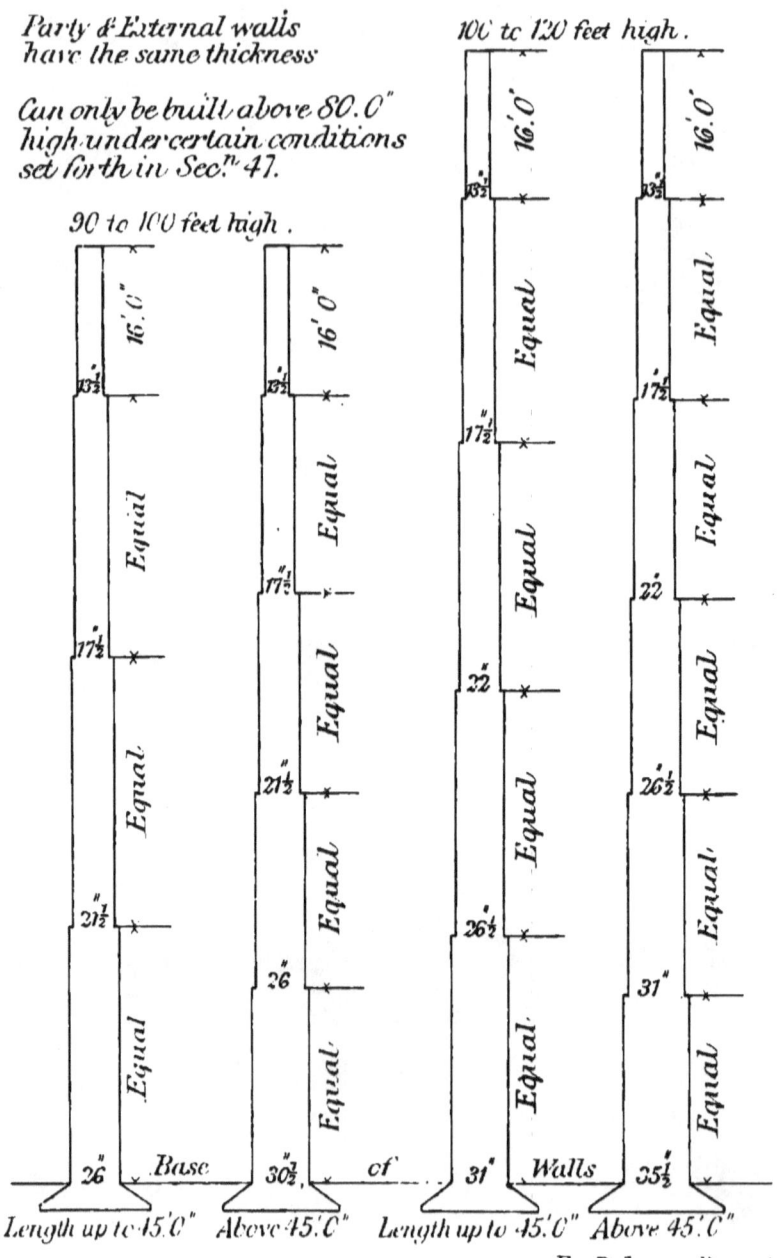

If the wall exceeds forty-five feet in length it shall be increased in thickness from the base up to within sixteen feet from the top of the wall by four inches and a half (subject to the provision in this Schedule respecting distribution in piers).

10. Where the wall exceeds one hundred feet but does not exceed one hundred and twenty feet in height it shall be at its base of the thickness following :—

If the wall does not exceed forty-five feet in length it shall be thirty-one inches thick at its base ;

If the wall exceeds forty-five feet in length it shall be increased in thickness from the base up to within sixteen feet from the top of the wall by four inches and a half (subject to the provision in this Schedule respecting distribution in piers).

11. The thickness of the wall at the top and for sixteen feet below the top shall be thirteen inches and a half, and the intermediate parts of the wall between the base and sixteen feet below the top shall not be of less thickness than would be the case if the wall were to be built solid throughout the space between straight lines drawn on each side of the wall and joining the thickness at the base to the thickness at sixteen feet below the top :

Nevertheless, in walls not exceeding thirty feet in height, the walls of the topmost storey may be nine inches thick provided the height of that story does not exceed ten feet.

12. If in any storey of a building of the warehouse class the thickness of the wall, as determined by the provisions of this schedule, is less than one-fourteenth part of the height of such storey, the thickness of the wall shall be increased to one-fourteenth part of the height of the storey, and the thickness of each external and party wall below that storey shall be increased to a like extent, but any such additional thickness may be confined to piers properly distributed, of which the collective widths amount to one-fourth part of the length of the wall. *Condition in respect of storeys exceeding a certain height.*

13. The thickness of any wall of a building of the ware- house class, if built of materials other than those before specified, shall be deemed to be sufficient if made of the thickness required by the provisions of this Schedule or of such other thickness as may be approved by the Council. *Thickness of walls built of materials other than such bricks, &c., as aforesaid.*

Miscellaneous.

1. The thickness of a cross-wall shall be two-thirds of the thickness hereinbefore required for an external or party wall of the same dimensions and belonging to the same class of buildings, but never less than eight and a half inches, and no wall subdividing any building shall be deemed to be a cross-wall unless it is carried up to the floor of the topmost storey, and unless in each storey the aggregate extent of the vertical faces or elevations of all the recesses and that of all the openings therein taken together does not exceed one-half of the whole extent of the vertical face or elevation of the wall.

2. Wherever a cross-wall becomes in any part an external wall, such cross-wall shall be of the thickness required for an external wall of the same height and length and belonging to the same class of buildings.

3. Where an increase of thickness is by any rule of Part I. or Part II. of this Schedule required in case of a wall exceeding sixty feet in height and forty-five feet in length, or in case of a storey exceeding in height sixteen times or fourteen times (as the case may be) the thickness prescribed for its walls, or in case of a wall below such storey the increased thickness may be confined to piers properly distributed, of which the collective widths amount to one-fourth part of the length of the wall.

THE SECOND SCHEDULE.

The following materials shall for the purposes of this Act be deemed to be fire-resisting materials:—

1. Brickwork constructed of good bricks, well burnt, hard and sound, properly bonded and solidly put together—

    (*a*) With good mortar compounded of good lime and sharp, clean sand, hard, clean, broken brick, broken flint, grit or slag; or

    (*b*) With good cement; or

    (*c*) With cement mixed with sharp, clean sand, hard, clean, broken brick, broken flint, grit or slag:

2. Granite and other stone suitable for building purposes by reason of its solidity and durability:

SECTION OF CROSS WALL
BUILDINGS NOT PUBLIC & NOT OF THE WAREHOUSE CLASS

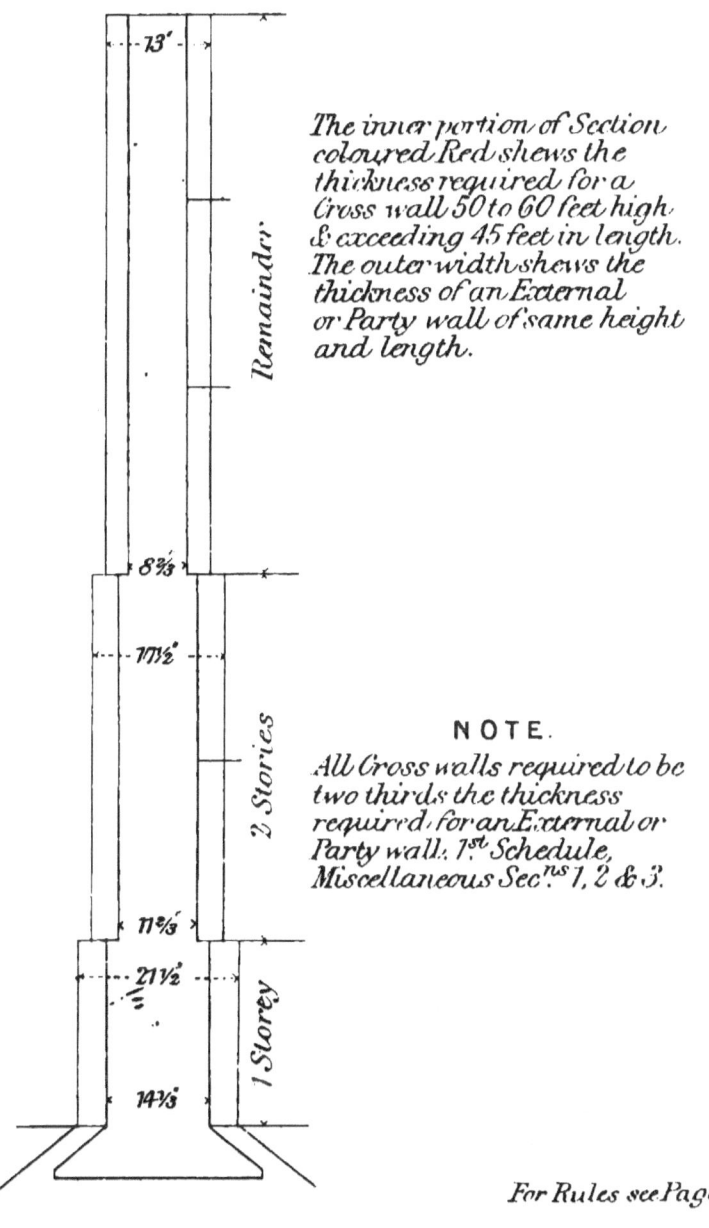

The inner portion of Section coloured Red shews the thickness required for a Cross wall 50 to 60 feet high & exceeding 45 feet in length. The outer width shews the thickness of an External or Party wall of same height and length.

NOTE.
All Cross walls required to be two thirds the thickness required for an External or Party wall. 1st Schedule, Miscellaneous Sec.ns 1, 2 & 3.

For Rules see Page 160

SECTION OF CROSS WALL
WAREHOUSE CLASS

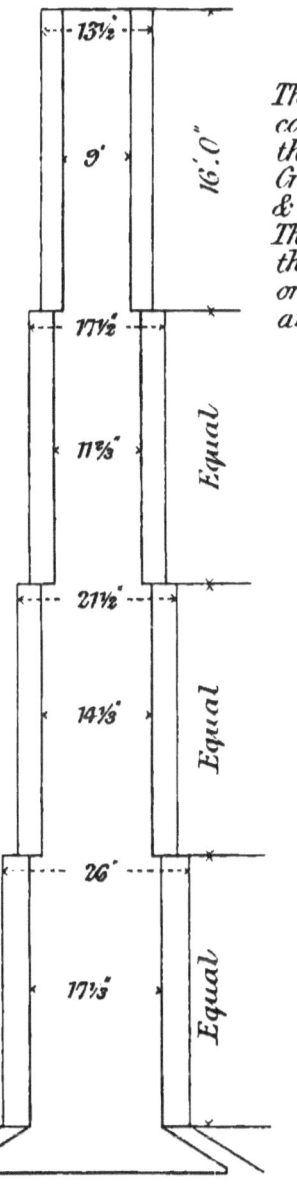

The inner portion of Section coloured Red shews the thickness required for a Cross wall 50 to 60 feet high & exceeding 45 feet in length. The outer width shews the thickness of an External or Party wall of same height and length.

NOTE.

All Cross walls required to be two thirds the thickness required for an External or Party wall. 1st Schedule, Miscellaneous Sec.ns 1, 2 & 3.

For Rules see Page. 110.

LONDON BUILDING ACT, 1894.   161

3. Iron, steel and copper:
4. Oak and teak and other hard timber when used for beams or posts or in combination with iron, the timber and the iron (if any) being protected by plastering in cement or other incombustible or non-conducting external coating;
  In the case of doors—
    Oak or teak or other hard timber, not less than two inches thick;
  In the case of staircases—
    Oak or teak or other hard timber, with treads, strings and risers not less than two inches thick:
5. Slate, tiles, brick and terra-cotta when used for coverings or corbels:
6. Flagstones when used for floors over arches, but not exposed on the underside and not supported at the ends only:
7. Concrete composed of broken brick, stone chippings or ballast, and lime cement or calcined gypsum when used for filling in between joists of floors:
8. Any material from time to time approved by the Council as fire-resisting.

THE THIRD SCHEDULE.

FEES PAYABLE TO DISTRICT SURVEYORS.

PART I.

On New Buildings.

	£	s.	d.
For any building not exceeding thirty square feet in area and not exceeding ten feet in height	0	10	0
For every building not exceeding four hundred square feet in area and not more than two storeys in height	1	10	0
For every additional storey	0	5	0
For every additional square or fraction of a square	0	2	6
For every building not exceeding four hundred square feet in area and of one storey only in height	0	15	0

On Additions, Alterations or other Works.

	£	s.	d.

For every addition or alteration or other work to which the provisions of this Act apply, made or done to or on any building after the roof thereof has been covered in—
    One-half of the fee charged in the case of a new building, calculated upon the area of the whole building.

For inspecting the arches or fire-resisting floors over or under public ways . . . 0 10 0

For inspecting the formation of openings in party walls (for each opening) . . . 0 10 0

For inspecting the closing of openings in party walls (for each opening) . . . 0 10 0

Provided that in the case of public buildings, buildings constructed of concrete and buildings divided into separate sets of chambers or tenements by party structures, the fees hereinbefore specified in this part of this Schedule shall in every case be increased by one-half.

On Chimneys and Flues.

On the construction of a furnace chimney-shaft or similar shaft for ventilation or other purposes, in addition to the fee for any other operation in progress at the same time, if not exceeding seventy-five feet in height . 2 0 0

    If exceeding seventy-five and not exceeding one hundred feet in height . . . 2 10 0

    For every additional ten feet or portion of ten feet in height 0 10 0

On the carrying of a flue from an oven, stove, steam boiler, furnace or close-fire into an old flue 0 10 0

On certifying that a chimney breast in a party wall may be cut away 0 10 0

On Certifying Plans.

For examining and certifying plans of an old building 2 2 0

LONDON BUILDING ACT, 1894.   163

On Wooden and Temporary Structures.

On inspection of any wooden structure or on
inspection of any structure or erection put
up on any public occasion the same amount
as for a new building, calculated on the area
of the structure or erection without reference
to the area of any building to which it may
be attached or in or on which it may be put
up.

Attending at Court.

For attending at a court when an order is made
for complying with notice of irregularity . 0 10 0

PART II.

On Dangerous Structures.

On each dangerous structure—
*Where there are not more than four adjoining or nearly
contiguous structures in the same ownership—*

1. For making a survey of the structure   £ s. d.
reported as dangerous and certifying
opinion thereon—
    If the structure do not exceed four
    squares in area and two storeys in
    height 0 7 6
    If exceeding four squares . . . 0 10 0
    For every additional storey above two 0 2 6
2. For each inspection of the structure and
report as to completion or progress of the
works 0 5 0
3. For inspecting the structure before the
hearing of the summons and attending
the court to give evidence—
    If one structure only . . . 0 10 0
    If more than one structure (for each
    structure) 0 5 0
4. For inspecting the structure before the
hearing of the summons against the
occupier (the owner having failed to
comply) and attending the court to give
evidence—

M 2

		£	s.	d.
If one structure only		0	10	0
If more than one structure (for each structure)		0	5	0
5. For every adjournment of the summons		0	5	0
6. For superintending the erection of shoring (including needling when requisite) and hoarding, whether done by the Council or not, and for certifying the account for the same when done by the Council		0	10	0
7. For shoring without hoarding or hoarding without shoring, and certifying the account		0	7	6
8. For supervision, including the report of the officer, in cases where it is necessary for the Council to execute works to ensure the safety of the public, under an order made by a court		0	5	0

When there are more than four adjoining or nearly contiguous structures in the same ownership—

	£	s.	d.
For Nos. 2, 3 and 4 in the above table	0	4	0
For No. 5	0	2	6
And for No. 8	0	4	0

PART III.

Fees Payable for Special Services.

The fees payable by a builder to the district surveyor for special services shall be the following:—

	£	s.	d.
For superintending the construction of floors and partition walls to stables under section 70 of this Act, per building	0	5	0
For superintending the construction of overhanging oriel windows, per building	0	5	0
For superintending the fixing of any oven, copper, steam boiler or stove to be used for trade purposes and not heated by gas	0	10	0
For superintending the fixing of pipes for conveying heated air or hot water or steam at high pressure (for each floor of a building on which pipes are fixed)	0	10	0
For services relating to the erection of buildings on low-lying lands, per building	0	5	0

PART IV.

FEES PAYABLE TO COUNCIL.

On Dangerous Structures.

For general services—

		£	s.	d.
1. For preparation of notices, forms for same, and postage		0	3	6
2. For service of notices (clerk's time)		0	2	6
3. For travelling per mile (one way)		0	0	3
4. For obtaining summonses and orders (clerk's time)		0	2	6
5. For cost of each summons or order		0	3	0

Where there are two or more adjoining or nearly contiguous structures in the same ownership—

	£	s.	d.
For Nos. 2 and 4 (above each)	0	2	0

The fees payable upon ten structures shall be the maximum fees.

On Dilapidated and Neglected Buildings or Structures.

	£	s.	d.
1. For each inspection of the building or structure and report	0	5	0
2. For obtaining summons and order (clerk's time)	0	2	6
3. For cost of each summons or order	0	2	0
4. For attendance at a court to give evidence	0	5	0
5. For every adjournment	0	2	6
6. For supervision of works, including report of officer in cases where the magistrate's order is executed by the Council	0	5	0
7. For travelling per mile (one way)	0	0	3

8. The cost of procuring local evidence to satisfy the magistrate that the condition of the structure is prejudicial to the property or to the inhabitants of the neighbourhood is to be considered separately in each case.

166   LONDON BUILDING ACT, 1894.

Where there are two or more adjoining or nearly contiguous structures in the same ownership—   £ s. d.
For Nos. 1, 4 or 6 (above) each . . . 0 3 0
For Nos. 2 or 5 (above) each . . . 0 2 0
The fees payable upon ten structures shall be the maximum fees.
For travelling per mile (one way) . . . 0 0 3

REGULATIONS.

1. The fees specified in this Schedule in respect of works to a party wall comprise the fees payable in respect of both sides of the wall.

2. No fee shall be charged in respect of the fixing of a chimney pot.

3. No fee shall be charged in respect of the repairing of a chimney top unless the top has been pulled down to a greater extent than twelve inches.

4. No fee shall be charged in respect of the repairing of a parapet unless the parapet shall have been pulled down to a greater extent than twelve inches.

5. In calculating the area of every new building for the purposes of this Schedule, the area of all outbuildings not exceeding thirty feet in area, whether attached or not, shall be included, provided such outbuildings be erected at the same time as the main building.

THE FOURTH SCHEDULE.

Session and Chapter.	Title or Short Title.	Extent of Repeal.
7 & 8 Vict. c. 84.	The Metropolitan Building Act, 1844.	So much as is unrepealed.
18 & 19 Vict. c. 120.	The Metropolis Management Act, 1855.	Section one hundred and forty-two, and in section two hundred and two the words "the plans, level, width, surface, inclination, and," and the words "and the plans and level of sites for building."
18 & 19 Vict. c. 122.	The Metropolitan Building Act, 1855.	The whole Act.

Session and Chapter.	Title or Short Title.	Extent of Repeal.
23 & 24 Vict. c. 52.	The Metropolitan Building Act (Amendment) 1860.	The whole Act.
24 & 25 Vict. c. 87.	The Metropolitan Building Amendment Act, 1861.	The whole Act.
25 & 26 Vict. c. 102.	The Metropolis Management Amendment Act, 1862.	Sections seventy-four, seventy-five, seventy-six, eighty-five, eighty-seven, ninety-eight and ninety-nine.
32 & 33 Vict. c. 82.	The Metropolitan Building Act, 1869.	The whole Act.
34 & 35 Vict. c. 39.	The Metropolitan Building Act, 1871.	The whole Act.
41 & 42 Vict. c. 32.	The Metropolis Management and Building Acts Amendment Act, 1878.	Sections four, six, seven, eight, nine, ten, fourteen, fifteen, sixteen, seventeen, eighteen, nineteen, twenty, twenty-one, from "and the district "surveyor" to "such house, "building, erection, or work," and the words " or surveyor," section twenty-two, so far as it relates to any notice or order served or made under any provision repealed by this Act, section twenty-three from "and every penalty imposed "by Part II." to " Acts amending "the same," section twenty-five, in section twenty-six the words "or in any byelaw of the board "thereunder," and in section twenty-seven the words " or in "any byelaw thereunder made."
45 & 46 Vict. c. 14.	The Metropolis Management and Building Acts (Amendment) Act, 1882	The whole Act.
53 & 54 Vict. c. ccxliii.	The London Council (General Powers) Act, 1890.	Sections twenty-seven to thirty-one, and sections thirty-three to thirty-seven.
54 & 55 Vict. c. lxxviii.	The London Sky Signs Act, 1891.	The whole Act.
56 & 57 Vict. c. ccxxi.	The London County Council (General Powers) Act, 1893.	Sections five to nine and section seventeen.

THE METROPOLIS MANAGEMENT ACT, 1855.

18 and 19 VICT. c. 120.

THIS Act is still in force, the portions repealed being—Sec. 142, and in Sec. 220 the words "the plans, level, width, surface, inclination, &c." and the words "and the plans and level of sites for building."

I give those clauses which relate to buildings.

<small>Gullyholes, &c., to be trapped.</small>

LXXI. Every District Board and Vestry shall, by providing proper traps or other coverings, or by ventilation, or by such other ways and means as shall be practicable for that purpose, prevent the effluvia of sewers from exhaling through gullyholes, gratings or other openings of sewers in any of the streets or other places within their district or parish.

<small>Vestry or District Board in certain cases may compel owners, &c., of houses to construct drains into the common sewer.</small>

LXXIII. If any house or building, whether built before or after the commencement of this Act, situate within any such parish or district, be found not to be drained by a sufficient drain communicating with some sewer and emptying itself into the same, to the satisfaction of the Vestry or Board of such parish or district, and if a sewer of sufficient size be within one hundred feet of any part of such house or building, on a lower level than such house or building, it shall be lawful for the Vestry or Board at their discretion, by notice in writing, to require the owner of such house or building forthwith, or within such reasonable time as may be appointed by the Vestry or Board, to construct and make from such house or building into any such sewer a covered drain, and such branches thereto, of such materials, of such size, at such level and with such fall as shall be adequate for the drainage of such house or building and its several floors or stories, and also of its areas, water-closets, privies and offices (if any), and for conveying the soil, drainage and wash therefrom into the said sewer, and to provide fit and proper paved or impermeable sloped surfaces for conveying surface water thereto, and fit and proper sinks, and fit and proper syphoned or otherwise trapped inlets and outlets for hindering stench therefrom, and fit and proper water supply and water-supplying pipes, cisterns and apparatus for scouring the same and for causing the same to convey away the soil, and fit and proper sand traps, expanding inlets and other apparatus for hindering the entry of improper substances therein, and all other such fit and proper works and arrangements as may appear to the Vestry or Board, or to their officers, requisite to secure the same and proper working of the said drain, and to prevent the same from obstructing or otherwise injuring or impeding the action of the sewer to which it leads; and it shall be lawful for the said Vestry or Board to cause the said works to be inspected while in progress, and from time to time during their execution to order such reasonable alterations therein, additions thereto, and abandonment of part or parts thereof, as may to the Vestry or Board or their officers appear, on the fuller knowledge afforded by the opening of the ground, requisite to secure the complete and perfect working of such works; and if the owner of such house or building neglect or refuse, during twenty-eight days after the said notice has been delivered to such owner, or left at such house or building, to begin to construct such drain and other works aforesaid, or any of them, or thereafter fail to carry them on and complete them with all reasonable despatch, it shall be lawful for the Vestry or Board to cause the same to be constructed and made, and to recover the expenses to be incurred thereby from such owner in the manner hereinafter provided. *Penalty on owner, &c., for neglect.*

LXXIV. If it appear to the Vestry or Board of any parish or district that a group or block of contiguous houses, or of adjacent detached or semi-detached houses, may be drained and improved more economically or advantageously in combination than separately, and a sewer of sufficient size already exist or be about to be constructed within one hundred feet of any part of such group or block of houses, whether contiguous, detached or semi-detached, it shall be lawful for such Board or Vestry to order that such group or block of houses be drained and *Provision for combined drainage of blocks of houses.*

improved, as hereinbefore provided, by a combined operation.

No house to be built without drains constructed to the satisfaction of the Vestry or District Board.

LXXV. It shall not be lawful to erect any house or other building in any parish mentioned in Schedule (A.) to this Act, or in any district mentioned in Schedule (B.) to this Act, or to rebuild any house or building within any such parish or district which has been pulled down to or below the floor commonly called the ground floor, or to occupy any house or building so newly built or rebuilt, unless a drain and such branches thereto, and other connected works and apparatus and water supply as hereinbefore mentioned, be constructed and provided to the satisfaction of the surveyor of the Vestry of such parish or Board of Works for such district, of such materials, of such size, at such level and with such fall as they may direct, so that the same shall be available for the drainage of the lowest floor of such house or building, and of its several floors or stories, and also of its areas, water-closets, privies and offices (if any), which drain shall lead from such house or building, or the intended site of such house or building, to such sewer, already made or intended to be constructed near thereto, as the Vestry or Board shall direct and appoint, or if there be no such sewer existing or intended to be constructed within one hundred feet of any part of the intended site of such house or building, then to such covered cesspool or other place, not being under any dwelling house, as the Vestry or Board shall direct; and whenever any house or building is rebuilt as aforesaid, the level of the lowest floor of such house or building shall be raised sufficiently to allow of the construction of such a drain and such branches thereto and other works and apparatus as are hereinbefore required, and for that purpose the levels shall be taken and determined under the direction of the Vestry or District Board.

Notice of buildings to be given to the Vestry or District Board before commencing the same.

LXXVI. Before beginning to lay or dig out the foundation of any new house or building within any such parish or district, or to rebuild any house or building therein, and also before making any drain for the purpose of draining directly or indirectly into any sewer under the jurisdiction of the Vestry or Board of or for any such parish or district, seven days' notice in writing shall be given to the Vestry or Board by the person intending to build or rebuild such house or building or to make such drain; and every such foundation shall be laid at such level as will permit the drainage of such house or building in compliance with this Act, and as the Vestry or Board shall order, and every such drain shall be made in such direction, manner and form, and of such materials and workmanship, and with such branches thereto and other connected works and apparatus and water supply as hereinbefore mentioned, and as the Vestry or Board shall order, and the making of every such drain shall be under the survey and control of the Vestry or Board; and the Vestry or District Board shall make their order in relation to the matters aforesaid, and cause the same to be notified to the person from whom such notice was received within seven days after the receipt of such notice, and in default of such notice, or if such house, building or drain, or branches thereto or other connected works and apparatus and water supply, be begun, erected, made or provided in any respect contrary to any order of the Vestry or Board made and notified as aforesaid, or the provisions of this Act, it shall be lawful for the Vestry or Board to cause such house or building to be demolished or altered, and to cause such drain or branches thereto and other connected works and apparatus and water supply to be relaid, amended, or re-made, or, in the event of omission, added, as the case may require, and to recover the expenses thereof from the owner thereof in the manner hereinafter provided.

LXXVII. It shall be lawful for any person, at his own expense, to make or branch any drain into any of the sewers vested in the Metropolitan Board of Works or any Vestry or District Board under this Act, or authorised to be made by them under this Act, such drain being of such a size, and of such conditions, and branched to such sewer, in such a manner and form of communication in all respects as the Vestry or Board shall direct or appoint; and in case any person make or branch any drain into any of the said sewers so vested in the Vestry or Board, or authorised to be made by them under this Act, of a larger size, or of different conditions, or in a different manner and

Power to branch drains into sewers constructed by Metropolitan Board or any Vestry or District Board under certain regulations.

172 THE METROPOLIS MANAGEMENT ACT, 1855.

form of communication than shall be directed or appointed by the Vestry or Board, every person so offending shall for every such offence forfeit a sum not exceeding fifty pounds.

Penalty.

Power for Vestries and District Boards to authorise inspection of drains, privies and cesspools.

LXXXII. It shall be lawful for any such Vestry or Board, or for their surveyor or inspector, or such other person as they appoint, to inspect any drain, water-closet, privy, cesspool, or water supply apparatus, or sinks, traps, syphons, pipes, or other works or apparatus connected therewith, within the parish or district of such Vestry or Board, and for that purpose, at all reasonable times in the daytime, after twenty-four hours' notice in writing has been given to the occupier of the premises to which such drain, water-closet, privy, cesspool or water supply apparatus, or other connected works or apparatus as aforesaid, is attached, or left upon the premises, or in case of emergency without notice to enter, by themselves, or their surveyor or inspector and workmen, upon any premises, and cause the ground to be opened in any place they think fit, doing as little damage as may be.

Vestry or District Board to cause drains, &c., to be put into proper condition, &c. where necessary.

LXXXV. If, upon such inspection as aforesaid, any drain, water-closet, privy or cesspool appear to be in bad order and condition, or to require cleansing, alteration or amendment, or to be filled up, the Vestry or Board shall cause notice in writing to be given to the owner or occupier of the premises upon or in respect of which the inspection was made, requiring him forthwith, or within such reasonable time as shall be specified in such notice, to do the necessary works; and if such notice be not complied with by the person to whom it is given the Vestry or Board may, if they think fit, execute such works, and the expenses incurred by them in so doing shall be paid to them by the owner or occupier of the premises.

Vaults and cellars under streets not to be made without the consent of the Vestry or Board.

CI. No vault, arch or cellar shall be made under any street without the consent of the Vestry or District Board of the parish or district in which the same is situate; and all such vaults, arches and cellars hereafter to be made within any parish or district mentioned in either of the Schedules (A.) and (B.) to this Act shall be substantially made, and so as not to interfere or communicate with any drain or sewer under the control of any Vestry or District

Board, or of the Metropolitan Board of Works, without their consents respectively first obtained; and if any vault, arch or cellar be made contrary to this provision it shall be lawful for the Vestry or District Board, or for the Metropolitan Board of Works, to fill up or alter the same, and the expenses incurred thereby shall be paid by the owner of such vault, arch or cellar.

CII. All vaults, arches and cellars made either before or after the commencement of this Act under any street in any parish or district mentioned in either of the Schedules (A.) and (B.) to this Act, and all openings into the same in any such street, shall be repaired and kept in proper order by the owners or occupiers of the houses or buildings to which the same respectively belong; and in case any such vault, arch or cellar be at any time out of repair, it shall be lawful for the Vestry or District Board of such parish or district to cause the same to be repaired and put into good order, and to recover the expenses thereof from such owner in the manner hereinafter provided. Vaults, &c., under streets to be repaired by owners or occupiers.

CV. In case the owners of the houses forming the greater part of any new street laid out or made or hereafter to be laid out or made, which is not paved to the satisfaction of the Vestry or District Board of the parish or district in which such street or district is situate, be desirous of having the same paved, as hereinafter mentioned, or if such Vestry or Board deem it necessary or expedient that the same should be so paved, then and in either of such cases such Vestry or Board shall well and sufficiently pave the same, either throughout the whole breadth of the carriageway and footpaths thereof, or any part of such breadth, and from time to time keep such pavement in good and sufficient repair; and the owners of the houses forming such street shall, on demand, pay to such Vestry or Board the amount of the estimated expenses of providing and laying such pavement (such amount to be determined by the surveyor for the time being of the Vestry or Board); and in case such estimated expenses exceed the actual expenses of such paving, then the difference between such estimated expenses and such actual expenses shall be repaid by the said Vestry or Board to the owners of houses by whom the said sum of Provisions for paving new streets.

money has been paid; and in case the said estimated expenses be less than the actual expenses of such paving, then the owners of the said houses shall, on demand, pay to the said Vestry or Board such further sum of money as, together with the sum already paid, amounts to such actual expenses.

Owners, &c., to remove future projections, on notice from Vestry or District Board.

CXIX. If any porch, shed, projecting window, step, cellar door or window, or steps leading into any cellar or otherwise, lamp, lamp post, lamp iron, sign, sign post, sign iron, showboard, window shutter, wall, gate, fence, or opening, or any other projection or obstruction placed or made against or in front of any house or building after the commencement of this Act, shall be an annoyance, in consequence of the same projecting into or being made in or endangering or rendering less commodious the passage along any street in their parish or district, it shall be lawful for the Vestry or District Board to give notice in writing to the owner or occupier of such house or building to remove such projection or obstruction, or to alter the same in such manner as the Vestry or Board think fit; and such owner or occupier shall, within fourteen days after the service of such notice upon him, remove such projection or obstruction, or alter the same in the manner

Penalty for neglect.

directed by the Vestry or Board; and if the owner or occupier of any such house or building neglect or refuse, within fourteen days after such notice, to remove such projection or obstruction, or to alter the same in the manner directed by the Vestry or Board, he shall forfeit any sum not exceeding five pounds, and a further sum not exceeding forty shillings for every day during which such projection or obstruction continues after the expiration of such fourteen days from the time when he may be convicted of any offence contrary to the provisions hereof.

Vestry or District Board may remove existing projections, and make compensation for the same.

CXX. It shall be lawful for every Vestry and District Board, if any projection or obstruction which has been placed or made against or in front of any house or building in any such street before the commencement of this Act shall be an annoyance as aforesaid, to cause the same to be removed or altered as they think fit. Provided always that the Vestry or Board shall give notice in

writing of such intended removal or alteration to the
owner or occupier against or in front of whose house or
building such projection or obstruction shall be, seven
days before such removal or alteration shall be commenced, and shall make reasonable compensation to every
person who shall incur any loss or damage by such removal, excepting in cases where the obstruction or projection may now be removable under any Act, in which case
no compensation shall be made.

CXXI. Every person who shall build or begin to build, Hoards to be erected dur-ing repairs.
or take down or begin to take down, any house, building
or wall, or alter or repair, or begin to alter or repair, the
outward part of any house, building or wall, shall, in all
cases in which the footway is thereby obstructed or rendered inconvenient, cause to be put up a proper and sufficient hoard or fence, with a convenient platform and
handrail, if there be room enough for the same, to serve
as a footway for passengers outside of such hoard or fence,
and shall continue such hoard or fence, in such cases as
aforesaid, with such platform and handrail, standing and
in good condition, to the satisfaction of the Vestry or
District Board of the parish or district in which such
house, building or wall is situate, during such time as
may be necessary for the public safety or convenience,
and shall, in all cases in which the same is necessary to
prevent accidents, cause such hoard or fence to be well
lighted during the night; and every such person who Penalty on not erecting hoards.
fails to put up such hoard or fence and such platform,
with such handrail as aforesaid, or who does not, whilst
the said hoard or fence is standing, keep the same well
lighted during the night, shall for every such offence
forfeit a sum not exceeding five pounds, and a further sum
not exceeding forty shillings for every day during the
continuance of such default.

CXXII. It shall not be lawful for any person to erect No hoard to be erected, without license from Vestry or District Board.
or set up in any street any hoard or fence or scaffold for
any purpose whatever, or any posts, bars, rails, boards or
other things by way of inclosure, for the purpose of
making mortar, or of depositing bricks, lime, rubbish or
other materials, without a license in writing first had
and obtained from the clerk or surveyor of the Vestry or

District Board of the parish or district in which such street is situate; and every such license shall state the place where and the purpose for which such hoard or fence, scaffold or inclosure is to be set up or made, and the size thereof, and the time for which it is to be permitted to continue.

If hoard be erected or materials be deposited in any manner otherwise than to the satisfaction of the Vestry or District Board, the same may be removed.

CXXIII. If any person erect or set up in any street any hoard or fence or scaffold for any purpose whatever, or any posts, bars, rails, boards, or other things by way of inclosure, for the purpose of making mortar, or of depositing bricks, lime, rubbish or other materials, without a license from the Vestry or District Board, or do any such act as aforesaid in any other manner than as permitted by such license, or continue the same beyond the time stated in such license, or fail to keep any hoard, fence, platform or handrail in good repair, he shall for every such offence forfeit a sum not exceeding five pounds, and a further sum not exceeding forty shillings for every day during the continuance of such offence; and it shall be lawful for the Vestry or Board to cause such hoard, fence, scaffold or inclosure to be pulled down, and the materials thereof, and also all the bricks, mortar, lime or other building materials, or other matters or things contained within any such inclosure, to be removed, and deposited in such place as the Vestry or Board may think fit, and to be kept until the charges of pulling down and removing the same be paid to the Vestry or Board; and in case the same be not claimed and the said charges paid within the space of eight days next after such seizure thereof, it shall be lawful for the Vestry or Board to order the same to be sold, and by and out of the proceeds of such sale to pay such charges, rendering any surplus to the owner or other person by law entitled thereto; and in case the proceeds of such sale be insufficient to cover such charges, and the charges of selling and disposing of such materials, matters and things, the deficiency shall be repaid by the owner of such materials, matters and things to the Vestry or District Board on demand.

Byelaws.

CCII. The Metropolitan Board of Works, and every District Board and Vestry respectively, may from time to time make, alter and repeal byelaws for all or any of the purposes following: (that is to say) for regulating the business and proceedings at their meetings and of committees appointed by them, the appointment and removal of their officers and servants, and the duties, conduct and remuneration of such officers and servants; and the said Metropolitan Board may also from time to time make, alter and repeal byelaws for regulating the material of the pavement and roadway of new streets and roads, and for regulating the dimensions, form and mode of construction, and the keeping, cleansing and repairing of the pipes, drains and other means of communicating with sewers, and the traps and apparatus connected therewith; for the emptying, cleansing, closing and filling up of cesspools and privies, and for other works of cleansing, and of removing and disposing of refuse, and for regulating the form of appeal and mode of proceeding thereon, and generally for carrying into effect the purposes of this Act; and every such Board and Vestry may thereby impose such reasonable penalties as they think fit, not exceeding forty shillings for each breach of such byelaws, and in case of a continuing offence a further penalty not exceeding twenty shillings for each day after notice of the offence from the Board or Vestry: provided always that under every such byelaw it shall be lawful for the Justices before whom any penalty imposed thereby is sought to be recovered, to order the whole or part only of such penalty to be paid, or to remit the whole penalty: provided also that no byelaws shall be repugnant to the Laws of *England* or to the provisions of this Act; and that no byelaw shall be of any force or effect unless and until the same be submitted to and confirmed at a subsequent meeting of the Board or Vestry: provided also that no penalty shall be imposed by any such byelaw unless the same be approved by one of Her Majesty's principal Secretaries of State.

Power to Metropolitan Board or Works to make byelaws.

Penalty for breach of byelaws.

Power to Justices to remit penalties.

CCIII. All byelaws made and confirmed as aforesaid in pursuance of this Act shall be printed, and hung up in

Publication of byelaws.

178   THE METROPOLIS MANAGEMENT ACT, 1855.

the principal office of the Board or Vestry, and be open to public inspection without payment, and copies thereof shall be delivered to any person applying for the same, on payment of such sum, not exceeding twopence, as the Board or Vestry shall direct; and such byelaws, when so published, shall be binding upon and be observed by all parties, and shall be sufficient to justify all parties acting under the same; and the production of a printed copy of such byelaws, authenticated by the seal of the Board or Vestry, shall be evidence of the existence, and of the due making, confirmation and publication of such byelaws, in all prosentions under the same, without adducing proof of such seal or of the fact of such confirmation or publication of such byelaws.

Evidence of byelaws.

Provisions for Protection of Property and Works of Metropolitan and District Boards and Vestries, and preventing Obstruction in Execution of Works.

Buildings not to be made over sewers without consent.

CCIV. No building shall be erected in, over or under any sewer vested in the Metropolitan Board of Works, or in any Vestry or District Board, without their consent first obtained in writing, and if any building be erected contrary to this provision the Board or Vestry in whom such sewer is vested may demolish the same, and the expenses incurred thereby shall be paid by the person erecting such building.

THE METROPOLIS LOCAL MANAGEMENT ACTS AMENDMENT ACT, 1862.

25 & 26 VICT. c. 102.

SECTIONS 74, 75, 76, 85, 87, 98 and 99 of this Act are repealed. I give the Clauses in force relating to building.

LXI. The seventy-seventh section of the firstly-recited Act is hereby repealed; and in lieu thereof be it enacted that no person shall make or branch any sewer or drain, or make any opening into any sewer vested in the Metropolitan Board of Works, or in any Vestry or District Board, without the previous consent in writing of such Board or Vestry: provided that it shall be lawful for any person with such consent, at his own expense, to make or branch any drain into any sewer vested in such Board or Vestry, or authorised to be made by them or either of them under the firstly-recited Act or this Act, such drain being of such size, materials and other conditions, and branched into such sewer in such manner and form of communication in all respects as the Board or Vestry shall direct or appoint: provided also that where any contribution to the cost of a sewer is payable in respect of drainage into the same, it shall not be lawful for any person to make or branch any drain into such sewer, except in conformity with the directions of the Board or Vestry in whom the same shall be vested with respect to payment of contribution under the provisions contained in the firstly-recited Act and this Act in that behalf; and in case any person, without the consent of the said Metropolitan Board, District Board or Vestry as aforesaid, make or branch, or cause to be made or branched, any sewer or drain, or make any opening into any of the sewers vested in any such Board or Vestry, or authorised to be made by them as aforesaid, or if any person make or branch, or cause to be made or branched, any drain of a different construction, size, material or other conditions,

Regulations respecting openings into sewers.

or in another manner or form of communication than shall be directed or appointed by such Board or Vestry, every person so offending shall for every such offence forfeit a sum not exceeding fifty pounds; and the Board or Vestry may cut off the connexion between such drain and their sewer, or if they shall see fit execute the necessary works for making the said drain conformable to their regulations or directions at the expense of the person making such drain or causing the same to be made, such expenses to be recovered either by action at law or in a summary manner before a Justice of the Peace, at the option of the Board or Vestry.

Where parties neglect to carry out works pursuant to order of Vestry, the Vestry may recover Penalty or do the works.

LXIV. Whereas by the seventy-third, seventy-fourth, seventy-sixth, eighty-first, eighty-fifth and eighty sixth sections of the firstly-recited Act, certain works, matters and things are required to be constructed, made or executed on the requisition of Vestries and District Boards by the owners or occupiers of the premises therein referred to; and in case any such owner or occupier refuse or neglect to commence, proceed with or complete the same, as the case may be, the Vestry or District Board are authorised to perform and execute such works, matters and things, and recover the costs incurred thereby in manner therein provided: be it enacted, that in case of any such neglect or default by any person or persons to comply with the order of any Vestry or District Board to execute any works, matters or things under any of the said provisions, the person or persons so offending shall forfeit and pay to the Vestry or District Board a sum not exceeding five pounds, and also a further sum not exceeding forty shillings for every day during which such offence shall continue, to be recovered by action at law or before a Justice of the Peace in a summary manner, at the option of the Vestry or District Board; and the Vestry or District Board may at their discretion either execute or perform any such works, matters or things, and recover the costs and expenses thereof from the owner of the property as aforesaid, or proceed for and recover the said penalty or penalties; but nothing herein contained shall render any person or persons liable to be proceeded against for the penalty as well as for the costs and expenses of the works.

LXVI. Whereas certain property within the limits of the metropolis is so situate as to render it impracticable, or practicable only at undue expense, to connect such property with covered sewers, and it is expedient that some temporary provision should be made for draining such property and abating the nuisances existing thereon or caused thereby: be it therefore enacted, that in any case in which any house or other building, whether erected before or after the passing of this Act, is without sufficient drainage, and there is no proper sewer within two hundred feet of any part of such house or building, it shall be lawful for the Vestry or District Board of the parish or district in which such house or building is situate, by notice in writing to require the owner of such house or building to construct and lay from such house or building a covered drain to lead therefrom into a covered water-tight cesspool or tank or other suitable receptacle, not being under a house or within such distance from a house as the Vestry or Board shall direct, and to construct such cesspool, tank or receptable; and the several provisions in the firstly-recited Act with respect to the laying of house drains at the expense of the owners of property, and the recovery of such expenses of, and the penalties for any omission in respect to the performance of any such works pursuant to the orders of Vestries or District Boards in accordance with the directions of the said Act, shall be extended to and apply to the making of such cesspools, tanks, receptacles and drains, and the orders of Vestries and District Boards in relation thereto and the expenses thereof.

Temporary provision for drainage of property where no proper sewer within 200 feet.

LXVIII. Every person who shall knowingly erect or place any building, wall, bridge, fence, obstruction, annoyance or encroachment in, upon, over or under any sewer under the Jurisdiction of the Metropolitan Board of Works, or of any Vestry or District Board, and every person obstructing, filling in or diverting any sewer or drain under the jurisdiction, survey or control of the Metropolitan Board, or of any Vestry or District Board, without the previous consent in writing of the Board or Vestry in whom the same may be vested, shall, in addition to any other proceeding to which he may be liable therefor, forfeit and pay to such respective Board or Vestry a sum

Penalty on persons placing buildings or encroachments on sewers.

not exceeding twenty pounds for every such offence; and the Board or Vestry may demolish and remove any such building, wall, bridge, fence, obstruction, annoyance or encroachment, and perform any works necessary for restoring or reinstating the sewer or other work or thing damaged; and the party erecting such building, wall, bridge, fence, or causing such obstruction, annoyance or encroachment, shall also pay the expense of removing and abating them respectively, and of re-opening, restoring, repairing or reinstating any sewer or drain obstructed, filled in, closed up or diverted; and in case of a continuing offence in any of the cases aforesaid the offender shall be liable to a further penalty, not exceeding five pounds, for each day after notice thereof from the Metropolitan Board of Works, or from the Vestry or District Board, to be recovered by action at law or before any Justice of the Peace by a summary proceeding, at the option of the Board or Vestry: provided always that nothing herein contained shall extend to prevent or impede the maintenance, repair or renewal of any buildings or works under which a sewer or drain has been constructed, but so, nevertheless, that such buildings or works shall not injure or obstruct the said sewer or drain.

Penalty on persons interfering with sewers.

LXIX. Any person who shall take up, remove, demolish or otherwise interfere with any sewer or part of a sewer vested in the Metropolitan Board of Works, or in any Vestry or District Board, without the previous permission in writing of such Board or Vestry, or who shall wilfully damage any sewer, bank, defence, wall, penstock, grating, gully, side entrance, tide valve, flap, work, or thing vested in the Metropolitan Board or any Vestry or District Board, or do any act by which the drainage of the metropolis or any part thereof may be obstructed or injured, shall for every such offence forfeit and pay to the said Metropolitan Board of Works, or to the Vestry or District Board aggrieved by any such act, for every such offence a sum not exceeding twenty pounds, and shall also pay to such Board or Vestry all the expenses of repairing, restoring, reinstating or amending any sewer or other work or thing so taken up, removed, demolished, damaged or interfered with, to be recovered by action at law or before a Justice of the Peace by a summary proceeding, at the option of the Board or Vestry.

LXXXVIII. If any person shall, without having given the notice directed by the seventy-sixth section of the firstly-recited Act, begin to lay the foundation of any new house or building within any parish mentioned in Schedule A of the said Act, or any district in Schedule B of the said Act, or to make any drain for the purpose of draining either directly or indirectly into any sewer under the jurisdiction of the Vestry or Board of such parish or district, he shall become liable to a penalty for every such offence not exceeding five pounds, and to a continuing penalty of forty shillings for each and every day during which he shall omit to give the notice directed by the said Act. *Persons omitting to give notice required by Section 76 of 18 & 19 Vict. c. 120 liable to penalty.*

XCVI. The two hundred and seventeenth, two hundred and eighteenth and two hundred and nineteenth sections of the firstly-recited Act are hereby repealed; and in lieu thereof be it enacted, that it shall be lawful for any Vestry or District Board, at their discretion, to require the payment of any costs or expenses which the owner of any premises may be liable to pay under the said recited Act or this Act, either from the owner or from any person who then or at any time thereafter occupies such premises, and such owner or occupier shall be liable to pay the same, and the same shall be recovered in manner authorised by the recited Act and this Act; and the owner shall allow such occupier to deduct the sums of money which he so pays out of the rent from time to time becoming due in respect of the said premises, as if the same had been actually paid to such owner as part of such rent: provided always that no such occupier shall be required to pay any further sum than the amount of rent for the time being due from him, or which, after such demand of such costs or expenses from such occupier, and after notice not to pay his landlord any rent without first deducting the amount of such costs or expenses, becomes payable by such occupier, unless he refuse, on application being made to him for that purpose by or on behalf of the Vestry or District Board, truly to disclose the amount of *Vestry or District Board may require payment of costs or expenses from Owner or occupier, and occupier paying to deduct from rent.*

his rent, and the name and address of the person to whom such rent is payable, but the burden of proof that the sum demanded from any such occupier is greater than the rent due by him at the time of such notice, or which has since accrued, shall lie upon such occupier: provided also that nothing herein contained shall be taken to affect any contract made or to be made between any owner and occupier of any house, building or other property whereof it is or may be agreed that the occupier shall pay and discharge all rates, dues and sums of money payable in respect of such house, building or other property, or to affect any contract whatsoever between landlord and tenant.

Agreements between landlord and tenant not to be affected.

XCVII. If the owner or landlord of any premises from whose rent any amount shall be deducted in respect of any costs, charges or expenses payable under the firstly-recited Act or this Act, shall hold the premises in respect of which the amount of such costs, charges or expenses shall be paid at a rent not less than the rack-rent, he shall be entitled to deduct the whole amount paid by him on account of such costs, charges or expenses from the rent payable by him to his superior landlord; and if he holds at a rent less than the rack-rent, he shall be entitled to deduct from the rent so payable by him a sum bearing the same proportion to the amount so paid by him on account of such costs, charges, or expenses as his rent shall bear to the rack-rent; and if the owner or landlord from whose rent any deduction be made under the provision last aforesaid be himself liable to the payment of rent for the premises in respect of which the deduction shall be made, and hold such premises for a term of which less than twenty-one years shall be unexpired, but not otherwise, he may deduct from the rent so payable by him a sum bearing the same proportion to the sum deducted from the rent payable to him as the rent payable by him shall bear to the rent payable to him, and so on in succession with respect to every landlord of the same premises both receiving and liable to pay rent in respect thereof, and holding the same for a term of which less than twenty-one years shall be unexpired as aforesaid: provided always that nothing herein contained shall be construed to entitle any person to deduct from the rent

Deduction by owner paying rent where amount of expenses deducted from rent paid to him.

payable by him more than the whole sum deducted from the rent payable to him: provided also that nothing herein contained shall be taken to affect any contract made or to be made between any owner or occupier of any house, building or other property whereof it is or may be agreed that the occupier shall pay and discharge all rates, dues and sums of money payable in respect of such house, building or other property, or to affect any contract whatsoever between landlord and tenant.

THE METROPOLIS MANAGEMENT AND BUILDING ACTS AMENDMENT ACT, 1878.

41 & 42 VICT. c. 32.

An Act to amend the Metropolis Management Act, 1855, the Metropolitan Building Act, 1855, and the Acts amending the same respectively.

[22nd July, 1878.]

WHEREAS the provisions of the several Acts now in force within the metropolis are insufficient for duly regulating the erection and extension of houses and buildings in close proximity to certain roads, passages and ways, and it is expedient that for such purpose further and better provisions should be made :

And whereas with a view to protect the public frequenting theatres and music halls within the metropolis from danger from fire it is expedient that provisions such as are in this Act contained should be made for empowering the Metropolitan Board of Works (in this Act referred to as "the Board") to cause alterations in existing theatres and music halls to be made in certain cases, and to make regulations with respect to the position and structure of new theatres and certain new music halls :

And whereas it is expedient to make provisions with respect to the making, filling up and preparation of the foundations and sites of houses and buildings to be erected within the metropolis, and with respect to the quality of the substances to be used in the formation or construction of the sites, foundations and walls of such houses and buildings with a view to the stability of the same, the prevention of fires and for purposes of health :

And whereas it is expedient to make further and better provisions with respect to the payment of expenses incurred by the Board in relation to dangerous structures :

And whereas for the purpose aforesaid it is expedient to amend the Metropolis Management Act, 1855, the Metropolitan Building Act, 1855, and the Acts amending the same respectively:

Be it therefore enacted by the Queen's most excellent Majesty, by and with the advice and consent of the Lords Spiritual and Temporal, and Commons, in this present Parliament assembled, and by the authority of the same, as follows; (that is to say)— *18 & 19 Vict c. 120. 18 & 19 Vict. c. 122.*

PRELIMINARY.

I. This Act may be cited for all purposes as the Metropolis Management and Building Acts Amendment Act, 1878. *Short Title.*

II. This Act shall extend and apply to the Metropolis as defined by the Metropolis Management Act, 1855. *Limits of Act 18 & 19 Vict. c. 120.*

III. This Act shall consist of three Parts. *Division of Act into three parts.*

PART I.

V. The Metropolis Management Act, 1855, and the Acts amending the same, and this Part of this Act shall be construed together as one Act: provided always that nothing in this Act shall be held to limit or restrict the powers now vested in the Commissioners of Sewers of the city of London, or in any body or person elsewhere within the metropolis, by an Act passed in the session of Parliament held in the fifty-seventh year of the reign of King George the Third, intituled "An Act for better paving, improving and regulating the streets of the Metropolis, and removing and preventing nuisances and obstructions therein." *Metropolis Management Acts and this part of Act to be construed as one Act. 18 & 19 Vict. c. 120. 57 Geo. III. c. xxx.*

XI. Whenever it appears to the Board that any house or other place of public resort within the metropolis which was at the time of the passing of this Act authorised to be kept open for the public performance of stage plays, and which is kept open for such purpose, under the authority of letters patent from Her Majesty, her heirs and successors or predecessors, or of a license granted by the Lord Chamberlain of Her Majesty's Household for the time being, or by Justices of the Peace, or that any house, room or other place of public resort within the metropolis, con- *Power to Board in certain cases to require proprietors of theatres and certain music halls in use at the time of the passing of this Act to remedy structural defects.*

taining a superficial area for the accommodation of the public of not less than five hundred square feet, which was at the time of the passing of this Act authorised to be kept open, and which is kept open, for dancing, music or other public entertainment of the like kind, under the authority of a license granted by any court of quarter sessions, is so defective in its structure that special danger from fire may result to the public frequenting the same, then, and in every such case the Board may, with the consent of the Lord Chamberlain in the case of theatres under his jurisdiction, and of Her Majesty's principal Secretary of State in all other cases, if in the opinion of the Board such structural defects can be remedied at a moderate expenditure, by notice in writing require the owner of such house, room or other place kept open for any of the purposes aforesaid, under such authority as aforesaid, to make such alterations therein or thereto as may be necessary to remedy such defects, within a reasonable time to be specified in such notice: and in case such owner fails to comply with the requirements of such notice within such reasonable time as aforesaid, he shall be liable to a penalty not exceeding fifty pounds for such default, and to a further penalty of five pounds for every day after the first day after the expiration of such reasonable time as aforesaid during which such default continues: provided always that any such owner may, within fourteen days after the receipt of any such notice as aforesaid, serve notice of appeal against the same upon the Board, and thereupon such appeal shall be referred to an arbitrator to be appointed by Her Majesty's First Commissioner of Works at the request of either party, who shall hear and determine the same, and may, on such evidence as he may think satisfactory, either confirm the notice served by the Board, or may confirm the same with such modifications as he may think proper, or refuse to confirm the same, and the decision of such arbitrator with respect to the requirements contained in any such notice, and the reasonableness of the same, and the persons by whom and the proportions in which the costs of such arbitration are to be paid, shall be final and conclusive and binding upon all parties.

In case of an appeal against any such notice, compliance with the requirements of the same may be postponed until after the day upon which such appeal shall be so decided as aforesaid, and the same, if confirmed in whole or in part, shall only take effect as and from such day.

XII. The Board may from time to time make, alter, vary and amend such regulations as they may think expedient with respect to the requirements for the protection from fire of houses or other places of public resort within the metropolis, to be kept open for the public performance of stage plays, and of houses, rooms or other places of public resort within the metropolis, containing a superficial area for the accommodation of the public of not less than five hundred square feet, to be kept open for public dancing, music or other public entertainment of the like kind, under the authority of letters patent from Her Majesty, her heirs or successors, or of licenses by the Lord Chamberlain of Her Majesty's Household, or by any Justices of the Peace, or by any court of quarter sessions, which may be granted for the first time after the passing of this Act; and may by such regulations prescribe the requirements as to position and structure of such houses, rooms or places of public resort which may, in the opinion of the Board, be necessary for the protection of all persons who may frequent the same against dangers from fires which may arise therein or in the neighbourhood thereof; provided that the Board may from time to time in any special case dispense with or modify such regulations, or may annex thereto conditions if they think it necessary or expedient so to do.

Power to Board to make regulations with respect to new theatres and certain new music halls for protection from fire.

The Board shall, after the making, altering, varying or amending of any such regulations, cause the same to be printed, with the date thereof, and a printed copy thereof shall be kept at the office of the Board, and all persons may at all reasonable times inspect such copy without payment, and the Board shall cause to be delivered a printed copy, authenticated by their seal, of all regulations for the time being in force to every person applying for the same, on payment by such person of any sum not exceeding five shillings for every such copy.

A printed copy of such regulations, dated and authenticated by the seal of the Board, shall be conclusive evidence of the existence and of the due making of the same in all proceedings under the same, without adducing proof of such seal or of the fact of such making.

From and after the making of any such regulations it shall not be lawful for any person to have or keep open any such house, room or any other place of public resort for any of the purposes aforesaid, unless and until the Board grant to such person a certificate in writing under their seal, to the effect that such house, room or other place was on its completion in accordance with the regulations made by the Board in pursuance of the provisions of this Act for the time being in force, and in so far as the same are applicable to such house or other place, and to the conditions (if any) annexed thereto by the Board.

In case any such house, room or place of public resort is opened or kept open by any person for any of the purposes aforesaid, contrary to the provisions of this enactment, such person shall be liable to a penalty not exceeding fifty pounds for every day on which such house or place of public resort is so kept open as aforesaid.

Provisional license for new premises.

XIII. A person interested in any premises about to be constructed, or in course of construction, which are designed to be licensed and used within the metropolis for the public performance of stage plays, or for public dancing, music or other public entertainment of the like kind, may apply to the licensing authority for the grant of a provisional license in respect of such premises. The grant of such provisional license shall, in respect of the discretion of the licensing authority and procedure, be subject to the same conditions as those applicable to the grant of a like license which is not provisional. A provisional license so granted shall not be of any force until it has been confirmed by the licensing authority; but the licensing authority shall confirm the same on the production by the applicant of a certificate by the Board that the construction of the premises has been completed in accordance with the regulations and conditions made by the Board as hereinbefore provided, and on being satisfied that no objection can be made to the character of the holder of such provisional license.

PART III.

Power for architects and persons authorised

XXI. The architect of the Board, and any other person authorised by the Board in writing under their seal, may, at all reasonable times after completion or during construction, enter and inspect any house, room or other place kept open or intended to be kept open for the public performance of stage plays, or for public dancing, music or other public entertainment of the like kind affected by any of the provisions of this Act, or of any regulations made in pursuance thereof; and if any person refuses to admit such architect or person, or to afford him all reasonable assistance in such inspection, in every such case the person so refusing shall incur for each offence a penalty not exceeding twenty pounds. *by Board and district surveyor to enter and inspect theatres, music halls, buildings, and works.*

XXII.* For the purpose of complying with the requirements of any notice or order served or made under the provisions of this Act, on any owner, builder or person, in respect of any house, building or other erection, room or place, such owner, builder or person, his servants, workmen and agents, may, after giving seven days' notice in writing to the occupier of such house, building or other erection, room or place, and on production of such notice or order, enter such house, building or other erection, room or place, and do all such works, matters and things therein or thereto, or in connection therewith, as may be necessary; and if any person refuses to admit such owner, builder or person, or his servants or workmen or agents, or to afford them all reasonable assistance, such person shall incur for each offence a penalty not exceeding twenty pounds. *Power to owners, &c., to enter houses,&c., to comply with notices or order.*

XXIII. Every penalty imposed by Part I. and Part III. of this Act may be recovered by summary proceedings before any Justice, in like manner and subject to the like right of appeal as if the same were a penalty recoverable by summary proceedings under the Metropolis Management Act, 1855, and the Acts amending the same; provided always that in any proceedings against any person for more than one penalty in respect of one or more breach or breaches of any provision of this Act or of any byelaw made in pursuance of this Act, it shall be lawful to include in one summons all such penalties, and the charge for such summons shall not exceed two shillings. *Recovery of penalties. 18 & 19 Vict. c. 120. 18 & 19 Vict. c. 122.*

XXIV. Her Majesty's royal palaces, and all buildings, works and ground excepted from the operation of the *Exceptions from Metropolis Management Acts extended to this Act. 18 & 19 Vict. c. 120.*

* This section is repealed so far as it relates to any notice or order served or made under any provision repealed by the London Building Act, 1894.

Metropolis Management Act, 1855, and the Acts amending the same, or of any of the said Acts, shall be excepted from the operation of the provisions of this Act which are to be construed with such Acts, and all exemptions from the provisions of any of the said Acts shall extend to such of the provisions of this Act as are to be construed as aforesaid with such Acts.

<small>Act not to apply to the Inner and Middle Temple, &c.</small>

XXVI. Nothing in this Act shall apply to the Inner Temple, the Middle Temple, Lincoln's Inn, Gray's Inn, Staple Inn, Furnival's Inn, or the close of the collegiate church of Saint Peter, Westminster.

<small>Saving rights of the Crown and the Duchy of Lancaster.</small>

XXVII. Nothing contained in this Act shall apply to or shall authorise or empower the Board, or any Vestry, District Board or district surveyor, to take, use, or in any manner interfere with any land, soil, tenements or hereditaments, or any rights of whatsoever nature belonging to or enjoyed or exercisable by the Queen's most Excellent Majesty in right of her Crown, or in right of her Duchy of Lancaster, without the consent in writing of the Commissioners for the time being of Her Majesty's Woods, Forests and Land Revenues, or one of them, on behalf of Her Majesty, in right of her Crown, first had and obtained for that purpose (which consent such Commissioners are hereby respectively authorised to give), or without the consent in like manner of the Chancellor of the said Duchy, on behalf of Her Majesty, in right of her said Duchy; neither shall anything contained in this Act, or in any byelaw thereunder made, extend to, divest, take away, prejudice, diminish or alter any estate, right, privilege, power, or authority vested in or enjoyed or exercisable by the Queen's Majesty, her heirs or successors, in right of her Crown, or in right of her said Duchy; and nothing contained in Part I. of this Act shall apply to the extension of Savoy Street or the bridge which the Chancellor and Council of the said Duchy are by the Metropolitan Board of Works (Various Powers) Act, 1875, empowered to make and construct, or to any house or building within the precinct of the Savoy, or upon the land mentioned in section six of the last-mentioned Act, constructed or extended after the passing of this Act, in or abutting upon any road, passage or way existing, formed or laid out at the time of the passing of this Act.

<small>38 & 39 Vict. c. 65.</small>

THE LONDON COUNCIL (GENERAL POWERS) ACT, 1890.

The following Section (32) of the London Council (General Powers) Act, 1890, 53 & 54 Vict. c. 218, is the only one remaining in force relating to Building.

XXXII. Every person who shall intend to build or take down any house, building or wall (not being within the City of London), within ten feet of any public thoroughfare, shall give notice of such intention to the Vestry or District Board of the parish or district in which such house, building or wall is situate, and shall, before commencing to build or take down any such house, building, or wall, cause to be put up such hoard or fence, with a convenient platform and handrail (if there be room enough), for the same to serve as a footway for passengers outside of such hoard or fence, as the Vestry or District Board may think to be proper and sufficient, and shall continue such hoard or fence, and such platform and handrail standing and in good condition to the satisfaction of the Vestry or District Board during the building or taking down of any such house, building or wall, unless the Vestry or District Board shall give their consent in writing to its previous removal, and shall, when required so to do by the Vestry or District Board, cause such hoard or fence, and such platform and handrail to be well lighted from sunset to sunrise:

Every person who fails to give such notice to the Vestry or district board, or who commences to build or take down any such house, building or wall, without causing to be put up such hoard or fence with or without such convenient platform and handrail, or who does not continue such hoard or fence with or without such convenient platform and handrail in good condition to the satisfac-

Notice to be given to Vestry or District Board of building or demolishing any house, building or wall.

tion of the Vestry or District Board as aforesaid, or who does not when required so to do cause such hoard or fence with or without such platform and handrail to be well lighted from sunset to sunrise, shall for every such offence be liable to a penalty not exceeding five pounds, and a further penalty not exceeding forty shillings for every day on which such offence shall continue after conviction thereof, such penalties to be recovered by summary proceeding.

THE METROPOLIS MANAGEMENT AMENDMENT ACT, 1890.

53 & 54 VICT. c. 66.

An Act to amend the Metropolis Management Acts.
[18th August, 1890.]

BE it enacted by the Queen's most Excellent Majesty, by and with the advice and consent of the Lords Spiritual and Temporal, and Commons, in this present Parliament assembled, and by the authority of the same as follows:

I. This Act may be cited for all purposes as the Metropolis Management Amendment Act, 1890. Short Title.

II. In this Act— Interpretation. 18 & 19 Vict. c. 20.
"The Metropolis Management Acts" includes the Metropolis Management Act, 1855, and any Acts amending the same.
Terms to which meanings are assigned by the Metropolis Management Acts have the same respective meanings.
"The Council" means the London County Council.

III. Any Vestry or District Board may from time to time execute any necessary works of repair upon any or any part of any carriage road within their parish or district which shall have been used for not less than six months for public traffic and which may not at the time of such repair have become repairable by them, and shall not by undertaking such repair prejudice or affect the powers of such Vestry or District Board to apportion and recover the expenses of paving such road or way if and when the same shall be paved as a new street under the Metropolis Management Acts. Power to Vestry or District Board to repair a road or way not being a street.
The expenses of and incident to such repair may in the

first instance be paid by the Vestry or District Board in the same manner as the expenses of repairing other streets repairable by them, and shall, as soon as may be thereafter, be apportioned upon and recovered from the owners of the houses and land bounding or abutting on such road or part thereof in the same manner as if such expenses were expenses of paving such road or part thereof as a new street under the provisions of the Metropolis Management Acts relative thereto, and the amount of the expenses so apportioned may be recovered by the Vestry or District Board in a court of competent jurisdiction.

Provided that no railway company shall be liable under this section to pay the proportion of the expenses of and incident to such works of repair apportioned upon them in respect of lands abutting on any such road, and used solely as part of their line of railway and sidings, and having no direct communication with such road, and the amount apportioned upon any such company in respect thereof shall be paid by the Vestry or District Board. But in the event of such company making a direct communication with such road before the same is taken over by the Vestry or District Board, a just share of the said expenses shall be payable by such company to the Vestry or District Board, and the amount of such share shall, in case of difference between the railway company and the Vestry or District Board, be fixed in a summary way by any metropolitan police magistrate in whose district such road shall be wholly or partly situate, and shall be payable on demand to the Vestry or District Board.

IV. Any person making any sewer, or branching any sewer or drain into any sewer vested in the Council, without the approval in writing of the Council first had and obtained, or otherwise than in accordance with a plan and section thereof approved by the Council, or causing any such sewer or drain to be so made or branched, shall be liable to a penalty not exceeding fifty pounds.

The Council may by notice in writing to the owner or owners of the premises connected with the sewer or drain so improperly made or branched, or (if there are no such premises) of the land in which it is placed, require such owner or owners forthwith to remove such sewer or drain or to reconstruct the same at his or their expense to the approval of the Council in accordance with the plan and section approved as aforesaid, and in the event of such owner or owners failing to comply with the terms of such requisition, such owner or owners, as the case may be, shall be severally liable to a penalty not exceeding five pounds for every day during which he or they shall fail to comply therewith. And the Council may execute the works required and recover the costs and expenses thereof in a court of summary jurisdiction from the person who shall have made or branched, or caused to be made or branched, the sewer or drain, or from the owner or owners of the premises connected therewith, or (if there are no such premises) of the land in which it is placed. Provided that if the premises of more than one owner are at the time of the commencement of the work by the Council connected with any such sewer, the costs and expenses thereof shall be apportioned amongst and recoverable from such owners in proportion to the rateable value of the premises respectively connected therewith.

Provided also that in the event of any such costs and expenses being paid to the Council by any such owner or owners, then such owner or owners shall be entitled to recover in a court of summary jurisdiction the amount so paid by them from the person who made or branched or caused such sewer or drain to be made or branched in manner aforesaid.

V. Any person making any sewer or branching any sewer or drain into any sewer vested in any Vestry or District Board without the approval in writing of such Vestry or District Board first had and obtained, or otherwise than in accordance with the plan and section thereof, if any, approved by the Council under the provisions of the Metropolis Management Acts relative thereto, or causing any such sewer or drain to be so made or branched, shall be liable to a penalty not exceeding fifty pounds. The Vestry or District Board concerned may, by notice in writing to the owner or owners of the premises connected with the sewer or drain so improperly made or branched, or (if there are no such premises) of the land in which it is placed, require such owner or owners forthwith to remove such sewer or drain, or to reconstruct the same at his or their expense to the approval of such Vestry or

Penalty in case of connections with local sewers.

District Board and in accordance with the plan and section approved as aforesaid, and in the event of such owner or owners failing to comply with the terms of such requisition, such owner or owners, as the case may be, shall be severally liable to a penalty not exceeding five pounds for every day during which he or they shall fail to comply therewith, and the Vestry or District Board may execute the works required and recover the costs and expenses thereof in a court of summary jurisdiction from the person who shall have made or branched, or caused to be made or branched the sewer or drain, or from the owner or owners of the premises connected therewith, or (if there are no such premises) of the land in which it is placed.

Provided that if the premises of more than one owner are at the time of the commencement of the work by the Vestry or District Board connected with any such sewer, the costs and expenses thereof shall be apportioned amongst and recoverable from such owners in proportion to the rateable value of the premises respectively connected therewith.

Provided also that in the event of any such costs and expenses being paid to the Vestry or District Board by any such owner or owners, then such owner or owners shall be entitled to recover in a court of summary jurisdiction the amount so paid by them from the person who made or branched or caused such sewer or drain to be made or branched in manner aforesaid.

Subsoil under a street, road, passage or way not to be removed without the consent of the Vestry or District Board or Council.

VI. Subject to the provisions of this Act, it shall not be lawful after the passing of this Act to form or lay out, or to commence to form or lay out any street, road, passage or way over land from which sand, gravel or other subsoil has been excavated or removed, until the site and subsoil of the street, road, passage or way has been properly levelled and made good to a sufficient depth with stones, gravel or other suitable material to form a sound foundation, to the satisfaction of the Vestry or District Board, to be expressed in writing, and it shall not be lawful to excavate, remove or take away any sand, gravel or subsoil from any land upon which any street, road, passage or way has been wholly or in part formed or laid out, or upon which it is intended to form or lay out any street, road, passage or way, except upon such conditions as to the levelling and making a proper foundation for the same as the Vestry of the parish or District Board of the district may in writing impose. Provided that this section shall not apply where no more sand, gravel or subsoil has been or is intended to be excavated, removed or taken away than is necessary to level or form a foundation for the paving, metalling or flagging of any street, road, passage or way. If the Vestry or District Board shall refuse their approval in writing, or shall impose conditions, any company or person dissatisfied with such refusal or with such conditions may, within seven days from the date of receiving notice of such refusal or of such conditions, appeal to the Council, and such appeal shall stand referred to such committee of the Council as the Council may appoint, and such committee shall have power to confirm or reverse such refusal, or to vary the conditions imposed, or impose such conditions as they may think fit, and their determination shall be final, and such committee may order any costs of such appeal to be paid to or by the Vestry or District Board or person appealing. Any company or person forming or laying out, or commencing to form or lay out, any street, road, passage or way, or excavating, removing or taking away any sand, gravel or subsoil contrary to the provisions of this Act, or to the conditions imposed by the Vestry or District Board, or on appeal by the Council, shall for every such offence be liable to a penalty not exceeding five pounds, and to a further penalty not exceeding twenty shillings for every day after the first during which the offence is continued, or during which such excavation shall be permitted to remain without the consent in writing of the Vestry or District Board or on appeal of the Council.

Provided always that nothing in this section contained shall apply to any road, passage or way formed or laid out or to be formed or laid out, and intended to be maintained as a road, passage or way not open to public use.

Provided also that nothing in this section contained shall prejudice or affect any existing rights of the owners of property fronting or abutting on any street, road, passage or way, to excavate subsoil for the purpose of forming or constructing cellars, vaults, subways or basements in connection with buildings erected on such property.

Surveyor or other officer to see that conditions are observed.

VII. The surveyor of the Vestry or District Board, or other officer of the Vestry or District Board, or any officer appointed for that purpose by the Council, shall take care that the provisions of the preceding section are complied with, and that any conditions imposed by the Vestry or District Board or the Council in giving their consent in writing thereunder are observed.

Limited application of Act to City of London.

VIII. Except so far as relates to any sewers vested in the Council, none of the provisions contained in this Act shall have any force or effect within the City of London.

Penalties and expenses.

IX. Penalties and expenses under this Act may be sued for and recovered either by the Council, or by the Vestry or District Board concerned, in the same manner as penalties under the Metropolis Management Act, 1855, and the Acts amending the same.

Expenses of Act.

X. Any costs, charges and expenses incurred by the Council of and incidental to the preparing, applying for and passing of this Act shall be paid by the Council.

THE PUBLIC HEALTH (LONDON) ACT, 1891.

The following Sections of the Public Health (London) Act, 1891, 54 & 55 Vict. c. 76, give provisions as to the occupation of underground rooms as dwellings.

Underground Rooms.

XCVI. 1. Any underground room, which was not let or occupied separately as a dwelling before the passing of this Act, shall not be so let or occupied unless it possesses the following requisites ; that is to say, <small>Provisions as to the occupation of underground rooms as dwellings.</small>

   (a) unless the room is in every part thereof at least seven feet high measured from the floor to the ceiling, and has at least three feet of its height above the surface of the street or ground adjoining or nearest to the room: provided that if the width of the area hereinafter mentioned is not less than the height of the room from the floor to the said surface of the street or ground, the height of the room above such surface may be less than three feet ; but it shall not in any case be less than one foot, and the width of the area need not in any case be more than six feet ;

   (b) unless every wall of the room is constructed with a proper damp course, and, if in contact with the soil, is effectually secured against dampness from that soil ;

   (c) unless there is outside of and adjoining the room and extending along the entire frontage thereof and upwards from six inches below the level of the floor thereof an open area properly paved at least four feet wide in every part thereof: provided that in the area there may be placed steps necessary for access to the room, and over and across such area there may be steps necessary for access to any building above the underground room, if the steps in each case be so placed as not to be over or across any external window;

(d) unless the said area and the soil immediately below the room are effectually drained;

(e) unless, if the room has a hollow floor, the space beneath it is sufficiently ventilated to the outer air;

(f) unless any drain passing under the room is properly constructed of a gas-tight pipe;

(g) unless the room is effectually secured against the rising of any effluvia or exhalation;

(h) unless there is appurtenant to the room the use of a water-closet and a proper and sufficient ash-pit;

(i) unless the room is effectually ventilated;

(j) unless the room has a fire-place with a proper chimney or flue;

(k) unless the room has one or more windows opening directly into the external air with a total area clear of the sash frames equal to at least one-tenth of the floor area of the room, and so constructed that one half at least of each window of the room can be opened, and the opening in each case extends to the top of the window.

2. If any person lets or occupies, or continues to let, or knowingly suffers to be occupied, any underground room contrary to this enactment, he shall be liable to a fine not exceeding twenty shillings for every day during which the room continues to be so let or occupied.

3. The foregoing provisions shall at the expiration of six months after the commencement of this Act extend to underground rooms let or occupied separately as dwellings before the passing of this Act, except that the sanitary authority, either by general regulations providing for classes of underground rooms, or on the application of the owner of such room in any particular case, may dispense with or modify any of the said requisites which involve the structural alteration of the building, if they are of opinion that they can properly do so having due regard to the fitness of the room for human habitation, to the house accommodation in the district, and to the sanitary condition

of the inhabitants and to other circumstances; but any requisite which was required before the passing of this Act shall not be so dispensed with or modified.

4. The dispensations and modifications may be allowed either absolutely or for a limited time, and may be revoked and varied by the sanitary authority, and shall be recorded together with the reasons in the minutes of the sanitary authority.

5. If the owner of any room feels aggrieved by a dispensation or modification not being allowed as regards that room, he may appeal to the Local Government Board, and that Board may refuse the dispensation or modification, or allow it wholly or partly, as if they were the sanitary authority. Such allowance may be revoked or varied by the Board, but not by the sanitary authority.

6. Where two or more underground rooms are occupied together, and are not occupied in conjunction with any other room or rooms on any other floor of the same house, each of them shall be deemed to be separately occupied as a dwelling within the meaning of this section.

7. Every underground room in which a person passes the night shall be deemed to be occupied as a dwelling within the meaning of this section; and evidence giving rise to a probable presumption that some person passes the night in an underground room shall be evidence, until the contrary is proved, that such has been the case.

8. Where it is shown that any person uses an underground room as a sleeping-place, it shall, in any proceeding under this section, lie on the defendant to show that the room is not separately occupied as a dwelling.

8. For the purpose of this section the expression "underground room" includes any room of a house the surface of the floor of which room is more than three feet below the surface of the footway of the adjoining street, or of the ground adjoining or nearest to the room.

XCVII. 1. Any officer of a sanitary authority appointed or determined by that authority for the purpose shall, without any fee or reward, report to the sanitary authority, at such times and in such manner as the sanitary authority may order, all cases in which underground rooms are occupied contrary to this Act in the district of such authority.

Enforcement of provisions as to underground rooms.

2. Any such officer or any other person having reasonable grounds for believing that any underground room is occupied in contravention of this Act may enter and inspect the same at any hour by day ; and if admission is refused to any other person other than an officer of the sanitary authority the like warrant may be granted by a Justice under this Act as in case of refusal to admit any such officer.

3. A warrant of a Justice authorising an entry into an underground room may authorise the entry between any hours specified in the warrant.

Provisions in case of two convictions for unlawfully occupying underground room.

XCVIII. Where two convictions for an offence relating to the occupation of an underground room as a dwelling have taken place within a period of three months (whether the person convicted were or were not the same), a petty sessional court may direct the closing of the underground room for such period as the court may deem necessary, or may empower the sanitary authority of the district permanently to close the same, in such manner as they think fit, at their own cost.

THE FACTORY AND WORKSHOP ACT, 1891.

54 & 55 Vict. c. 75.

An Act to amend the Law relating to Factories and Workshops.
[5th August, 1891.]

VII. 1. Every factory of which the construction is com- Provision against fire.
menced after the first day of January, one thousand eight
hundred and ninety-two, and in which more than forty
persons are employed, shall be furnished with a certificate from the sanitary authority of the district in
which the factory is situate, that the factory is provided
on the storeys above the ground floor with such means of
escape in case of fire for the persons employed therein as
can reasonably be required under the circumstance of each
case, and a factory not so furnished shall be deemed not
to be kept in conformity with the principal Act, and it
shall be the duty of the sanitary authority to examine
every such factory, and on being satisfied that the factory
is so provided to give such a certificate as aforesaid.

2. With respect to all factories to which the foregoing
provisions of this section do not apply, and in which more
than forty persons are employed, it shall be the duty of
the sanitary authority of every district, as soon as may
be after the passing of this Act, and afterwards from time
to time, to ascertain whether all such factories within
their district are provided with such means of escape as
aforesaid, and, in the case of any factory which is not so
provided, to serve on the person being, within the meaning
of the Public Health Act, 1875, the owner of the factory
a notice in writing specifying the measures necessary for
providing such means of escape as aforesaid, and requiring
him to carry out the same before a specified date, and
thereupon such owner shall, notwithstanding any agreement with the occupier, have power to take such steps

as are necessary for complying with the requirements, and, unless such requirements are so complied with, such owner shall be liable to a fine not exceeding one pound for every day that such non-compliance continues. In case of a difference of opinion between the owner of the factory and the sanitary authority, the difference shall, on the application of either party, be referred to arbitration, and thereupon the provisions of the First Schedule to this Act shall have effect, except that the parties to the arbitration shall be the sanitary authority on the one hand and the owner on the other, and the award on the arbitration shall be binding on the parties thereto. If the owner alleges that the occupier of the factory ought to bear or contribute to the expenses of complying with the requirement, he may apply to the county court having jurisdiction where the factory is situate, and thereupon the county court, after hearing the occupier, may make such order as appears to the court just and equitable under all the circumstances of the case.

3. All the expenses incurred by a sanitary authority in the execution of this section shall be defrayed—
    (*a*) in the case of an authority of an urban district, as part of their expenses of the general execution of the Public Health Act, 1875; and
    (*b*) in the case of an authority of a rural district, as special expenses incurred in the execution of the Public Health Act, 1875; and such expenses shall be charged to the contributory place in which the factory is situate.

4. In the application of this section to the administrative County of London the London County Council shall take the place of the sanitary authority, and their expenses in the execution of this section shall be defrayed as part of their expenses in the management of the Metropolitan Building Act, 1855, and the Acts amending the same.

LONDON COUNTY COUNCIL.

BYELAWS AND REGULATIONS IN FORCE.

BYELAWS MADE BY THE COUNCIL UNDER SEC. 16 OF THE METROPOLIS MANAGEMENT AND BUILDINGS ACTS AMENDMENT ACT, 1878.

I. The heretofore subsisting byelaws made by the Metropolitan Board of Works on the 3rd of October 1879, and the 22nd of January 1886, and confirmed by the Secretary of State for the Home Department on the 6th of October 1879, and the 23rd of June 1886, are hereby repealed, and in lieu thereof the following are made:— Repeal of previous byelaws.

II. No house, building or other erection shall be erected upon any site or portion of any site which shall have been filled up or covered with any material impregnated or mixed with any fæcal, animal or vegetable matter, or which shall have been filled up or covered with dust, or slop, or other refuse, or in or upon which any such matter or refuse shall have been deposited, unless and until such matter or refuse shall have been properly removed, by excavation or otherwise, from such site. Any holes caused by such excavation must, if not used for a basement or cellar, be filled in with hard brick or dry rubbish, or concrete or other suitable material to be approved by the District Surveyor. Foundations and sites of buildings.

The site of every house or building shall be covered with a layer of good concrete, at least 6 inches thick, and smoothed on the upper surface.

The foundations of the walls of every house or building shall be formed of a bed of good concrete, not less than 9 inches thick, and projecting at least 4 inches on each side of the lowest course of footings of such walls. If the site be upon a natural bed of gravel, concrete may be omitted from the foundations of the walls, with the approval of the District Surveyor.

The concrete must be composed of clean gravel, broken hard brick, properly burnt ballast, or other hard material to be approved by the District Surveyor, well mixed with freshly burnt lime or cement in the proportions of one of lime to six, and one of cement to eight of the other material.

Description and quality of the substances of walls.

III. The external walls of every house, building or other erection shall, except in the case of concrete buildings, be constructed of good, hard, sound, well-burnt bricks, or stone.

Similar bricks shall be used in the portions of party and cross-walls below the surface or level of the ground, and above the roof, including the chimney stacks. Cutters or malms may be used in arches over recesses and openings in, or for facings of, external walls.

Stone used for the construction of walls must be free from vents, cracks and sand-holes, and be laid on its natural bed.

All brick and stone work shall be put together with good mortar or good cement.

The mortar to be used must be composed of freshly burned lime and clean sharp sand or grit, without earthy matter, in the proportions of one of lime to three of sand or grit.

The cement to be used must be Portland cement, or other cement of equal quality, to be approved by the District Surveyor, mixed with clean sharp sand or grit in proportions of one of cement to four of sand or grit.

Burnt ballast or broken brick may be substituted for sand or grit, provided such material be properly mixed with lime in a mortar mill.

Every wall of a house or building shall have a damp course composed of materials impervious to moisture, to be approved by the District Surveyor, extending throughout its whole thickness at the level of not less than 6 inches below the level of the lowest floor. Every external wall or inclosing wall of habitable rooms or their appurtenances or cellars which abuts against the earth shall be protected by materials impervious to moisture to the satisfaction of the District Surveyor.

The top of every party-wall and parapet-wall shall be finished with one course of hard, well-burnt bricks set on edge in cement, or by a coping of any other waterproof and fire-resisting material, properly secured.

Whenever concrete is used in the construction of walls, the concrete shall be composed of Portland cement and of clean Thames or pit ballast, or gravel, or broken brick or stone, or furnace clinkers, with clean sand in the following proportions, viz. one part of Portland cement, two parts of clean sand, and three parts of the coarse material, which is to be broken up sufficiently small to pass through a 2-inch ring.

The proportions of the materials to be strictly observed, and to be ascertained by careful admeasurement; and the mixing either by machine or hand to be most carefully done with clean water, and, if mixed by hand, the material to be turned over dry before the water is added.

The walls to be carried up regularly and in parallel frames of equal height, and the surface of the concrete filled in the frame to be left rough and uneven to form a key for the next frame of concrete.

The thicknesses of concrete walls to be equal at the least to the thicknesses for walls to be constructed of brickwork prescribed by the 12th section of the Metropolitan Building Act, 1855, and the first schedule referred to therein.

Such portions of concrete party-walls and chimney stacks as are carried above the roofs of buildings to be rendered externally with Portland cement.

IV. It shall be the duty of each District Surveyor, on receiving notice of the commencement of any house, building or other erection, or of any alteration or addition, or on his becoming aware that any house, building or other erection, or any alteration or addition, is being proceeded with, to see that the provisions of the foregoing byelaws are duly observed (except in cases where the London County Council may have dispensed with the observance thereof), and to see that the terms and conditions upon which any dispensation may have been granted are complied with.

Duties of District Surveyors.

V. The District Surveyor shall, in respect of the erection of any house or other building, be entitled to receive the sum of five shillings, the same to be taken and deemed to be a fee due to such District Surveyor in respect of the

Fees to be paid to District Surveyors.

duties imposed upon him by the Metropolis Management and Building Acts Amendment Act, 1878, and these byelaws; such fees to be payable in the manner and at the time prescribed by section 51 of the Metropolitan Building Act, 1855. The District Surveyor shall also, in every case where, in respect of any breach of these byelaws, or of the above Act of Parliament, an application shall have been made by him to a Justice, and an order made thereon, be in like manner entitled to receive the sum of ten shilllings in addition to the before-mentioned fee of five shillings.

There shall be paid to the District Surveyor, in respect of his supervision of any building constructed wholly or in part with concrete walls, a fee one-half more in amount than the fee to which he would be entitled under the Metropolitan Building Act, 1855, for a new building or addition. No additional fee is, however, to be charged in respect of any alteration to a concrete building.

Deposit of plans and sections.

VI. On notice being given to a District Surveyor of the intended erection, re-erection, alteration of, or addition to a public building or a building to which section 56 of the Metropolitan Building Act, 1855, applies, it shall be the duty of the person giving such notice to deposit plans and sections of such erection, re-erection, alteration or addition with the District Surveyor. Such plans and sections shall be of sufficient detail to show the construction.

On notice being given to the District Surveyor of the intended erection or alteration of or addition to any house, building or other erection, other than a public building, or one to which section 56 of the Metropolitan Building Act, 1855, applies, the District Surveyor may, if he think fit so to do, by notice in writing, require the person giving such notice to produce a plan or plans and sections of any such house, building or other erection, or of the intended alterations or additions thereto, for his inspection.

Penalties and dispensation.

VII. In case of any breach of any of the provisions contained in these byelaws, the offender shall be liable for each breach to a penalty not exceeding five pounds, and in each case of a continuing offence, to a further penalty not exceeding forty shillings for each day after notice of such offence from the London County Council or District Surveyor.

In any case in which the Council think it expedient

they may dispense with the observance of any of the foregoing byelaws, or any part thereof, upon such terms and conditions as they may think proper, and in case of the non-observance of any terms and conditions upon which the Council may have dispensed with the observance of any of the foregoing byelaws, then such proceedings may be taken, and such liabilities shall be incurred, as if the same had been enacted by such byelaws.

The Seal of the London County Council
was hereto affixed on the 13th day of (L. S.)
October, 1891.

H. DE LA HOOKE,
Clerk of Council.

I hereby confirm the foregoing Byelaws.

HENRY MATTHEWS,
One of Her Majesty's principal Secretaries of State.

WHITEHALL,
19th October, 1891.

LONDON COUNTY COUNCIL.

BYELAWS MADE BY THE COUNCIL UNDER SEC. 31 OF THE LONDON COUNCIL (GENERAL POWERS) ACT, 1890.

Description and quality of the substances of which plastering is to be made.

I. All laths used for plastering shall be sound laths free from sap, but iron or other incombustible laths, wire netting or other suitable material to the satisfaction of the District Surveyor may be used.

Plastering or coarse stuff shall be composed of lime and sand in the proportion of 1 of lime to 3 of sand, mixed with water and hair, but Portland cement, Keene's cement, Parian cement, Martin's cement, Selenitic cement, or other approved cement or plaster of Paris, may also be used for plastering.

The lime to be used must be freshly burned lime.

The sand to be used must be clean, sharp sand, free from loam or earthy matter.

The hair to be used must be good and sound, and free from grease or dirt; 1 lb. of hair to be used to every 3 cubic feet of coarse stuff. Fibrous material to the satisfaction of the District Surveyor may be used instead of hair, and ground brick or furnace slag to the satisfaction of the District Surveyor may be used instead of sand.

The setting coat shall be composed of lime or cement mixed with clean washed sand, or of cement only.

Clear water only is to be used in mixing the material.

The Portland cement to be used must weigh not less than 90 lbs. to the imperial bushel.

Fibrous slab or other slab plastering of sufficient thickness and securely fixed, may be used on ceilings, partitions and walls to the satisfaction of the District Surveyor.

As to the mode in which and the materials with which any excavation outside

II. Any excavation made within a line drawn outside the site of a house, building, or other erection, and at an uniform distance therefrom of 3 feet, shall not be filled up otherwise than with the natural soil or with brick or dry rubbish or other suitable material to be approved by the

District Surveyor, not consisting of, nor impregnated or mixed with any fæcal, animal or vegetable matter, or with dust or slop or other refuse, and shall be properly rammed.

the site of a building is to be filled up.

III. It shall be the duty of each District Surveyor on receiving notice of the commencement of any house, building or other erection, or on his becoming aware that any house, building or other erection is being proceeded with, or that any excavation is being made within a line drawn outside the site of a house, building or other erection, and within 3 feet therefrom, to see that the plastering is of the description and quality prescribed by, and that any excavation be filled up with the material and in the manner specified in the foregoing byelaws.

Duties of District Surveyors.

IV. There shall be paid to the District Surveyor in respect of his supervision of the plastering of any house, building or other erection, and in respect of the filling in of any excavation made outside the site of any house, building or other erection, and within a distance of 3 feet therefrom, an inclusive fee of five shillings, such fee to be payable in the manner and at the time specified in Section 51 of the Metropolitan Building Act, 1855.

Fees to be paid to District Surveyors.

V. In case of any breach of the provisions contained in these byelaws, the offender shall be liable for each offence to a penalty not exceeding five pounds, and, in each case of a continuing offence, to a further penalty not exceeding forty shillings for each day after notice of such offence from the London County Council or the District Surveyor.

Penalties.

The Seal of the London County Council
was hereto affixed on the 13th day of   (L. S.)
October, 1891.

M. DE LA HOOKE,
Clerk of the Council.

I hereby confirm the foregoing Byelaws.

HENRY MATTHEWS,
One of Her Majesty's principal Secretaries of State.

WHITEHALL,
19th October, 1891.

LONDON COUNTY COUNCIL.

THE METROPOLIS MANAGEMENT AND BUILDING ACTS AMENDMENT ACT, 1878.

REGULATIONS MADE BY THE COUNCIL ON THE 9TH OF FEBRUARY, 1892, WITH RESPECT TO THE REQUIREMENTS FOR THE PROTECTION FROM FIRE OF THEATRES, HOUSES, ROOMS AND OTHER PLACES OF PUBLIC RESORT WITHIN THE ADMINISTRATIVE COUNTY OF LONDON.

Limits of regulations

These regulations shall, unless otherwise specified, apply to all theatres, houses, rooms or other places of public resort within the Administrative County of London, to be kept open for the public performance of stage plays, and to all houses, rooms or other places of public resort within the said County, to be kept open for public dancing, music or other public entertainment of the like kind, under the authority of letters patent from Her Majesty the Queen, her heirs or successors, or of Licenses by the Lord Chamberlain of Her Majesty's Household, or by the London County Council, other than letters patent, or licenses which may have been granted for the first time before the passing of the above-mentioned Act.

Interpretation of "such premises."

In these regulations the expression "such premises" means a theatre, house, room or other place of public resort to be kept open for any of the purposes aforesaid.

PART I.—STRUCTURAL.

Applications and drawings.

1. Every person who for the first time after the making of these regulations shall be desirous of obtaining authority to open any such premises within the said County, shall first make an application in writing to the Clerk of the Council for a certificate under the above Act.

Such application shall contain a statement as to the nature and extent of the interest of such person in such premises, and the character of the entertainment for which such premises are proposed to be used, and be accompanied by complete plans, elevations and sections, drawn on tracing linen, to a scale of one-eighth of an inch to a foot; and by a block plan showing the position of such premises in relation to any adjacent premises, and to the public thoroughfares upon which the site of such premises abuts, drawn to a scale of not less than one-twentieth of an inch to a foot.

Such drawings shall be coloured to distinguish the materials employed in the construction of the building; the width of all staircases, corridors, gangways and doorways, together with the heights of the tiers and other parts of the building.

The thicknesses of the walls, and scantlings of the various materials, shall be clearly shown by figured dimensions; and the cardinal points shall be marked upon each plan.

Such drawings shall be accompanied by a specification of the works to be executed, describing the materials to be employed and the mode of construction to be adopted, together with such other particulars as may be necessary to enable the Council to judge whether the requirements of these regulations will, when such premises have been completed, have been complied with.

Such drawings shall also show the respective numbers of persons to be accommodated in the various parts of such premises, and the area to be assigned to each person, which shall not be less than 1 foot 8 inches by 1 foot 6 inches in the gallery, and not less than 2 feet 4 inches by 1 foot 8 inches in other parts of such premises.

Such drawings and specification to be deposited with the Council. A duplicate copy of approved drawings and specifications shall be signed by the Chairman of the Committee and returned to the applicants.

II. One-half at least of the total length of the boundaries of the site of any such premises which consist of an entire building, and in case of a room or other such premises not consisting of an entire building, one-half at least of the total length of the boundaries of the site of the building of which such room or other such premises form part, shall abut upon public thoroughfares, of which one thoroughfare at least shall be not less than 40 feet wide, and of the remainder none shall be less than 30 feet wide if a carriage way, or 20 feet wide if a footway.

If, in compliance with Regulation No. 10, an additional passage or way should be necessary, it may be provided by means of a private passage or way.

Such passage or way shall not be less than 10 feet in width, and under the complete control of the owner of such premises, and no doors, windows or other openings of the adjoining premises shall communicate therewith, or overlook any portion of such passage or way.

Windows overlooking site.

III. No such premises shall be erected upon a site within 20 feet of any windows or other openings belonging to any other premises overlooking the site.

Walls.

IV. All such premises shall be enclosed with proper external or party walls of brick or stone.

The thickness of such walls shall not be less than the thickness prescribed by the Metropolitan Building Act, 1855, for walls of similar height and length in buildings of the warehouse class.

Dressing-rooms.

V. Dressing-rooms shall be arranged in a separate block of buildings, or divided from the place of public resort by party walls, with only such means of communication therewith as may be approved by the Council.

All such dressing-rooms shall be constructed of fire-resisting materials, and connected with an independent exit leading directly into a thoroughfare or way.

All such dressing-rooms shall be ventilated to the outer air by windows in the external walls.

The walls of all such dressing-rooms shall be hung, for decorative purposes, only with materials completely adhering to the surface of such walls.

No such dressing-rooms shall be situated more than one storey below the street level.

Sufficient and separate water-closet and urinal accommodation, properly ventilated to the outer air, shall be provided for the use of the male and female artistes.

No theatre under or over any other building.

VI. No theatre shall be constructed underneath, or on the top of, any part of any other building.

VII. No such premises shall have more than three tiers or horizontal divisions, including the gallery, above the level of the pit. *Number of tiers.*

Where the front seats of the gallery are separated from the gallery by a partition, such seats shall not count as a separate tier.

VIII. When the first tier or balcony extends over the pit, stalls or area, the height between the floor of the pit and the first tier shall not be at any part less than 10 feet, and the height between the floor of the highest part of the gallery and the lowest part of the ceiling over the same shall not be less than 12 feet. *Height of tiers.*

IX. In all such premises the floor of the highest part of the pit, or of the stalls where there is no pit, shall not be more than 6 inches above the level of the street adjoining the principal entrance to the pit, and the lowest part of the floor of the pit or stalls shall not be more than 15 feet below such level. *Floor of pit.*

X. Two separate exits, not leading into the same thoroughfare or way, shall be provided to every tier or floor of such premises. *Entrances and exits.*

If any tier or floor shall be divided into two parts, two separate exits, not leading into the same thoroughfare or way, shall be provided to each of such parts.

Such exits shall be arranged so as to afford a ready means of egress from both sides of each tier or floor, and shall lead directly into a thoroughfare or way.

XI. Where vestibules are provided, not more than three tiers or floors (or where such tiers or floors are divided into two or more parts, such parts of tiers or floors) shall communicate with one vestibule. *Vestibules.*

The width of each vestibule shall be at least one-third greater than the united width of all the doorways or passages that lead thereto.

The united widths of all the doorways or passages that lead from a vestibule towards a thoroughfare or way, shall be at least of the same width as such vestibule.

Not more than one exit from each separate part of a tier or floor shall be used as an entrance.

XII. In all such premises where a stage with a pro- *Proscenium wall.*

scenium shall be erected, such stage shall be separated from the auditorium by a brick proscenium wall not less than 13 inches in thickness, and such wall shall be carried up the full thickness to a height of at least 3 feet above the roof, such height being measured at right angles to the slope of the roof, and shall be carried down below the stage to a solid foundation.

Not more than three openings shall be formed in the proscenium wall, exclusive of the proscenium opening.

No such opening shall exceed 3 feet in width and 6 feet 6 inches in height, and each of such openings shall be closed by a wrought-iron door not less than one-fourth of an inch in thickness in the panel, hung in a wrought-iron frame so as to close of itself without a spring.

No openings formed in the proscenium wall shall at the lowest part be at a higher level than the floor of the stage.

All the decorations around the proscenium shall be constructed of fire-resisting materials.

Proscenium opening.

XIII. The proscenium opening shall be provided with a fire-resisting screen to be used as a drop curtain, of such pattern, construction and gearing, and with such arrangements for pouring water upon the surface of the screen which is towards the stage as may be approved by the Council.

Roof over stage.

XIV. The height of the wall plate carrying the rafters of the roof over the stage shall not be less than twice the height of the proscenium opening, such height being measured from the level of the stage at the curtain line.

An opening shall be formed in the roof near the back of the stage, of a superficial area at the base of at least one-tenth of the superficial area of the stage. Such opening shall be covered with a lantern light, glazed on the top and sides, and be fitted with suitable exhaust cowls.

Corridors, passages and staircases.

XV. Every staircase, landing, lobby, corridor or passage intended for the use of not more than 400 persons of the audience, shall be formed of fire-resisting materials, and shall not be less than 4 feet 6 inches wide; but if communicating with any portion of the house intended for the accommodation of a larger number of the audience than 400 persons, it shall be increased in width by

6 inches for every additional 100 persons until a maximum width of 9 feet be obtained.

XVI. Every staircase for the use of the audience shall have solid square (as distinguished from spandril) steps of York or other stone or fire-resting materials, to be approved by the Council, with treads not less than 11 inches wide and with risers not more than 6 inches high, without winders, in flights of not more than 12 or less than 3 steps each. {Staircases.}

The treads of each flight of steps shall be of uniform width, and be pinned into brick walls at both ends.

The several flights of such steps shall be supported and enclosed upon all sides by brick walls not less than 9 inches thick, to be carried down to the level of the footings.

No staircase shall have more than two flights of twelve steps each without a turn.

All landings shall be 6 inches thick, be square upon plan, and have brick arches 9 inches deep turned under them in the middle of such landings.

Every staircase shall have a roof of fire-resisting materials to be approved by the Council.

A continuous handrail shall be fixed on both sides of all steps and landings, supported by strong metal brackets built into the wall.

Such handrails shall be chased into the walls where the thickness of the walls will permit, but in all cases where the flights of steps return, the newel wall shall be chased so as to allow the handrail to turn without projecting on the landing.

XVII. A clear passage or gangway not less than 3 feet wide shall be formed at the sides and in the rear of the seating in every part of such premises. {Gangways.}

Such passages or gangways shall at all times be kept entirely free from chairs, flap seats or other obstructions, whether permanent or temporary.

XVIII. All constructional ironwork in such premises shall be embedded in fire-resisting materials in a manner to be approved by the Council. {Ironwork.}

XIX. All workshops, store-rooms, wardrobe or painting rooms in connection with such premises, shall be separated {Workshops, etc.}

from such premises by brick walls not less than 9 inches thick.

All openings in such walls shall be closed with self-closing wrought-iron doors, hung in a wrought-iron frame.

All such doors, if consisting of a single fold, shall be made to overlap, when closed, the door frame at least 3 inches; and, if made in two folds, such folds shall overlap each other when closed, at least 3 inches on each side.

All floors and ceilings of such rooms shall be formed of fire-resisting materials.

All such rooms shall be ventilated by windows in the outer walls.

Limelight tanks, boilers and dynamos.

XX. All limelight tanks, boilers with engines, and dynamos with engines, shall be each placed in a ventilating chamber or building of fireproof construction.

Such chambers or buildings shall be separated from such premises, and from each other, by brick walls and fireproof floors without openings, and shall be enclosed upon one or more sides by external walls.

Scene dock.

XXI. All scene docks or stores, and property rooms in connection with such premises shall be enclosed by brick walls not less than 9 inches thick, and shall have floors and ceilings of fire-resisting materials.

All openings from such docks, stores or rooms to such premises shall be closed by self-closing wrought-iron doors, hung in wrought-iron frames.

All such doors, if consisting of a single fold, shall be made to overlap, when closed, the door frame at least 3 inches; and, if made in two folds, such folds shall overlap each other, when closed, at least 3 inches on each side.

Enclosures.

XXII. No enclosure shall be allowed in any such premises where the public can assemble for any other purpose than to view the performance, except so far as the Council shall consider necessary for the provision of refreshment bars, or in the case of a theatre for the provision of a foyer.

Skylights.

XXIII. All skylights, and the sloping sides of lantern lights, shall be protected by galvanised iron-wire guards, securely fixed on the outside of such skylights or lantern lights.

XXIV. All such premises when lighted by gas shall have separate and distinct gas services and meters as follows:— *Gas.*
  (a) To the stage;
  (b) To the auditorium;
  (c) To the staircases, corridors and exits.

Such meters shall be placed in properly ventilated chambers of fireproof construction.

All gas brackets shall be fixed without joints; and all burners within reach of the audience shall be fitted with secret taps, and be efficiently protected by glass or wire globes.

All gas burners within 3 feet of the ceiling shall have hanging shades of uninflammable material to distribute the heat.

All gas pipes shall be made of iron or brass.

Where there is a stage or wings with scenery, the footlights or floats shall be protected by fixed iron-wire guards, and the burners shall be provided with glass chimneys.

The rows and lines, and gas burners in the wings (which must commence 4 feet at least from the level of the stage) shall be protected by fixed iron-wire guards.

All battens shall be hung by at least three wire ropes, and be protected at the back by a solid metal guard and wire fixed to a stiff iron frame at such a distance from the gas jets that no part of the scenery or decoration can become heated.

All movable lights shall be fitted with flexible tubes, and the gas in every case shall be turned off by the tap on the stage as well as by that on the flexible tube.

All flexible tubes shall be of sufficient strength to resist pressure from without.

An indicating glass plate shall be provided at a convenient place at the side of the stage.

XXV. All doorways used by the public shall be at least 4 feet 6 inches wide in the clear, with doors hung in two folds made to open outwards towards the thoroughfare or way. *Doors and fastenings.*

All internal doors shall be so hung as not to obstruct, when open, any gangway, passage, staircase or landing.

No door shall open immediately upon a flight of steps, but a square landing at least the width of the doorway shall be provided between such steps and such doorway.

All exit doors having fastenings shall be fastened by automatic bolts only, of a pattern to be approved by the Council; but where such doors are also to be used by the public for entrances, they shall be fastened with espagnolette or lever bolts only, of a pattern to be approved in each case by the Council, and fitted with lever handles at a height of 3 feet 6 inches from the floor.

All doors used for entrances, and all gates, shall be made to open both ways, and shall, when opened inwards, be locked back against the wall in such a manner as to require a key to release them.

All barriers and internal doors shall be made to open outwards, with no other fastenings than automatic bolts.

No locks, monkey-tail, flush or barrel bolts, or locking bars, or other obstructions to exit, shall be used on any doors, gates or barriers.

Ventilation. — XXVI. All parts of such premises shall be properly and sufficiently ventilated in a manner to be approved by the Council.

All openings for ventilation shall be shown on the plans, and described in the specification, which shall be submitted to the Council for its approval.

Warming. — XXVII. No fire-place shall be formed in any portion of the auditorium or stage of such premises.

All open fire-places or stoves in any other part of such premises shall be protected by strong fixed iron-wire guards and fenders, part of which may be made to open for all necessary purposes.

All heating apparatus shall be placed in a position to be approved by the Council, and enclosed upon all sides by brick walls not less than 9 inches thick, and shall be properly ventilated.

All hot-water pipes or coils shall, where necessary, be recessed in the walls, or otherwise arranged so as not to diminish the clear width of the gangways.

Where such premises are heated by artificial means, the high pressure hot-water system with sealed pipes will be inadmissible, and either hot-air or the low pressure hot-water circulation system shall be adopted, having an open cold water supply cistern, and the pipes throughout the system shall be of galvanised wrought iron, with the exception of those in immediate contact with the boiler, which may be either of galvanised wrought iron or copper.

The boiler shall be made of wrought iron, copper or mild steel, and shall be provided with a dead weight or other approved safety valve, which must be attached to the boiler by an independent galvanised wrought iron or copper pipe, and must not under any circumstances be fixed to the circulating pipes, and must be placed in such a position as will ensure protection from soot and dirt.

The term low pressure shall be understood to mean the pressure due to the vertical head of water between the boiler and the supply cistern.

XXVIII. All such premises containing a superficial area for the accommodation of the public of 1000 feet and upwards shall be provided with a sufficient number of hydrants, each of a diameter of not less than 2½ inches, to be connected by a 3-inch main with a Water Company's high-pressure street main. Water Supply.

Each of such hydrants shall be provided with at least a 30-feet length of hose, with fittings of the Metropolitan Fire Brigade pattern.

In all such premises where there is no constant supply of water, there shall be provided on the top of the proscenium wall, or at some other place to be approved by the Council, two cisterns, to be kept always filled with water.

Such cisterns shall be each capable of containing at least 250 gallons of water for every 100 persons of the audience to be accommodated in the building.

Such cisterns shall be properly protected from all danger from frost.

Fire mains shall be connected with such cisterns to hydrants to be fixed in such places and manner as may be approved by the Council.

XXIX. Notice shall be given to the Clerk of the Council of any intended structural addition to, or alteration of, any such premises, in respect of which the Council may have granted a certificate under the said Act of 1878, to the effect that such premises were, on their original completion, in accordance with the Council's regulations. Addition or alteration to premises.

Such notice shall be accompanied by plans, elevations

and sections, block plan and specification of the works to be executed similar to those required in the case of premises to be certified for the first time by the Council, and showing such intended addition or alteration.

The Council will, if necessary, cause a fresh survey of such premises to be made.

No doors, bolts or other fastenings, obstructions to the means of egress, flap seats or other means of diminishing or stopping up the gangways, shall be put, nor shall any alterations of a like nature be made to such premises without the previous consent of the Council being obtained thereto.

Part II.—General.

Oil or candle lamps.

XXX. Additional means of lighting, for use in the event of the gas or the electric light being extinguished, shall be provided for the auditorium, corridors, passages, exits, and staircases, by a sufficient number of oil or candle lamps, of a pattern to be approved by the Council, properly secured to an uninflammable base out of the reach of the public.

Such lamps shall be kept alight during the whole time the public are in such premises.

No mineral oils shall be permitted to be used in such lamps.

Fire alarm.

XXXI. Every theatre, and, where considered necessary by the Council, all other premises licensed by the Council, shall be connected with the nearest Fire Brigade Station by telephone.

Notices.

XXXII. All exit and other doors used by the public shall be indicated by painted notices in 3-inch white block letters upon a black ground.

Such notices shall be painted on the doors and walls at least 6 feet 9 inches above the floor.

The words "no exit" shall be painted at least 6 feet 9 inches above the floor, in 3-inch white block letters upon a black ground, upon all doors, in sight of the audience, which do not lead to exits.

Precautions against fire.

XXXIII. Wet blankets or rugs, and buckets filled with water shall be always kept on the stage or in the flies, scene docks, or wings, and attention shall be directed to them by placards legibly printed or painted, and fixed immediately above them.

Some person shall be held responsible by the management for keeping the wet blankets or rugs and buckets ready for immediate use.

Hatchets, hooks and other appliances, for taking down hanging scenery in case of fire, shall be always kept in readiness for immediate use.

The regulations as to fire shall be always posted in some conspicuous place in such premises, so that all persons connected with such premises may be acquainted with such regulations.

Part III.—Electric Lighting.

XXXIV. Where the electric light is permitted in such premises, it shall be on condition that a competent electrical engineer do certify in writing to the satisfaction of the Council once in six months that the system is in proper working order. *Certificate*

1. All such premises when lighted by electric light shall have at least three separate and distinct circuits (*a*) for the stage (*b*) and (*c*) for the auditorium, corridors and exits. *Circuits.*

    The circuits referred to in (*b*) and (*c*) shall be so arranged that half the lights in each division of the auditorium and half those in each corridor and exit shall be on (*b*) and the other half on (*c*) circuit.

    When the current is supplied by a public lighting company these circuits shall be taken separately from the street mains.

    Under all circumstances complete metallic circuits must be employed.

    Gas and water pipes shall never form part of any circuit.

    The number of lamps shall be so sub-divided that no sub-circuit shall carry more than 65 ampères; and each sub-circuit shall start from a distributing board.

2. All conductors used within buildings shall be of *Conductors.*

copper having a conductivity equal to not less than 98 per cent. of that of pure copper, and shall be so proportioned to the work they have to do that, if double the normal current be transmitted, their temperature shall not rise to above 150 degrees Fahr.

The conductors shall be insulated with pure and vulcanised india-rubber.

The insulation resistance shall not be less than 300 megohms per statute mile, at 60 degrees Fahr., after one minute's electrification, when tested with at least 400 volts, and after 48 hours' immersion in water.

The insulated conductors shall be protected on the outside by stout tape or braiding impregnated with preservative compound.

If it is desired to use any other means of insulation than that above specified, special permission shall be obtained from the Council, and no material shall be used which is not waterproof, or which will soften at a temperature below 170 degrees Fahr.

In all cases conductors conveying currents of high electromotive force inside buildings shall be specially and exceptionally insulated, and cased in, and the casing made fireproof.

The positive and negative terminals connected to such conductors shall not be nearer to each other than 12 inches, and shall be efficiently protected from risk of contact.

Flexible conductors in connection with movable lights shall be insulated with vulcanised india-rubber, and protected on the outside by a stout braiding; should any of these flexible conductors be damaged, it shall be at once replaced.

No circuit of this nature shall carry more than 10 ampères, and each circuit shall be protected by a double pole fuse.

Conductors, fixing and protection.

3. All conductors shall be efficiently protected from mechanical injury.

Where conductors pass through walls, fireproof floors or ceilings, they shall be protected by iron pipes or by glazed stoneware or porcelain tubes, and precautions shall be taken to prevent the possibility of fire or water passing along the course of the conductors.

In special cases, or where necessary for protection from the depredations of rats, mice, or other vermin, armour cables may be used. These need receive no further mechanical protection.

Lead-covered cables shall not be used unless protected by external armour of iron or steel.

Metal fastenings for fixing conductors shall be avoided, but when unavoidable some additional covering shall be used to protect the conductor, unless armoured, from mechanical injury at the points of support.

If casing be used, it shall be of hard wood, and each conductor shall be laid in a separate groove the cover shall be secured with screws.

Casings shall, as far as possible, be placed in sight, and the conductors shall always be accessible.

Joints in conductors shall be avoided, but when unavoidable they shall be electrically and mechanically perfect. Soldering fluids shall not be used in making such joints.

4. All external conductors shall be specially insulated and laid in iron pipes properly jointed, and of ample size. *External conductors.*

Such iron pipes shall be protected where necessary, and securely fixed and supported when not underground.

5. All exposed metal work, such as fittings, switch and fuse covers, &c., shall be efficiently insulated from the circuits. *Switches, cut-outs, &c.*

All switches, cut-outs, ceiling roses, wall and floor sockets and lamp-holders, shall have uninflammable bases.

All switches shall be of ample size to carry the currents for which they are intended without heating, and shall be so constructed that it will be impossible for them to remain in any position intermediate between the "on" and the "off" positions, or to permit of a permanent arc.

All circuits shall be efficiently protected by cut-outs, placed in positions easily accessible to the staff, but inaccessible to the public.

The main cut-outs shall be of such pattern and be fixed in such a position as to admit of quick replacement.

All circuits carrying a current of 20 ampères or more shall be provided with a cut-out on each conductor, and the two cut-outs shall not come in the same compartment.

All cut-outs shall be so constructed that fused metal in falling cannot cause a short circuit or an ignition.

All cut-outs shall be so marked as to show what circuit or lamps they control.

All wall or floor sockets shall be provided with fuses in their fixed portions.

The sockets for the stage shall be of hard wood with metal guards, care being taken to avoid risk of ignition, and they shall be of specially substantial construction.

6. Resistances for regulating the power of the lights shall be mounted on incombustible bases, and shall be so protected and placed at such a distance from any combustible material that no part of the resistance, if broken, can fall on such material.

Principal resistances shall be placed in a fire-proof room reserved for the purpose.

7. Arc lamps shall not be used inside buildings without special permission from the Council.

When they are used special precautions shall be taken to guard against danger from falling glass or incandescent particles of carbon.

All parts of the lamps, lanterns and fittings which are liable to be handled (except by the persons employed to trim them) shall be insulated.

8. Where there is a stage, special care shall be taken that all works in connection with the lighting of the stage are carried out in as substantial a manner as possible.

No metal work in connection with the circuits shall be exposed or so fixed or constructed as to be liable to cause a short circuit.

Lamps on battens, footlights, &c. shall be protected by stiff wire guards, so arranged that no

scenery or other inflammable material can come
in contact with the lamps.

No readily combustible material shall be used in
connection with any lamps on the stage in such
a manner that it might come in contact with the
lamps.

No soft or readily inflammable wood shall be used
in connection with the lamps on the stage, and
all wood shall be protected by uninflammable
material from the possibility of ignition by an
arc between any two parts of the two conductors,
or by heated particles from any conductor or
part of a conductor which may connect together
the two main conductors.

Where a number of lights, as in the footlights,
battens, &c., are supplied under control of one
switch, and protected by one single or double
pole cut-out, as the case may be, the conductors
shall be maintained throughout of such a section
that they will be effectually protected by the
cut-outs against heating.

The leads to the battens shall be specially guarded,
particularly at the points where they join on
to the battens, and a sufficient length shall be
allowed to prevent the leads receiving any
injury through any movement of the battens.

The battens shall be suspended by at least three
wire ropes attached to insulators on the battens.

On no account shall the same battens be adapted
for both gas and electric light.

9. A switchboard, containing all the necessary switches, *Stage switch-*
cut-outs, and other fittings for the control and *board.*
regulation of the stage lighting shall be fixed in
some convenient position overlooking the stage.
This board shall be inaccessible to all but the
persons employed at such premises to work it.

10. Boilers, steam engines, gas engines and dynamos, *Generating*
when used for the supply of electricity to such *plant.*
premises, shall be placed in such positions as
shall be sanctioned by the Council.

Gas engines shall be placed in rooms so adequately
and continuously ventilated that no explosive
mixture of gas can accumulate by any leakage

through the engine in the event of any of the gas cocks being left turned on.

A hood, connected with a pipe carried into the external air, shall be fixed over the ignition tube when this is used.

11. Primary or secondary batteries shall be placed in rooms so adequately ventilated that no fan shall be necessary.

The batteries shall be well insulated.

12. Transformers used to transform either direct or alternating currents, together with the switches and cut-outs connected therewith, shall be placed in a fire and moisture-proof structure.

Where the primary current is of high potential, such structure should be preferably outside the building.

No part of such apparatus shall be accessible except to the person in charge of its maintenance.

No transformer which, under normal conditions of load, heats above 130 degrees Fahr. shall be used.

Transformer circuits shall be so arranged that under no circumstances shall a contact between the primary and the secondary coils lead an electromotive force of high pressure into the building. The term high pressure means in all cases pressure above 200 volts.

13. The insulation resistance of a system of distribution shall be such that the greatest leakage from any conductor to earth, when all branches are switched on, the lamps and motors being removed, shall not exceed one fifteen-thousandth part of the total current intended for the supply of the said lamps and motors; the test being made at the usual working electro-motive force. Provided that this rule shall not be held to justify a lower insulation resistance than 5000 ohms, nor to require one higher than 5 megohms.

14. The generating plant and switching gear shall be in the hands of thoroughly competent manipulators, and the engine room (if any) shall be inaccessible to the general public, and shall where possible have an independent entrance.

15. A plan of the wiring shall be always kept in a prominent position in the office of the manager of such premises. *Plan of wiring.*

Part IV.

XXXV. The Council reserves to itself the right from time to time, in any special case, to modify or dispense with these regulations. *Power to modify or dispense with these regulations.*

All applications for dispensations or modifications shall be made in writing, addressed to the Clerk of the Council, and contain a statement of the facts of the particular case, and the reasons why it is desired to modify or dispense with these regulations as applicable thereto.

XXXVI. The person or persons in whose name the license is granted will be held responsible by the Council for the carrying out of the above regulations, for the due management of such premises, and for the safety of the public and his or their employées in the event of fire. *Person responsible.*

NOTE.—*Every person who receives a certificate under the Act of 1878 shall be informed that the issue of the certificate does not preclude the Council from considering, on its merits, any application which may hereafter be made with respect to the licensing of the building.*

LONDON COUNTY COUNCIL.

REGULATIONS MADE BY THE COUNCIL ON NOV. 23, 1891,
UNDER THE LONDON BUILDING ACT, 1894.

3. (*a*) That on and after the 1st of January 1895, the following be the regulations of the Council in relation to applications for sanction or consent under the London Building Act, 1894, in substitution for the regulations now existing in relation to the same subject matter—

I.—GENERAL.

All applications are to be addressed to the Superintending Architect, County Hall, Spring Gardens, S.W.

All applications must be in writing on foolscap paper, and all drawings (including plans, sections and elevations) must be on tracing linen of sufficient size to permit of the approval of the Council being endorsed thereon.

The scale to which drawings are made must be drawn thereon and not expressed in words; the north point must be indicated on all plans.

The site must be coloured pink, the proposed building red, existing buildings grey, and any land to be dedicated and left open for the use of the public blue.

The name of the person on whose behalf the application is made must be stated. Reference must be made to the section of the Act under which sanction is sought, and particulars must be furnished as to the nature of the application and the situation of the street, building or structure.

All drawings must be sent in duplicate.

II.—PARTICULARS AS TO DRAWINGS REQUIRED IN
EACH CASE.

(1) *New Streets, &c.,* Section 7 *and* Section 10.

Plans must be to a scale of 88 feet to the inch, and must be accompanied by longitudinal sections to the same horizontal scale, but to a vertical scale of 11 feet to the inch, showing the natural and intended surface levels of the streets (computed from ordnance or some other fixed datum), and by cross sections to a scale of 22 feet to the inch.

A key plan of the locality, showing the surrounding property, must also be sent.

The names proposed to be given to the streets must be submitted; they must be such as are not already in use.

In the event of the application being sanctioned, two additional copies of the plans will be required.

In the case of the widening of streets under Section 10 (4) sections will not be required.

(2) *Buildings within prescribed distances, lines of frontage, &c.,* Section 13, Section 17 *and* Section 22.

Plans must be to a scale of 22 feet to the inch, and must show the situation of the building in relation to others adjacent. The height and precise distance from the centre of the roadway of the proposed building and the width of the street are to be figured.

The names and addresses of the owners and occupiers of the nearest building on each side of the proposed building must also be sent.

In the event of an application being approved, an additional copy of the drawings will be required.

In the case of applications under Section 13 (5), the extent and height of the old buildings on the site must be shown to the same scale.

(3) *Space at rear of domestic buildings*, Section 41, *and open space about working-class dwellings not on the public way*, Section 42.

Plans and Sections must be to the scale of one-eighth of an inch to the foot; they must indicate the height of the proposed buildings in every part; there must also be a block plan to the scale of 22 feet to 1 inch, showing the adjoining premises, with the approximate height of any buildings thereon.

(4) *Open space at rear of domestic buildings on old sites.* Section 43.

Plans and sections to the scale of one-eighth of an inch to a foot, showing the height and extent of the previously existing buildings and certified by the District Surveyor, must be sent, together with plans and sections of the proposed new buildings to the same scale. The position and approximate height of any adjacent buildings must be indicated on a block plan to the scale of 22 feet to 1 inch.

(5) *Laying out new streets on a cleared area.* Section 44.

In addition to the plans required under Regulation II. (1) and (so far as any relaxation or modification of the rules of Part V. of the Act may be asked for) under II. (3) a plan will be required to the scale of 88 feet to 1 inch, showing the width of old streets on the area, and the extent and approximate height of all old buildings thereon, as well as of the proposed new streets and buildings.

(6) *Height of buildings.* Section 47 and Section 49.

A block plan to a scale of 22 feet to an inch, showing the position of the proposed building and of any adjacent buildings, and the width of the street.

Also a plan and sections to the scale of one-eighth of an inch to the foot, showing the height of the several parts of the building.

(7) *Timber in external walls*, Section 55, *and furnace chimney shafts*, Section 65.

Plans, sections and elevations to the scale of one-eighth of an inch to a foot, together with such details to a larger scale as may be necessary to show the construction.

A block plan to the scale of 22 feet to the inch, showing the position of the building.

(8) *Projections*, Section 73.

In addition to the drawings, &c. required by Regulation II. (2), a plan, section and side elevation to the scale of one-eighth of an inch to a foot. In the case of the application being approved, an additional copy of the drawings will be required.

(9) *Additional cubical extent*, Section 76, *and buildings for the supply of electricity*, Section 203.

A block plan to the scale of 22 feet to the inch, showing the position of the building and buildings adjacent.

Plans and sections to the scale of one-eighth of an inch to the foot, showing the height of the building in its various parts.

The use to which the various parts of the building are intended to be put are to be indicated, and any points bearing upon the question of liability to fire.

(10) *Special and temporary buildings and wooden structures.* Part VII.

Applications must be accompanied by a block plan of the premises, showing the position of the building or structure, and also by a plan, elevation and section to a scale of one-eighth of an inch to the foot, together with such details to a larger scale as may be necessary to show the construction.

A fee of 5s. must be paid to the cashier of the Council on depositing the application, and a further fee of 5s. on obtaining a notification of the order of the Council, and in no case will the work be allowed to proceed until the fees are paid.

Every application for an extension of the period for which the Council has allowed the use of a temporary building, must be accompanied by a certificate from the District Surveyor as to its condition, and as to its stability for such further period as may be applied for, and also as to any repairs which may be requisite.

In cases where the structure has existed for less than three years, and if the inspection be merely to ascertain that the building has not been altered as to condition or position, and to certify that an extension of time may be allowed, a fee of 10s. may be demanded and received by the District Surveyor.

In cases where the structure has existed for three years or more, and a certificate with regard to structural stability is required, a fee of 20s. may be demanded and received by the District Surveyor.

Naming of streets and numbering of houses. Part IV.

Persons laying out new streets or building rows of houses would facilitate their own operations with reference to leases and the numbering of houses required by the Council under the statute, by observing the following rules—

St. Paul's Cathedral is recognised as a central point, and the numbering of houses begins at the end or entrance of the street nearest to that building, except where a street leads from a main thoroughfare to a less important street, and then the numbering must start from the main thoroughfare.

Taking, therefore, the sides of a street as left and right (assuming that the back is towards St. Paul's) the odd numbers will be assigned to the left-hand side, and the even numbers to the right-hand side.

No name is to be used for a street unless with the approval of the Council; and it must be a name consisting, if possible, of one word, with the addition of "street," "road," or other like term, and not already in use within the county.

Only such streets as are leading thoroughfares of considerable length can be designated "roads."

No street under 50 feet in width can be called an "avenue."

The names "gardens" and "groves" can only be used when the terms seem appropriate.

Names in some way associated with the locality are preferred.

Names for terraces or places, or other blocks of houses, and sections of streets, usually known as subsidiary names are not recognised.

Any person interested in property affected by any order of the Council for re-naming streets or re-numbering houses is permitted, on application, to make a copy of the order and a tracing of the plan attached thereto; or a certified copy of the order and plan may be furnished to him on his paying the cost of making the same.

A fee of 1s. is to be charged to all persons seeking information involving a reference to the records with regard to orders for re-naming streets or re-numbering houses.

If a copy of an order and plan be required, there will be a further fee of not less than 1s. 6d.

A more extended plan may be obtained for a larger payment.

Copies of orders and plans are to be made in the superintending architect's department.

LONDON COUNTY COUNCIL.

BYELAWS MADE BY THE COUNCIL UNDER SECTION 39 (1) OF THE PUBLIC HEALTH (LONDON) ACT, 1891.

With respect to water-closets, earth-closets, privies, ashpits, cesspools and receptacles for dung, and the proper accessories thereof in connection with buildings, whether constructed before or after the passing of this Act.

I. Every person who shall hereafter construct a water-closet or earth-closet in connection with a building, shall construct such water-closet or earth-closet in such a position that, in the case of a water-closet, one of its sides at the least shall be an external wall, and in the case of an earth-closet two of its sides at the least shall be external walls, which external wall or walls shall abut immediately upon the street, or upon a yard or garden, or open space of not less than one hundred square feet of superficial area, measured horizontally at a point below the level of the floor of such closet. He shall not construct any such water-closet so that it is approached directly from any room used for the purpose of human habitation, or used for the manufacture, preparation or storage of food for man, or used as a factory, workshop or workplace, nor shall he construct any earth-closet so that it can be entered otherwise than from the external air.

He shall construct such water-closet so that on any side on which it would abut on a room intended for human habitation, or used for the manufacture, preparation or storage of food for man, or used as a factory, workshop or workplace, it shall be enclosed by a solid wall or partition of brick or other materials, extending the entire height from the floor to the ceiling.

He shall provide any such water-closet that is approached from the external air with a floor of hard smooth impervious material, having a fall to the door of such water-closet of half an inch to the foot.

He shall provide such water-closet with proper doors and fastenings.

Provided always that this byelaw shall not apply to any water-closet constructed below the surface of the ground and approached directly from an area or other open space available for purposes of ventilation, measuring at least forty superficial feet in extent, and having a distance across of not less than five feet, and not covered in otherwise than by a grating or railing.

II. Every person who shall construct a water-closet in connection with a building, whether the situation of such water-closet be or be not within or partly within such building, and every person who shall construct an earth-closet in connection with a building, shall construct in one of the walls of such water-closet or earth-closet which shall abut upon the public way, yard, garden or open space, as provided by the preceding byelaw, a window of such dimensions that an area of not less than two square feet, which may be the whole or part of such window, shall open directly into the external air.

He shall in addition to such window, cause such water-closet or earth-closet to be provided with adequate means of constant ventilation by at least one air-brick built in an external wall of such water-closet or earth-closet, or by an air-shaft, or by some other effectual method or appliance.

III. Every person who shall construct a water-closet in connection with a building, shall furnish such water-closet with a cistern of adequate capacity for the purpose of flushing, which shall be separate and distinct from any cistern used for drinking purposes, and shall be so constructed, fitted and placed as to admit of the supply of water for use in such water-closet so that there shall not be any direct connection between any service pipe upon the premises and any part of the apparatus of such water-closet other than such flushing cistern

Provided always that the foregoing requirement shall be deemed to be complied with in any case where the apparatus of a water-closet is connected for the purpose of flushing with a cistern of adequate capacity, which is used solely for flushing water-closets or urinals.

He shall construct or fix the pipe and union connecting such flushing cistern with the pan, basin or other receptacle with which such water-closet may be provided, so that such pipe and union shall not in any part have an internal diameter of less than one inch and a quarter.

He shall furnish such water-closet with a suitable apparatus for the effectual application of water to any pan, basin or other receptacle with which such apparatus may be connected and used, and for the effectual flushing and cleansing of such pan, basin or other receptacle, and for the prompt and effectual removal therefrom and from the trap connected therewith of any solid or liquid filth which may from time to time be deposited therein.

He shall furnish such water-closet with a pan, basin or other suitable receptacle of non-absorbent material, and of such shape, of such capacity, and of such mode of construction as to receive and contain a sufficient quantity of water, and to allow all filth which may from time to time be deposited in such pan, basin or receptacle, to fall free of the sides thereof and directly into the water received and contained in such pan, basin or receptacle.

He shall not construct or fix under such pan, basin or receptacle, any "container" or other similar fitting.

He shall construct or fix immediately beneath or in connection with such pan, basin or other suitable receptacle an efficient siphon trap, so constructed that it shall at all times maintain a sufficient water seal between such pan, basin or other suitable receptacle and any drain or soil pipe in connection therewith. He shall not construct or fix in or in connection with the water-closet apparatus any D trap or other similar trap.

If he shall construct any water-closet or shall fix or fit any trap to any existing water-closet or in connection with a soil pipe, which is itself in connection with any other water-closet, he shall cause the trap of every such water-closet to be ventilated into the open air at a point as high as the top of the soil pipe, or into the soil pipe at a point above the highest water-closet connected with such soil pipe, and so that such ventilating pipe shall have in all parts an internal diameter of not less than two inches, and shall be connected with the arm of the soil pipe at a point not less than three and not more than twelve inches from the highest part of the trap, and on that side of the water seal which is nearest to the soil pipe.

IV. Any person who shall provide a soil pipe in connection with a building to be hereafter erected, shall cause such soil pipe to be situated outside such building, and any person who shall provide or construct or refit a soil pipe in connection with an existing building shall, whenever practicable, cause such soil pipe to be situated outside such building, and in all cases where such soil pipe shall be situated within any building, shall construct such soil pipe in drawn lead, or of heavy cast iron jointed with molten lead and properly caulked.

He shall construct such soil pipe so that its weight in proportion to its length and internal diameter shall be as follows:—

Diameter.	Lead. Weight per 10-feet length. Not less than	Iron. Weight per 6-feet length. Not less than
3½ inches.	65 lbs.	48 lbs.
4 ,,	74 ,,	54 ,,
5 ,,	92 ,,	69 ,,
6 ,,	110 ,,	84 ,,

Every person who shall provide a soil pipe outside or inside a building shall cause such soil pipe to have an internal diameter of not less than three and a half inches, and to be continued upwards without diminution of its diameter, and (except where unavoidable) without any bend or angle being formed in such soil pipe to such a height and in such a position as to afford by means of the open end of such soil pipe a safe outlet for foul air, and so that such open end shall in all cases be above the highest part of the roof of the building to which the soil pipe is attached, and, where practicable, be not less than three feet above any window within twenty feet, measured in a straight line from the open end of such soil pipe.

He shall furnish the open end of such soil pipe with a wire guard covering, the openings in the meshes of which shall be equal to not less than the area of the open end of the soil pipe.

In all such cases where he shall connect a lead trap or

pipe with an iron soil pipe or drain he shall insert between such trap or pipe and such soil pipe or drain, a brass thimble, and he shall connect such lead trap or pipe with such thimble by means of a wiped or overcast joint, and he shall connect such thimble with the iron soil pipe or drain by means of a joint made with molten lead, properly caulked.

In all such cases where he shall connect a stoneware trap or pipe with a lead soil pipe, he shall insert between such stoneware trap or pipe and such soil pipe a brass socket or other similar appliance, and he shall connect such stoneware trap or pipe by inserting it into such socket, making the joint with Portland cement, and he shall connect such socket with the lead soil pipe by means of a wiped or overcast joint.

In all cases where he shall connect a stoneware trap or pipe with an iron soil pipe or drain, he shall insert such stoneware trap or pipe into a socket on such iron soil pipe or drain, making the joint with Portland cement.

He shall so construct such soil pipe that it shall not be directly connected with the waste of any bath, rain-water pipe, or of any sink other than that which is provided for the reception of urine or other excremental filth, and he shall construct such soil pipe so that there shall not be any trap in such soil pipe or between the soil pipe and any drain with which it is connected.

V. A person who shall newly fit or fix any apparatus in connection with any existing water-closet shall, as regards such apparatus and its connection with any soil pipe or drain, comply with such of the requirements of the foregoing byelaws as would be applicable to the apparatus so fitted or fixed if the water-closet were being newly constructed.

VI. Every person who shall construct an earth-closet in connection with a building shall furnish such earth-closet with a reservoir or receptacle, of suitable construction and of adequate capacity, for dry earth, and he shall construct and fix such reservoir or receptacle in such a manner and in such a position as to admit of ready access to such reservoir or receptacle for the purpose of depositing therein the necessary supply of dry earth.

He shall construct or fix in connection with such reservoir or receptacle suitable means or apparatus for the frequent and effectual application of a sufficient quantity of dry earth to any filth which may from time to time be deposited in any receptacle for filth constructed, fitted or used in, or in connection with, such earth-closet.

He shall construct such earth-closet so that the contents of such reservoir or receptacle may not at any time be exposed to any rainfall or to the drainage of any waste water or liquid refuse from any premises.

VII. Every person who shall construct an earth-closet in connection with a building shall construct such earth-closet for use in combination with a movable receptacle for filth.

He shall construct such earth-closet so as to admit of a movable receptacle for filth, of a capacity not exceeding two cubic feet, being placed and fitted beneath the seat in such a manner and in such a position as may effectually prevent the deposit upon the floor or sides of the space beneath such seat, or elsewhere than in such receptacle, of any filth which may from time to time fall or be cast through the aperture in such seat.

He shall construct such receptacle for filth in such a manner and in such a position as to admit of the frequent and effectual application of a sufficient quantity of dry earth to any filth which may be from time to time deposited in such receptacle for filth and in such a manner and in such a position as to admit of ready access for the purpose of removing the contents thereof.

He shall also construct such earth-closet so that the contents of such receptacle for filth may not at any time be exposed to any rainfall or to the drainage of any waste water or liquid refuse from any premises.

VIII. Every person who shall construct a privy in connection with a building shall construct such privy at a distance of twenty feet at the least from a dwelling-house or public building, or any building in which any person may be or may be intended to be employed in any manufacture, trade or business.

IX. A person who shall construct a privy in connection with a building shall not construct such privy within the distance of one hundred feet from any well, spring or stream of water used, or likely to be used, by man for drinking or domestic purposes, or for manufacturing drinks for the use of man, or otherwise in such a position as to render any such water liable to pollution.

X. Every person who shall construct a privy in connection with a building shall construct such privy in such a manner and in such a position as to afford ready means of access to such privy, for the purpose of cleansing such privy and of removing filth therefrom, and in such a manner and in such a position as to admit of all filth being removed from such privy, and from the premises to which such privy may belong, without being carried through any dwelling-house or public building, or any building in which any person may be or may be intended to be employed in any manufacture, trade or business.

XI. Every person who shall construct a privy in connection with a building, shall provide such privy with a sufficient opening for ventilation as near to the top as practicable and communicating directly with the external air.

He shall cause the floor of such privy to be flagged or paved with hard tiles or other non-absorbent material, and he shall construct such floor so that it shall be in every part thereof at a height of not less than six inches above the level of the surface of the ground adjoining such privy, and so that such floor shall have a fall or inclination towards the door of such privy of half an inch to the foot.

XII. Every person who shall construct a privy in connection with a building shall construct such privy for use in combination with a movable receptacle for filth, and shall construct over the whole area of the space immediately beneath the seat of such privy a floor of flagging or asphalte or some suitable composite material, at a height of not less than three inches above the level of the surface of the ground adjoining such privy; and he shall cause the whole extent of each side of such space between the floor and the seat, other than any part that may be occupied by any door or other opening therein, to be constructed of flagging, slate or good brickwork, at least nine inches thick, and rendered in good cement or asphalted.

He shall construct the seat of such privy, the aperture in such seat, and the space beneath such seat, of such dimensions as to admit of a movable receptacle for filth, of a capacity not exceeding two cubic feet, being placed and fitted beneath such seat in such a manner and in such a position as may effectually prevent the deposit upon the floor or sides of the space beneath such seat, or elsewhere than in such receptacle, of any filth which may from time to time fall or be cast through the aperture in such seat.

He shall construct such privy so that for the purpose of cleansing the space beneath the seat, or of removing therefrom or placing or fitting therein an appropriate receptacle for filth, there shall be a door or other opening in the back or one of the sides thereof capable of being opened from the outside of the privy, or in any case where such a mode of construction may be impracticable, so that for the purposes aforesaid the whole of the seat of the privy or a sufficient part thereof may be readily moved or adjusted.

XIII. A person who shall construct a privy in connection with a building shall not cause or suffer any part of the space under the seat of such privy, or any part of any receptacle for filth in or in connection with such privy, to communicate with any drain.

XIV. Every person who shall intend to construct any water-closet, earth-closet or privy, or to fit or fix in, or in connection with, any water-closet, earth-closet or privy, any apparatus or any trap or soil pipe, shall, before executing any such works, give notice in writing to the clerk of the Sanitary Authority.

XV. Every owner of an earth-closet or privy existing at the date of the confirmation of these byelaws shall, before the expiration of six months from and after such date of confirmation, cause the same to be reconstructed in such manner that its position, structure and apparatus shall comply with such of the requirements of the foregoing byelaws as are applicable to earth-closets or privies newly constructed.

XVI. When any person shall provide an ashpit in connection with a building, he shall cause the same to consist of one or more movable receptacles sufficient to contain the house refuse which may accumulate during any period not exceeding one week. Each of such receptacles shall be constructed of metal and shall be provided with one or more suitable handles and cover. The capacity of each of such receptacles shall not exceed two cubic feet.

Provided that the requirement as to the size of each of such receptacles shall not apply to any person who shall construct such receptacle or receptacles in connection with any premises to which there is attached as part of the conditions of tenancy the right to dispose of house refuse in an ashpit used in common by the occupiers of several tenancies, but in no case shall such ashpit be of greater capacity than is required to enable it to contain the refuse which may accumulate during any period not exceeding one week.

XVII. The occupier of any premises who shall use any ashpit shall, if such ashpit consist of a movable receptacle, cause such receptacle to be kept in a covered place or to be properly covered, so that it shall not be exposed to rainfall, and if such ashpit consist of a fixed receptacle, he shall cause the same to be kept properly covered.

XVIII. Where the Sanitary Authority have arranged for the daily removal of house refuse in their district, or in any part thereof, the owner of any premises in such district or part thereof shall provide an ashpit which shall consist of one or more movable receptacles, sufficient to contain the house refuse which may accumulate during any period not exceeding three days, which the Sanitary Authority may determine, and of which the Sanitary Authority shall give notice by public announcement in their district. Each of such receptacles shall be constructed of metal, and provided with one or more suitable handles and cover. The capacity of each of such receptacles shall not exceed two cubic feet.

Provided always that this byelaw shall not apply to the owner of any premises until the expiration of three months after the Sanitary Authority have publicly notified their intention to adopt a system of daily collection of house refuse in that part of their district which comprises such premises.

XIX. Where any receptacle shall have been provided as

an ashpit for any premises in pursuance of any byelaw in that behalf, no person shall deposit the house refuse which may accumulate on such premises in any ashpit that does not comply with the requirements of these byelaws.

XX. Every person who shall construct a cesspool in connection with a building shall construct such cesspool at a distance of one hundred feet at the least from a dwelling-house or public building, or any building in which any person may be, or may be intended to be, employed in any manufacture, trade or business.

XXI. A person who shall construct a cesspool in connection with a building shall not construct such cesspool within the distance of one hundred feet from any well, spring or stream of water.

XXII. Every person who shall construct a cesspool in connection with a building shall construct such cesspool in such a manner and in such a position as to afford ready means of access to such cesspool, for the purpose of cleansing such cesspool and of removing the contents thereof, and in such a manner and in such a position as to admit of the contents of such cesspool being removed therefrom, and from the premises to which such cesspool may belong, without being carried through any dwelling house or public building, or any building in which any person may be, or may be intended to be, employed in any manufacture, trade or business.

He shall not in any case construct such cesspool so that it shall have, by drain or otherwise, any means of communication with any sewer or any overflow outlet.

XXIII. Every person who shall construct a cesspool in connection with a building shall construct such cesspool of good brickwork bedded and grouted in cement, properly rendered inside with cement, and with a backing of at least nine inches of well-puddled clay around and beneath such brickwork, and so that such cesspool shall be perfectly watertight.

He shall also cause such cesspool to be arched or otherwise properly covered over, and to be provided with adequate means of ventilation.

XXIV. A person shall not use as a receptacle for dung any receptacle so constructed or placed that one of its sides shall be formed by the wall of any room used for human habitation, or under a dwelling-house, factory, workshop or workplace, and he shall not use any receptacle in such a situation that it would be likely to cause a nuisance or become injurious or dangerous to health.

XXV. Every owner of any existing receptacle for dung shall, before the expiration of six months from the date of the confirmation of these byelaws, and every person who shall construct a receptacle for dung, shall cause such receptacle to be so constructed that its capacity shall not be greater than two cubic yards, and so that the bottom or floor thereof shall not, in any case, be lower than the surface of the ground adjoining such receptacle.

He shall so construct such receptacle that a sufficient part of one of its sides shall be readily removable for the purpose of facilitating cleansing,

He shall also cause such receptacle to be constructed in such a manner and of such materials, and to be maintained at all times in such a condition as to prevent any escape of the contents thereof, or any soakage therefrom, into the ground or into the wall of any building.

He shall cause such receptacle to be so constructed that no rain or water can enter therein, and so that it shall be freely ventilated into the external air.

Provided that a person who shall construct a receptacle for dung, the whole of the contents of which are removed not less frequently than every forty-eight hours, shall not be required to construct such receptacle so that its capacity shall not be greater than two cubic yards.

And provided that a person who shall construct a receptacle for dung, which shall contain only dung of horses, asses or mules with stable litter, and the whole of the contents of which are removed not less frequently than every forty-eight hours, may, instead of all other requirements of this byelaw, construct a metal cage, and shall beneath such metal cage adequately pave the ground at a level not lower than the surrounding ground, and in such a manner and to such an extent as will prevent any soakage into the ground; and if such cage be placed near to or against any building he shall adequately cement the wall of such building in such a manner and to such an extent as will prevent any soakage from the dung within or upon such receptacle into the wall of such building.

XXVI. The occupier of any premises shall cause every water-closet belonging to such premises to be thoroughly cleansed from time to time, as often as may be necessary for the purpose of keeping such water-closet in a cleanly condition.

The occupier of any premises shall once at least in every week cause every earth-closet, privy and receptacle for dung belonging to such premises to be emptied and thoroughly cleansed.

The occupier of any premises shall once at least in every three months cause every cesspool belonging to such premises to be emptied and thoroughly cleansed.

Provided that where two or more lodgers in a lodging house are entitled to the use in common of any water-closet, earth-closet, privy, cesspool or receptacle for dung, the landlord shall cause such water-closet, earth-closet, privy, cesspool or receptacle for dung to be cleansed and emptied as aforesaid.

The landlord or owner of any lodging-house shall provide and maintain in connection with such house, water-closet, earth-closet or privy accommodation in the proportion of not less than one water-closet, earth-closet or privy for every twelve persons.

For the purposes of this byelaw "a lodging-house" means a house or part of a house which is let in lodgings or occupied by members of more than one family. "Landlord" in relation to a house or part of a house which is let in lodgings, or occupied by members of more than one family, means the person (whatever may be the nature or extent of his interest) by whom or on whose behalf such house or part of a house is let in lodgings or for occupation by members of more than one family, or who for the time being receives or is entitled to receive the profits arising from such letting. "Lodger" in relation to a house or part of a house which is let in lodgings or occupied by members of more than one family, means a person to whom any room or rooms in such house or part of a house may have been let as a lodging or for his use or occupation.

Nothing in this byelaw shall extend to any common lodging-house.

XXVII. The owner of any premises shall maintain in proper condition of repair every water-closet, earth-closet, privy, ashpit, cesspool and receptacle for dung, and the proper accessories thereof belonging to such premises.

PENALTIES.

XXVIII. Every person who shall offend against any of the foregoing byelaws shall be liable for every such offence to a penalty of five pounds, and in the case of a continuing offence to a further penalty of forty shillings for each day after written notice of the offence from the Sanitary Authority. Provided, nevertheless, that the Court before whom any complaint may be made or any proceedings may be taken in respect of any such offence may, if the Court think fit, adjudge the payment as a penalty of any sum less than the full amount of the penalty imposed by this byelaw.

INDEX.

A.

ABSTRACT of Building Act, 1-27

ACCESSES AND STAIRS, 74

ACT, LONDON BUILDING, 1894, 29-167
    abstract of portion relating to building, 1-27
    commencement of operation, 31
    differences between, and previous Acts, xxi
    extent, 31
    list of sections, vii-xviii
    regulations as to applications for sanction under, 232

ACTS repealed, 29
    still in force, xix
    supplementary, xix

ADDITIONS to buildings, 145, 147

ADJOINING OWNER liable for expenses, 99
    rights of, 87, 90, 91
    to have account of expenses, 99

AGREEMENT between landlord and tenant as to payment of expenses, 184

ALTERATION of names of streets, 52, 53

ALTERATIONS in buildings, 147

APPEAL, TRIBUNAL OF, 131
    duration of office, 131
    enforcement of decision, 133
    fees to be paid over to Council, 133
    may state case for High Court, 132
    officers and assistants, 131
    power of Council to support decisions of its officers before, 132
    procedure and fees, 132
    removal of members, 131
    remuneration of members, 131
    vacancies, 131

APPLICATION of Building Act, 143

APPLICATION to Council, regulations as to, 232

APPROVAL to plans, mode of giving, 135

ARCHES UNDER PUBLIC WAYS, 76

ARCHITECT, SUPERINTENDING, appointment, 115
    applications under Building Act to be made to, 232

ARC LAMPS in theatres, 228
AREAS, dimensions permissible, 201
ASHPITS, byelaws as to, 215, 216
AUDIT OF ACCOUNTS of surveyors' fees, 124
AVENUE, requisite width for street so called, 237

B.

BANK OF ENGLAND exempt, 142
BARGEBOARDS, xxviii
BASEMENTS, lighting and ventilation of, 54
BATTERIES, electric lighting, in theatres, 229
BOILERS in theatres, 220, 223
BREACH OF BYELAWS, penalty for, 177
    rules as to, 67
BRESSUMMERS, xxvii
BRICK AND STONE WALLS, byelaw as to construction, 208
BRIDGES, 142
BUILDING, definition of, xxi
    frontages, lines of, 49-51, 233
    setting back on re-erection, 49
BUILDING OWNER, may recover expenses from adjoining owner, 99
    rights of, 88, 94
    to underpin adjoining building, 94
BUILDINGS, cubical extent of, 80, 235
    domestic, thickness of walls, 153
    erected before commencement of Building Act, 147
    in progress, 148
    not public or of warehouse class, thickness of walls, 153
    not to be made over sewers without consent, 178
    one-storey, xxix
    separation of, xxix, 79
    uniting, 81
    warehouse class, thickness of walls, 157
BYELAWS, Council may make, 125
    dispensation from, 210
    exemption of City, 127
    evidence of, 178
    existing, Plates 13 to 19
    in force, 207
    penalties under, 210
    power of vestries, &c., to make, 177
    publication of, 177
    repeal of, 207
    under Building Act, 125
    under Public Health Act, 238
    under repealed Acts, 149
    water-closets, &c., 238

INDEX. 253

C.

CANAL works, exemption of, 143
CASES FOR PLANTS, 145
CATTLE MARKETS, 143
CELLARS under streets, regulations as to, 172
    to be repaired by owners or occupiers, 173
CENTRE OF ROADWAY, xxvi
    buildings within prescribed distance, 233
CESSPOOLS, byelaws as to, 247
    cleansing, byelaw as to, 248
CHAMBERS, SETS OF, limitation of area, xxix
CHIMNEYS, xxix
    and flues, rules as to, 69, Plate 15
    furnace, 72, 235
    openings, xxx, 70
    rendering on outside face, xxx, 70.
    shafts, xxx, 235
CHURCHES, &c., staircases in, 83
CITY, exemption of, 51, 127, 200
CLEARED AREA, rearrangement of streets on, 61, 234
COMBINED DRAINAGE of blocks of houses, 169
CONCRETE BUILDINGS, byelaws as to construction, 209, 210
CONDITIONS, power of Council to impose, 134
CONDUCTORS, electric lighting, 225, 226
CONSERVATORS OF THAMES, buildings of, 143
CONSTRUCTION OF BUILDINGS, 65-87
CONVERSION OF BUILDINGS, 147
    into public buildings, 83
COPIES of orders and plans, 237
CORNICES, wood, xxviii
CORRIDORS in theatres, 218
COSTS AND EXPENSES, payment by owner or occupier, 183, 184
COUNCIL, COUNTY, byelaws and regulations in force, 207
    byelaws as to water-closets, &c , 238
    fees payable to, 165
    fire authority, 205
    (General Powers) Act, 1890, 193
    power to impose conditions, 134
    regulations under Building Act, 232
COUNTY COURT, powers and appeal, 127
COURTS within building, 61
COVENT GARDEN MARKET, 143
CROSS WALLS, 160
CUBICAL EXTENT of buildings, 80, 235
    consent to increased, 81

D.

Damp course, byelaw as to, 208
Dangerous and noxious businesses, 105
   building near, 105
Dangerous structures, 100
   Court may make order, 102
   expenses, 102
   fees to surveyor, 103
   notice to owner, 101
   proceedings, 101
   recovery of expenses and fees, 103, 104, 105
   removal of inmates, 103
   sale of, 1, 2. 103
   to be surveyed, 100
   surveyor's certificate, 100
   within City, 100
Deduction by owner paying rent where expenses deducted from rent paid to him, 184
Definitions, 31
   building, xxi
   domestic building, 54
   front or rear of building, 62
   general line of buildings, 50
      appeal against, 50
   what street a building is in, 51
Demolition of buildings by Council, 128
Detached buildings, exemption of, 144
Dispensation from byelaws, 210
Dilapidated Structures, removal of, 103
Disagreement between district surveyor and builder, 234
Distillery not noxious business, 108
District surveyors, Council may appoint assistant, 117
   Council may proceed on behalf of, 123
   duties as to byelaws, 209
   disagreement between, and builder, 234
   duties with regard to excavations, 213
   examinations for, 117
   fees to, by builders and owners, 122
      by Council, 122
      periods when entitled to, 122
      for new buildings, 161
      for additions or alterations, 162
      for chimneys, 162
      for certifying plans, 162
      for wooden and temporary structures, 163

DISTRICT SURVEYORS—*continued*
  fees for dangerous structures, 163
    for special services, 164
    for inspection under byelaws, 209
  may appoint deputy, 117
  may give notice to produce plans, &c., 210
  must have an office, 117
  notice of irregularity, 120
  notice of objection, 120
  not to act in case of buildings under own superintendence, 117
  power of Council to pay salaries, 123
  power of entry, 119
  powers of Council with regard to, 116
  returns by, 124
  to enforce Act, 118
  to notify irregularities, 124
  to supervise buildings, 116

DOCK COMPANIES' BUILDINGS, 144

DOMESTIC BUILDING, definition of, 54
  height of, 54-61
  on old sites, 60, 234
  open spaces at rear, 54-61, 234, Plate 19

DOORS in theatres, 221

DRAINAGE, approval of, by vestry or district board, 171
  combined, provision for, 169
  temporary, 181

DRAINING INTO SEWER, 171
  in unauthorised manner, and penalty, 171, 172

DRAINS, faulty, notice of, 172
  inspection of, power to authorise, 172
  no house to be built without, 170
  power of vestry to execute works, 172
  vestry or district board may compel construction, 168

DRAWINGS, regulations as to, 232, 233
  copies, 237

DRESSING-ROOMS in theatres, 216

DUNG, RECEPTACLES FOR, byelaws as to, 248
  cleansing, byelaw as to, 249

DWELLING-HOUSES, height of rooms, xxxi

E.

EARTH-CLOSETS, byelaw as to, 238, 240, 241
  cleansing, byelaw as to, 249
  reconstruction of, byelaw as to, 245
  proposed, notice to be given, 245

EASEMENTS, interference with, 99

ELECTRIC LIGHTING in theatres, 225
   certificate, 225
   plant, 229
   supervision, 230
ELECTRICITY, buildings for supply of, 146, 235
EMBANKMENT WALLS, 142
ENCLOSURES in theatres, 220
ENCROACHMENTS ON SEWERS, 181
   penalty for, 182
ENGINES AND BOILERS in theatres, 220
ENTRANCES AND EXITS in theatres, 217
ENTRY, power of owner, 191
EXCAVATIONS, byelaw as to filling up, 212
   fee to district surveyor, 213
   penalty for breach of byelaw as to, 213
EXEMPTION, duration of, 147
EXEMPTIONS from Building Act, 142
   from Acts, 191, 192
   School Board buildings, 49
EXHIBITION BUILDINGS, 142
EXPENSES, account to be delivered to adjoining owner, 99
   agreement between landlord and tenant as to payment of, 181
   as to party structures, 96
   building owner may recover, 99
   incurred by Council, 134
   may be required from owner or occupier, 183
   payment by owners, 129
   with regard to dangerous and neglected structures, recovery of, 104
EXTERNAL AND PARTY WALLS, height of, 152
   timber in, 235

F.

FACTORY AND WORKSHOP ACT, 1891, 205
FACTORIES, provision against fire, 205
FEES for inspection under byelaws, 209
   payable to Council, 165
   to district surveyors, 122, 161
      audit of accounts of, 124
FILLING UP EXCAVATIONS, byelaw as to, 212
FIRE ALARM in theatres, 224
FIRE, means of escape from, to be provided in high buildings, 69
   precautions in theatres, 224
   prevention, authority for, 204, 205
      in theatres, &c., regulations as to, 214

FIRE, provision against, in factories, 205
  recovery of expenses, 206
FIRE-RESISTING materials, what to be deemed, 160
FLOOR of pit in theatres, 217
  under and over ovens, &c., 73, 74
FLUES, xxix
FLUSHING CISTERN, byelaw as to, 239
FOOTINGS of walls, 152
FOUNDATIONS, byelaw as to, 207
FURNACES, chimneys of, 72, 235
  floors under and above, 73, 74

G.

GANGWAYS in theatres, 219
GAS in theatres, 221
GAS COMPANIES, saving rights of, 146
GASWORKS, buildings, 143
  not noxious business, 108
GENERAL LINE of buildings, conditions as to building in front of, 50, 51
  notice of definition, 50
GOVERNMENT BUILDINGS, exemption of, 145
GRADIENT, fixing of, xxvii
GRAVEL SUBSOIL, byelaw as to, 207
GREENHOUSES, 145
GUILDHALL, 142
GULLY HOLES, 168

H.

HABITABLE ROOMS, rules, 74, Plate 16
HANDRAILS in theatres, 219
HEARTHS, xxx, 70
HEIGHT OF BUILDINGS, limitation of, 55, 62-65, 234
  procedure where increased, 63
HEIGHT of storey, 152
HISTORICAL BUILDINGS, 134
HOARDINGS, xxxi
  lighting, 193
  penalty for not erecting, 175
  to be licensed by vestry or district board, 175
  to be lighted, 175

HOARDINGS—*continued*
    to be erected during repairs, 175
    to be erected and maintained, 193
    unauthorised or inadequate, may be removed and sold by vestry, 176
HOLLOW WALLS, xxx, 151
HOUSES, numbering, 236

I.

INNS OF COURT, buildings belonging to, 146
INSPECTION OF DRAINS, power to authorise, 172
INSULATION RESISTANCE in theatres, 230
INTERFERING WITH SEWERS, 182
    penalty for, 182
IRON BUILDINGS, 235
IRONWORK in theatres, 219

J.

JETTIES, 142

L.

LAMPS, OIL, in theatres, 224
LANTERN LIGHTS, xxxii, Plate 14
LEGAL PROCEEDINGS, 127
    by surveyor, 127
    county court, powers and appeal, 127
LENGTH OF WALLS, 152
LICENSE, provisional, for new theatre premises, 190
LIMELIGHT TANKS, 220
LINE OF BUILDING FRONTAGE, 49–51
    general, plans, &c., regulations as to, 232
    when exceeded, proceedings by local authority, 129
LOCAL AUTHORITIES, saving powers of, 148
LODGER, definition of, 249
LODGING HOUSE, definition of, 249
    water-closets, &c., in, byelaws as to, 249, 250
LOW-LYING LAND, dwelling-houses on, regulations for, 108

M.

MANSION HOUSE, 142
METROPOLIS MANAGEMENT AND BUILDING ACTS AMENDMENT ACT, 1878, 186
    regulations with respect to prevention from fire in theatres, &c., 214

INDEX.

METROPOLIS LOCAL MANAGEMENT AMENDMENT ACT, 1862, 179
METROPOLIS MANAGEMENT ACT, 1855, 168
   clauses still in force, relating to buildings, 168
   portions repealed, 168
METROPOLIS MANAGEMENT AMENDMENT ACT, 1890, 195
MEWS, 64
MUSIC-HALLS AND THEATRES, power to require remedy of structural defects, 187
   (*See* THEATRES)

N.

NAMES OF STREETS, affixing by local authority, 52
   alteration of, 52, 53
   choice of, 236
   register of, 53
   regulations as to, 233, 236
   renaming, 237
NAMING AND NUMBERING STREETS, 52
   copies of orders, 235
   regulations for, 233, 235
NEGLECT to carry out works on order of vestry, 180
NEGLECTED STRUCTURES, 103
   removal of, 103
NEW BUILDINGS, erection of, at less than prescribed distance, 17
   notice to comply with section 13, 45
   position with reference to streets, 43
   sanction to construction at less than prescribed distance, 48
NEW STREETS, appeal, 48
   compensation to owners, 46
   naming, regulations as to, 236
   on cleared area, 234
   plans, &c., regulations as to, 237
   paving, 173
   supply of regulations, 48
NOTICE as to proposed water-closet, &c., 215
   by builder to surveyor, 118
   of definition of general line of buildings, 56
   of objection to proposed works, 119
   proceedings on non-compliance with, 121
   to be evidence of intended works, 119
   to comply with section 13, 45
   to produce plans, &c., 210
   to remove projections, 175
   to vestry or district board before commencing building or drain, 171
   to vestry or district board of new building or taking down, 193
   penalty for failure to give, 193
   works may be commenced without, in case of emergency, 119
   of irregularity, 120
   penalty for not giving, 183
   service of, 133
   to be in writing, 133

NOXIOUS BUSINESS, building near, 106
    old, 106
NUMBERING HOUSES, 236
    copies of orders and plans, 236
    Council may carry out, 53

O.

OBSTRUCTIONS IN STREETS, preventing, 137
OCCUPIER, conditions of payment of costs or expenses by, 183
OFFENCES AGAINST BUILDING ACT, 137
OFFICERS UNDER REPEALED ENACTMENTS, 150
OIL LAMPS in theatres, 224
OLD SITES, domestic buildings on, 234
ONE-STOREY BUILDINGS, xxix
OPENINGS in roof, xxviii
    into sewers, 179
OWNERS not to be found, consent on behalf of, 135
    payment of expenses by, 129
    power of entry, 135
    power to enter houses, &c., to comply with notices, 191
    rights of, 87
    security to be given by, 95
    settlement of difference between, 91
    (*See* ADJOINING AND BUILDING OWNER)

P.

PARAPETS, height and thickness of, 67
PARTY ARCHES over passages, &c., 75
PARTY STRUCTURE, ownership, 99
    rule as to expenses, 96
PARTY FENCE WALLS, exemption of, 144
PARTY WALLS, chases in, 68
    easements relating to, 99
    height above roof, 67
    partially destroyed, 147
    rights of owners, and procedure with regard to, 87 *et seq.*
    top of, byelaw as to, 208
    when so deemed, 67
PASSAGES in theatres, 218
PAVING NEW STREETS, provisions for, 173
PENALTIES and expenses, recovery of, 200
    application of, 128
    breach of byelaw as to plastering and excavations, 213
    breach of byelaws, 177

PENALTIES—*continued*
    breach of byelaws to be approved by Secretary of State, 177
    building near dangerous or noxious business, 140
    commencing or altering street without sanction, 137
    contravening building regulations, 138
    contravening regulations as to buildings in low-lying land, 110
    contravention by workmen, &c., 141
    draining into sewer in unauthorised manner, 172
    failure to give notice to vestry of new building, &c., 193
    encroachments on sewers, 182
    erecting obstruction, 138
    establishing dangerous or noxious business, 140
    failure to carry out drainage, 169
    failure to make good, 139
    failure to serve building notice, &c., 141
    general rule, 142
    hindering builder, 141
    hindering district surveyor, 141
    hindering persons from complying with order, 141
    hindering traffic, 138
    hindrance and wilful damage, 139
    illegal conversion or employment of building, 142
    interfering with sewers, 182
    making sewers without or contrary to plans approved, 196, 197
    neglecting notices, 138
    neglect to carry out works on order of vestry, 180
    non-compliance with conditions imposed by Council, 110
    non-compliance with order of County Court, 141
    non-compliance with requirements with regard to theatres, &c., 188, 190
    non-removal of projections, 174
    not erecting hoards, 175
    not giving certain notices, 183
    offences against Building Act, 137 *et seq.*
    offences against byelaws under Public Health Act, 1891, 250
    recovery of, 191
    refusing to admit or hindering purchaser of materials sold under Act, 139
    remission of, by Justices, 177
    removing subsoil, 199
        surveyor of vestry to see that conditions are observed, 200
    sky signs, unauthorised, 140
    under byelaws, 210
    underground rooms, unauthorised, 202
PERMISSIVE POWERS, objectionable, xxvii
PIERS, 142
PIPES for hot air, &c., 73
PLANS AND DOCUMENTS, ownership of, 135
PLANS AND SECTIONS, byelaw as to deposit of, 210
PLASTERING, byelaw as to, 212
    duties of district surveyor, 213
    fee to district surveyor, 213
    penalty for breach of byelaw as to, 213

PLANT, electric lighting, in theatres, 229
POWER OF ENTRY TO OWNER, 155
PRIVATE BUILDINGS, thickness of walls, xxxiii
    exempted, Plate 18
PRIVATE ROADS of railway company, 48
PRIVIES, byelaw as to reconstruction of, 245
    cleansing, byelaw as to, 249
    proposed, notice to be given, 245
    regulations as to, 242
PROCEEDINGS, limitation of time for, 135
PROJECTIONS, 76, 235
    additional drawings required, 235
    compensation for removal of, 175
    limitation of, xxviii
    notice to remove, 174
    penalty for non-removal, 174
    vestry or district board may remove, 174
    when owners to remove, 174
PROSCENIUM wall, 217
    opening, 218
PUBLIC BUILDINGS, construction, 82
    conversion into, 83
    thickness of walls, xxxiv
PUBLIC HEALTH (LONDON) ACT, 1861, 201
PUBLIC HEALTH ACT, 1891, byelaws under, 238
    penalties for offences against, 250
PUBLIC RESORT, places of. See THEATRES

Q.

QUAYS, 142

R.

RAILWAY ARCHES, buildings under, 84
RAILWAY BUILDINGS, exempt from Parts of Act, 87, 143
RAILWAY COMPANIES, exemption from Act, 51
    position with regard to repairs of road not being a street, 196
RAISING STOREY to comply with Act, 64
REARRANGEMENT OF STREETS on cleared area, 61
RECESSES AND OPENINGS in walls, xxxi, 65, Plate 13
REGISTER OF ALTERATIONS in names of streets, 53
REGISTER OF CONDITIONAL CONSENTS, 51
RESISTANCES in theatres, 228
REPEAL of previous enactments, 149

INDEX. 263

REPEALED ACTS, references to, 150
REPEALED ENACTMENTS, schedule of, 166
   officers under, 150
RIGHTS OF OWNERS, 87
RIVER WORKS, 142
ROAD, not being a street, vestry may repair, 195
   railway companies and, 196
   use of designation, 237
ROADWAY, centre of, xxvi
ROOFS, construction of, 69
   inclination of, xxix, 69
   limitation of number of storeys in, xxviii, 69
   openings in, compulsory, xxviii
   over stage, 218
   removal of, not to affect proceedings, 137
   storeys in, 69
ROYAL EXCHANGE, 142

S.

SALE OF MATERIALS of demolished buildings by Council, 128
SANITARY AUTHORITY, certificate and inspection of fire provision by, 205
SANITARY OFFICERS, duties as regards underground dwellings, 203
SCENE DOCK, 220
SCHOOL BOARD BUILDINGS, exemption of, 49
SECURITY TO BE GIVEN BY OWNERS, 95
SEPARATION OF BUILDINGS, xxix, 70
SESSIONS HOUSES, 143
SETTING BACK BUILDING on re-erection, 49
SEWERS, apportionment of costs among owners, 198
   buildings over, 178
   encroachments on, 181
      penalty for, 182
   interfering with, 182
   openings into, 179
   penalty for making without or contrary to plans approved, 196, 197
SHEDS, xxvii, 151
SHOP FRONT PROJECTIONS, 77, Plate 17
SITES OF BUILDINGS, byelaw as to, 207
SKYLIGHTS in theatres, 220
SKY SIGNS, alteration of, 113
   appeal against refusal, 114
   definition, 110
   district surveyor to report on, 111
   forfeiture of license, 114

SKY SIGNS—*continued*
 prohibition of future, 111
 regulation of existing, 111
 removal, 114
 renewal of license, 111
 surveyor's certificate, 112
  notice of refusal, 113
 within City, 115

SMALL BUILDINGS, exemption of, 144

SPECIAL BUILDINGS, 235

SOIL PIPES, byelaw as to, 241

SPACE AT REAR of domestic buildings, 54, Plate 19

STABLES, 64

STAGE, lighting, 228
 switchboard, 229

STAIRCASES in churches, 83
 in theatres, 218
 ventilation of, 74

STOREYS, height of, 152
 above 60 feet, 69
 limitation of number, xxviii, 69
 of exceptional height, 156
 raising, to comply with Act, 64
 restriction of height in relation to thickness of walls, 156, 159

STRUCTURE defined, 100

STREETS, adaptation of ways for, 40
  grounds for refusing, 41
 formation and widening of, 38–49
 greater width may be required, 42
 grounds for refusal to sanction plans, 38
 naming and numbering of, 52, 236
 new, xxvii, 38
 position of new buildings, 43
 sanction to formation of, 38
 evidence of commencement of, 38

SUBSOIL OF STREET, regulations as to removal of, 198

SUPERINTENDING ARCHITECT, appointment of, 115
 may appoint deputy, 116
 applications under Building Act to be made to, 232

SURPLUS OF SALE, payment into court, 129

SWITCHBOARD, stage, 229

SWITCHES in theatres, 227

T.

TEMPORARY BUILDINGS, 85, 86, 235
TEMPORARY DRAINAGE, 181
TERRACES, naming, 237

THEATRES, &c., additions to, 223
  alterations to, 223
  boilers, 220, 223
  doors, 221
  dressing-rooms, 216
  certificate, control of, 231
  corridors, 218
  electric lighting, 225 *et seq.*
    certificate, 225
    supervision, 230
  enclosures, 220
  engines and boilers, 220
  entrances and exits, 217
  fire alarm, 224
  fire precautions, 224
  floor of pit, 217
  gangways, 219
  gas, 221
  handrails, 219
  ironwork, 219
  lamps and candles, 224
  limelight tanks, 220
  new, regulations concerning, 189
  notices on exits and non-exits, 224
  not to be constructed beneath or above any other building, 216
  passages, 218
  person responsible for carrying out regulations, 231
  plan of electric wiring, 231
  power to enter and inspect, 190
    modify regulations, 231
    require remedy of structural defects, 187
      penalty, 188
      appeal, 188
  proscenium wall, 217
    opening of, 218
  provisional license for, 190
  regulations as to fire prevention in, 214
  roof, 218
  scene dock, 220
  site, 215
  skylights, 220
  staircases, 219
  structural regulations, 214
  tiers, number and height of, 217
  ventilation, 222
  vestibules, 217
  walls, 216
  warming, 222
  water supply, 223
  windows overlooking, 216
  workshops, 219

THICKENING OF WALLS, 153

THICKNESS, extra, of certain walls, 151
    of walls in buildings not public nor of warehouse class, 153
TIERS in theatres, number and height of, 217
TIMBER in external walls, 66
    piles of loose, 87
TOP OF PARTY WALL, byelaw as to, 208
TRANSFORMERS in theatres, 230

U.

UNDERGROUND DWELLINGS, closing of, 204
    definition of, 203
    duty of sanitary officer, 203
    regulations as to, 201
    relief from regulations, 202
    unauthorised, penalty for letting, 202
UNDERPINNING by building owner, 94
    rules for, 153
UNITING BUILDINGS, 81

V.

VACATIONS, expiry of periods in, 130
VAULTS UNDER STREETS, regulations as to, 172
    to be repaired by owners or occupiers, 173
VENTILATING VALVES, 145
VENTILATION of staircases, 74
    theatres, 222
VESTIBULES IN THEATRES, 217

W.

WALLS, classification of, xxxii
    construction of, 151
    cross, 160
    external and party, height of, 152
    external, timber in, 66
    extra thickness of certain, 151
    footings of, 152
    hollow, xxx, 151
    length of, 152
    materials, byelaw as to, 208
    of exceptional materials, warehouse class, 159
    of public buildings, xxxiv
    other than brick or stone, 151
    of underground rooms, 201
    recesses and openings, 65
    structure and thickness, 65

WALLS—*continued*
    theatres, &c., 216
    thickening of, 153
    thickness of, xxxiii, Plates 1 to 12
    in buildings not public, nor of warehouse class, xxix, 153
    warehouse class, xxxiv, 157

WAREHOUSE class of buildings, increase of cubical extent of, xxviii
    rules concerning walls, xxxiv, 157

WARMING APPARATUS in theatres, 222

WATER-CLOSETS, byelaw as to, 236
    cleansing, byelaw as to, 247
    in lodging-houses, byelaws as to, 249, 250
    proposed, notice to be given, 245

WATER SUPPLY in theatres, 223

WHARVES, 142

WORKING CLASS DWELLINGS, re-erected on old site, 64
    open space about, 58, 231

WINDOWS in roofs, xxxii
    overlooking theatres, 216

WOOD AND TIMBER, storing of, 136

WOODEN STRUCTURES, 86, 235

WORKSHOPS IN THEATRES, 219

Y.

YARD SPACE, XXXV

www.ingramcontent.com/pod-product-compliance
Lightning Source LLC
Chambersburg PA
CBHW031859220426
43663CB00006B/686